The Practitioner In\

Marilyn Cochran-Smith and Susan L. Lytle, SERIES EDITORS

Tensions of Teaching:
Beyond Tips to Critical Reflection
JUDITH M. NEWMAN

John Dewey and the Challenge of
Classroom Practice
STEPHEN M. FISHMAN &
LUCILLE McCARTHY

"Sometimes I Can Be Anything":
Power, Gender, and Identity
in a Primary Classroom
KAREN GALLAS

Learning in Small Moments:
Life in an Urban Classroom
DANIEL R. MEIER

Interpreting Teacher Practice:
Two Continuing Stories
RENATE SCHULZ

Creating Democratic Classrooms:
The Struggle to Integrate Theory and Practice
LANDON E. BEYER, Editor

ACKNOWLEDGMENTS

As a teacher educator I have been privileged to work with many outstanding classroom teachers. They have taught me a great deal. I know that writing is scary for many of them, but I believe their voices should be heard, their words should be read. I also believe they should tell their own stories. Consequently, whenever possible, I have encouraged them to see themselves as writers and to write with publication in mind. For persisting when it seemed this work would never be done, I wish to thank Jim Albright, Jim Beveridge, Kimberly Crass, Marcia Harding, Elizabeth Hughes, Pattie Kimpton, Rosemary Manning, Janie McTavish, Sandra Millen, Susan Wastie, and Veronica Yeung.

I also wish to thank Susan Church, Diane Stephens, and Wayne Serebrin whose responses to early drafts of this manuscript encouraged me to believe these were stories worth sharing. Thanks, also, to Nan Campbell, Matt Meiers, Tannis Nishibata, Claire Sutton, Edie Wilde and Zoë Thompson for their candid reactions to these teachers' stories.

Thanks to Brad Lambertus for his editorial assistance. My special thanks to Ann Nicholson for seeing something worthwhile in these stories and doing her utmost to bring *Tensions of Teaching* to publication.

Tensions of Teaching
Beyond Tips to Critical Reflection

Judith M. Newman
with

Jim Albright
James Beveridge
Kimberley Crass
Marcia Harding
Elizabeth Hughes
Patty Kimpton

Rosemary Manning
Janie McTavish
Sandra Millen
Wendy Peters
Susan Wastie
Veronica Leung

Teachers College
Columbia University
New York and London

Published in the United States of America by Teachers College Press
1234 Amsterdam Avenue, New York, NY 10027

Published in Canada by Canadian Scholars' Press

Library of Congress Cataloging-in-Publication Data

Newman, Judith, 1943—
    Tensions of teaching : beyond tips to critical reflection / Judith
M. Newman with Jim Albright . . . [et. al.].
        p.   cm.— (The practitioner inquiry series)
    Includes bibliographical references.
    ISBN 0-8077-3736-4
    1. Teaching—United States. 2. Educational change—United
States. 3. Action research in education—United States. I. Title.
II. Series
LB1025.3.N49 1998
371.102'0973—dc21   97-39274
                                                              CIP

ISBN 0-8077-3736-4

Manufactured in Canada

02 01 00 99 98   1   2   3   4   5

Page layout and cover design by Brad Horning

TABLE OF CONTENTS

The Contributors

Jim Albright has been an English Language Arts teacher with the Halifax Regional School Board for twenty-three years. He is also currently a doctoral student at Pennsylvania State University.

Jim Beveridge is principal of Transcona Collegiate in Winnipeg. He lives with his wife Patti and their three children, Alexandra, Ian and Andrew. His interests include reading, traveling and physical fitness.

Susan Church works with the Halifax Regional School Board as a researcher and teaches at Mount Saint Vincent University. She is currently pursuing her doctorate at the University of South Australia.

Kimberly Crass is a Grade One teacher at Queenston School, Winnipeg, Manitoba. She is in the final stages of completing her thesis for a Master of Education Degree.

Marcia Harding has spent most of her twenty-five years teaching Grade Three students in Queens County, Nova Scotia. She believes each child is a treasure and learning is an adventure.

Elizabeth Hughes is a Resource Teacher at Prince Andrew High School in Dartmouth, Nova Scotia. The dynamics of classroom power and their effects on learning continue to intrigue her daily.

Patti Kimpton is currently teaching English/Language Arts a t Quesnel Secondary School, in Quesnel BC. She considers herself a woman of the world, is a mother of two, and a student of life.

Rosemary Manning is currently a learning centre teacher for elementary children with learning disabilities with the Halifax Regional School Board. She has been teaching for seven years. All of her teaching experience has been with special needs children.

Sandra Millen has bee teaching junior high in Winnipeg for twenty-five years. She is currently teaching language arts and science to Grade

Eight students at Ecole River Heights Middle School. Her educational interests include the politics of education and professional growth.

Janie McTavish is currently seconded to the Manitoba Department of Education and Training. As a regional curriculum consultant she is involved in implementing new English Language Arts curricula with an emphasis on differentiated instruction.

Judith Newman, formerly Dean of the Faculty of Education, University of Manitoba, is now writing and consulting in Halifax Nova Scotia. She teaches graduate courses on teacher action research and various aspects of literacy and computers in education. Her current research includes ways of helping teachers engage in critical reflection. She is author of several books and numerous articles on literacy and critical inquiry into teaching. *Interwoven Conversations: Learning* and *Teaching Through Critical Reflection* has recently been republished by Canadian Scholars' Press.

Wendy Peters operates a private music studio in Winnipeg, Manitoba where she teaches piano and musicianship to children of all ages.

Susan Wastie has worked with preschool children and their families in the UK and Canada since 1972. Currently, she is a senior speech-language pathologist for the Vancover-Richmond Health Board, BC. She recently completed a MA Degree in Education at Simon Fraser University.

Veronica Yeung works as a special needs teacher assistant in an elementary school in Winnipeg, Manitoba. She also runs a graphic design business.

Foreword

❖

THE TENSIONS OF TEACHING

Susan Church

For the past decade or more there has been a veritable frenzy of educational reform efforts initiated within individual schools and school districts and by provincial and state governments across North America. Many commissions, panels and working groups have issued reports and recommendations for how to "fix" public education. From site-based management to national curriculum and standards, each new initiative has brought with it the promise of improved student learning. As I write, yet another panel has published its solution for the future. A headline in the February/March, 1997 Reading Today, the newspaper of the International Reading Association, announced that the U.S. National Commission on Teaching and America's Future has concluded that "teachers are the key." The commission's report, What Matters Most: Teaching for America's Future sets out what they call "an audacious goal for America's future" and an ambitious agenda through which teacher education and professional development would be transformed in order to ensure that every student in America has access to competent, caring, qualified teaching in schools organized for success by the year 2006.

While I applaud this panel's recognition that teachers play a central role in the education process and while I do not dispute their conclusion that both teacher education and professional development practices need to be transformed, their call for more rigorous licensing standards, tougher accreditation requirements for teacher education institutions and regular performance reviews for licensed teachers is yet another example of a regulatory approach to educational change, much like the development of national curriculum and standards and other top-down reform efforts. I want to ask the commission members "Why more regulations?" when research evidence cited by Sizer (O'Neil, 1995) and many others shows that this approach to reform has not resulted in improved student learning. Hargreaves (1997) argues that,

> ...our change efforts have been so preoccupied with skills and standards that they have not gotten to the heart of what a great deal of teaching is about: establishing bonds and forming relationships with students, making classrooms into places of excitement and wonder, ensuring that all students are included and no one feels an outcast, and so on. This involves a lot of emotional labor for teachers—a labor of love to be sure, but hard labor all the same. Change strategies that are preoccupied with standards, targets, checklists and form-filing can leave teachers with no time to care for or to connect with their students. When this happens, teachers feel that their fundamental purposes have been lost—with catastrophic results for their commitment and effectiveness (ix).

I talk to many teachers and administrators these days who feel that their sense of purpose has been lost. I am alarmed by the increase in the numbers of educators who are feeling this way; even those who are the most creative, caring and talented are telling me that the personal costs of their work are becoming too high—that they do not know how much longer they can sustain the energy and spirit it takes to be a teacher or principal in the current context. The last thing these people need is more regulations; they are already buried under an avalanche of reforms. Yet, it is clear that there need to be transformations in the working lives of these individuals if we expect them to provide the kind of teaching and learning environments needed by our increasingly diverse and challenging student population. The goal the Commission on Teaching and America's Future has set is clearly a worthy one; it is their proposed means of achieving that goal that I question.

Judith Newman and the teachers who have shared their struggles with the "tensions of teaching" provide an alternative perspective on teacher change. They show that ongoing critical reflection is a powerful means through which teachers transform their beliefs and practices. Each of these writers grappled with real questions that emerged directly from their work and then effected changes based upon what they were learning about themselves, their students and the context within which they were working. Once teachers take this kind of critical stance m their own work, they can never go back. They become engaged in a continual process of self- questioning and self-renewal. They do not need outside experts and well-intentioned reformers to tell them how to be better teachers; ongoing self-reform is central to their work. They do not need to be coerced to make connections with the professional community outside their classroom; they seek out and value the perspectives others can bring to their inquiries.

Clearly, critiquing one's own practice is a risky business. These authors have made themselves vulnerable by publishing their writing but they also have opened possibilities for their audience. Their reflections and insights have the potential to provoke further inquiry as readers consider the questions about their own beliefs and practices that these stories raise. Like these writers, I have grappled with how to engage resistant learners and with when to intervene and when to back off in the classroom. I have become angry about the systemic inequities in public education, and I have learned difficult and sometimes painful lessons about the politics of education. The connections I made as I read these narratives were often with the most difficult and frustrating situations I have experienced in my own teaching. Nevertheless, the collection left me with a sense of hope. These writers show that the incidents that cause us the greatest discomfort also can lead to the greatest positive change if we are open to learning from them. As Judith Newman points out in the Preface, that learning is most likely to occur if teachers are part of a supportive community in which there is ongoing individual and collective inquiry and in which a leader, such as Judith, fosters critical reflection. Having been part of several of the groups that have coalesced under her tutelage, I am aware of the central role she has played in helping educators both to become more critically aware and to write the stories of their experiences.

The writers featured in this collection were fortunate to have the opportunity to be part of one of those communities of learning. Their experiences provide powerful evidence that these kinds of professional communities provide a context within which teachers and administrators can sustain meaning and purpose in their work and, as a result, better meet the needs of students. If those interested in improving public education were to take the messages of this collection seriously, they would give up on the quest for ever more rigorous and demanding regulations and devote their time, energy and resources to the much more complex, yet potentially much more rewarding, task of supporting teacher inquiry. Of course, that would mean shifting power to teachers by inviting them to give voice to the kinds of concerns that engage the authors of *The Tensions of Teaching*. The resulting challenges to many of the assumptions that underlie dominant practices in public education would undoubtedly cause discomfort, and even anger, in some. Yet, I believe it is only through those kinds of challenges that genuine educational reform will occur. With this engaging and readable collection, Judith Newman and her co-authors have made a significant contribution to the ongoing conversation about educational change. I hope that teachers, administrators, policy makers and others involved in reform will listen to what they have to say.

Hargreaves, A. (1997). "Introduction." In A. Hargreaves, (Ed.) *Rethinking Educational Change with Heart and Mind,* 1997 ASCD Yearbook. Alexandria, VA: ASCD: vii-xv.

O'Neil, J. (1995). "On Lasting School Reform: A Conversation with Ted Sizer." *Educational Leadership,* 52 (3): 4-9.

Preface
❖

KEEPING THE DORY AFLOAT

I began my academic career in 1976 at Dalhousie University. As the only "literacy" person on faculty, I needed to search for colleagues with other theoretical and professional interests. That turned out to be fortuitous. These colleagues introduced me to a whole new world of political questions. Ruth Gamberg, a Marxist sociologist; Edgar Friedenberg, a social critic; and Doug Myers, a political historian, all pushed me to critically examine my role as a teacher educator.

I recall one particularly fractious meeting shortly after I joined the education department during which Friedenberg self-righteously described himself as "sitting on the shore recording the sinking of the *Titanic*." I immediately thought to myself, "I own a dory; perhaps I can rescue some survivors." Notice that I didn't dispute Freidenberg's analysis of education as a floundering institution, only his passive role as critic. In spite of his pessimism about education and his contention that its sinking was inevitable, I believed it was possible to institute change and as teacher educators we had a responsibility to try. That realization marked the beginning of my political activism with educators.

I began by challenging the assumptions of the classroom teachers taking my courses. I set them tasks that encouraged them to see their students in new ways. It wasn't long before a number of teachers were asking me questions about implementing new literacy curriculum initiatives. Luckily I didn't have extensive classroom experience with young children learning to read so I was unable to offer any prescriptions. Instead, I invited the teachers to meet with me as a group—the first of a number of teacher study groups that I subsequently helped launch.

The study group served a number of purposes. It afforded a safe haven in which teachers could reveal their insecurities, where they could share tentative instructional ideas with one another, where they could critique one another's professional practice. The conversation often veered to "nifty tips;" my role was to challenge the teachers' complacency, to push them to ground their instruction within a theoretical framework. The teachers' prime concern was what they were going to do in the classroom; I was insisting that they reflect on why they chose certain activities over others and how those choices affected their students. All of us, I believed, needed continually to rethink our assumptions and re-examine our practice.

I understood from the outset that we were challenging the status quo, that we were engaged in a political activity that could leave the teachers vulnerable, that we had to work together and put what we were doing into writing in order to legitimize it professionally. As it turned out we didn't begin by writing. We started by holding a series of annual summer institutes for other local teachers. For three years the core study group planned and delivered experiences for colleagues based on what they themselves had been learning about literacy learning and instruction. The members of this first study group also became involved in the local reading association and began offering inservices around the province. As a collective we worked hard to help other teachers examine literacy instruction.

But there was a naiveté to all of our efforts. We thought that if we told people about an alternate view of literacy learning and instruction, showed them examples of what children could do, then literacy instruction in the province would suddenly change. Not so. As Susan Church (1996) writes:

> ...As I reflected on my own leadership role, I recognized that I had not invited dialogue within the context of staff development experiences. There were few opportunities for teachers to question why they were being asked to change when they believed they were already doing a competent job. In working with the teachers, I had been guilty of perpetuating practices that controlled and silenced teachers—at the very same time that I was promoting the development of student voice, choice and self-direction within their classrooms. Ironically, the top-down effort to institutionalize whole language, and thus liberate students from the shackles of traditional teacher-directed instruction, resulted in many teachers feeling disempowered, angry and anything but liberated. (p.25-26)

Some teachers thought differently about what they were doing in their classrooms; most, however, felt pressured to adopt a few new literacy activities, but they did so without changing their underlying beliefs.

Our first foray into writing was a collaborative effort—*Whole Language: Theory in Use* (Newman, 1985). The anthology consisted of narrative accounts of classroom experiences. The teachers were attempting to "show," not "tell," about student-centered language instruction. The subtitle was chosen to signal that we were writing about more than language instruction activities. We intentionally chose the subtitle to alert readers to the need for theoretically grounded practice. No one noticed the connection.

Reading through the anthology a decade later I can see the political character of each teacher's writing. Issues of power and control, of gender, of the impact of labeling students, although not spelled out explicitly, are certainly evident in these articles. But the education community received the book as a collection of "how-to" pieces. In spite of my efforts to help educators grasp that our inquiry into literacy learning goes far beyond reading and writing to a need to articulate beliefs about teaching and learning, the political nature of the enterprise was missed completely.

I continued exploring, and helping teachers explore, the political agenda of language and literacy instruction. A few years later, with a graduate class at Mount Saint Vincent University, I once again had an opportunity to engage teachers in writing. The specific course dealt with writing; my focus—to help the teachers explore writing by becoming writers themselves. The course examined conflicting theories of writing as well as the research on writing development and instruction. We paid particular attention to reading/writing relationships. We also explored various writing strategies by engaging in numerous writing activities. I didn't know we had a publishable work until I had compiled the teachers articles at the end of the course.

Finding Our Own Way (Newman, 1987) went a bit further than *Whole Language: Theory in Use*. The teachers' narratives were more overtly about the tensions of teaching. Some of them were accounts based on experiences long past, others were more recent. In all of them the teachers took a reflective look at some problematic aspect of their teaching. They looked at making the shift from traditional transmission classrooms to open, learner-directed environments. They explored the relationship between learning and teaching, examined assumptions underlying instructional decisions in the process, discovering that every teaching act, every decision, is based on a what are often contradictory beliefs. They delved into the conflicting messages they send students and wrote about the impact of attempting to change their assumptions. They took risks as they considered what was involved in learning from students.

Again, the political nature of these inquiries wasn't explicitly spelled out. In large measure, that was because I hadn't shaped the class discussion adequately. While we read widely in the research literature on writing and writing instruction, I failed to include articles, chapters, and books by critical theorists such as Stanley Aronowitz (Aronowitz and Giroux, 1985), Michael Apple (1990), Stephen Ball (1990), Henry Giroux (1981, 1989), Maxine Greene (1978), and Roger Simon (1992). Although I was familiar with the writings and arguments of these authors, I hadn't yet figured out how to include them in the class conversation. We were so busy reading material intended to help teachers question their assumptions about writing and writing instruction, and exploring our own writing, that I had difficulty introducing any critical analysis of education that would have helped the teachers name and situate the issues that were the basis of their emerging narratives. An astute reader might detect in these pieces the seeds of a political critique by classroom teachers. Unfortunately, most readers don't perceive the subtext.

My next attempt to examine the tensions of teaching appeared in a narrative account of my own teaching. *Interwoven Conversations: Learning and Teaching Through Critical Reflection* (Newman, 1991) was a reflective look at my own practice. I used the story of a two-week summer institute to raise questions about inquiry into one's own practice and to examine the theoretical underpinnings of my own professional work. I was attempting to make more explicit for myself and for readers the political agenda of teaching. Using critical incidents from my own teaching and from the teachers who participated in the institute, I ventured to show reflection-in-action and to examine the tensions that affect what and how I teach.

Interwoven Conversations was followed by an anthology of poetry by teachers—*In Our Own Words: Poems by Teachers* (Newman, 1993). I had been using poetry for a number of years as a reflective tool. I had accumulated a substantial collection of poems written by teachers; many of them about the tensions of teaching and the constraints of classroom life. I sorted through what I had and compiled the book.

Then I moved from Mount Saint Vincent University to the University of Manitoba as Dean of the Faculty of Education. The political constraints

I found myself dealing with were no longer covert. Suddenly I was confronted with the politics of education, both at the university and in public schools, at every working moment.

I began a new graduate course—Action Research: Educating as Inquiry. The first year I successfully built a working collaborative. I was better at helping the teachers name and explore the political issues they were confronting in their practice, but I was unsuccessful at helping them bring their writing to closure.

The following year I was better organized. The participants (elementary, junior high, and senior high teachers, a program assistant, a principal, a curriculum supervisor, and a music teacher) began with inquiries into their professional practice. "Start with a critical incident—an experience as a learner or teacher that stands out for you, something that's caught your attention this week or last—and see where it gets you." I was asking these educators to capture some moments from ongoing activity to discover what they might learn from them.

As individual inquiries began taking shape, I suggested readings to help the participants identify emerging issues and to think about their professional practice in a more overtly political way. Through their inquiries they learned to notice critical incidents and record them, they struggled for connections, they read to discover how others made sense of experience, they found new ways of naming and interpreting their own experience. As writers they had to push beyond their concerns for fluency to struggle with clarity in their writing. They had to learn how to write personal narratives which showed, instead of told, about their experiences. They had to discover how to help one another make sense of their inquiries. They had to find ways of answering the question all readers ask, "So what?"

An important aspect of the learning that occurred during the writing of these pieces was the discovery that teaching and learning are always journeys. The educators learned a great deal about the political nature of teaching. Each critical incident opened unexpected doors on issues that face teachers everyday. They discovered that every action, every decision in a classroom carries with it the potential both to support and to interfere with a student's learning. They discovered how their decisions make them vulnerable and fearful. They learned, as they explored, how teaching is fraught with tensions. The action research, and the writing which brings it to fruition, allowed them to put names to those tensions, to better understand the constraints under which they work.

The product of their venture into action research is this anthology. In addition to the pieces written by the participants of the 1994-95 action research course, I have included two pieces from the Summer Institute for Teachers at Simon Fraser University where I taught in 1994, as well as four pieces from my last writing course at Mount Saint Vincent in 1992-93. I elected to include these pieces in this compilation because they deal explicitly with the tensions of teaching and I felt they deserved a wider audience than the limited one our class publication afforded.

Tensions of Teaching, then, is the culmination of inquiries into our own practice. In it the practitioners reflect on issues which their various critical incidents raise for their professional practice. They have pushed themselves beyond an immediate concern for "tips" to an exploration of the tensions that arise from the communal life of classrooms and schools. They grapple with constraints which impact from outside and they examine the political ramifications of inaction and a reliance on others for making classroom decisions. They have all come to understand that there are no simple solutions to the problems educators face. Each practitioner must confront the complexity of the endeavor we call teaching.

Twenty years ago I recognized that as a teacher educator I had a dual responsibility—not only to help educators critique schools and schooling but also to provide leadership and support for their efforts to change themselves. For twenty years I have worked to keep my dory afloat. Every year I have collected a crew of educators willing to sail hazardous seas. Together we have gone fishing, keeping eyes peeled for icebergs and other unexpected dangers, we have returned safely with our catch. With each voyage I have become more experienced at sailing and fishing.

Long ago I realized I wasn't likely to change the institution of schools, but I believed I might be able to help others think about their professional activity in new ways. I have kept my dory seaworthy and done what I could to help public school educators identify and understand the tensions and constraints which impact on them. We offer *Tensions of Teaching* in the hope that others are able, through our insights, to see and understand their own experiences differently.

Judith Newman
Halifax, NS

Aronowitz, Stanley and Henry Giroux. (1985). *Education Under Siege: The Conservative, Liberal, and Radical Debate Over Schooling.* Westport, Conn: Bergin & Garvey.

Apple, Michael. (1990). *Ideology and Curriculum.* 2nd ed. London, Boston: Routledge & Kegan Paul.

Ball, Stephen. (1990). *Politics and Policy Making in Education: Explorations in Policy Sociology.* London, New York: Routledge.

Church, Susan. (1996). *The Future of Whole Language: Reconstruction or Self-destruction?* Portsmouth, NH: Heinemann Educational Books.

Giroux, Henry. (1981). *Ideology, Culture and the Process of Schooling.* London: Falmer.

Giroux, Henry. (1989). *Critical Pedagogy, the State, and Cultural Struggle.* Albany: State University of New York Press.

Greene, Maxine. (1978). *Landscapes of Learning.* New York: Teachers College Press.

Newman, Judith M. (Ed.). (1985). *Whole Language: Theory in Use.* Portsmouth, NH: Heinemann Educational Books.

Newman, Judith M. (Ed.). (1987). *Finding Our Own Way: Teachers Examining their Assumptions.* Portsmouth, NH: Heinemann Educational Books.

Newman, Judith M. (1991). *Interwoven Conversations: Learning and Teaching Through Critical Reflection.* Toronto: OISE Press.

Newman, Judith M. (Ed.). (1993). *In Our Own Words: Poems by Teachers.* Halifax, NS: Braeside Books.

Simon, Roger. (1992). *Teaching Against the Grain: Texts for a Pedagogy of Possibility.* Toronto: OISE Press.

ACTION RESEARCH:
EXPLORING THE TENSIONS OF TEACHING

Judith M. Newman

> "You were sitting on the roof?" Lieutenant Joe
> Leaphorn kept the tone of the question neutral.
> "Yessir," Jim Chee said. "You can see the whole
> plaza from up there."
> That was the advantage, of course. The
> disadvantage being that you couldn't catch the kid
> once you saw him. But Leaphorn didn't press that
> point. It was obvious from Chee's slightly abashed
> expression that he was aware of it. Leaphorn put the
> first page of Chee's report facedown on his desk and
> reread the second and terminal page. It was neatly
> typed but—by Leaphorn's standards—sadly
> incomplete.... (p. 22) *

I'm an avid mystery reader. I always have a stack of crime novels beside my
bed. There's something about the genre I find very compelling—I can't say
what for sure, but I definitely find mysteries satisfying to read, certainly
more than just a cheap escape.

One of my favorite detective writers is Tony Hillerman. His novels are
cast in the American southwest, in a locale referred to as "the four
corners"—the intersection of Utah, Colorado, Arizona, and New Mexico.
Find Flagstaff in northern Arizona on the map and you're in the general
region. What I find so very interesting and appealing about Hillerman's
country and the stories he tells is that people go about their normal lives,
not troubled greatly by what's happening in the rest of the world. Hillerman
develops great plots and you would expect considerable action with stories
that have murder at their core, but this is not so—in Hillerman's novels
very little happens. They are contemplative; they unfold slowly, in Navajo
time.

---

* Hillerman, Tony. (1993). *Sacred Clowns*. Toronto: Harper Collins

Lieutenant Joe Leaphorn, a middle-aged officer of the Navajo Tribal Police stationed in Window Rock, does most of his detecting by cogitating on details, attempting to construct connections among apparently unrelated events. The territory is large and unpopulated; he has lots of time, as he drives from one location to another, to think about people and why they do things. Leaphorn is a subtly drawn character, and his investigations reveal powerful glimpses of Navajo and other local cultures.

It's late spring and I'm preparing for a new course on action research for teachers. I browse my book shelves, choosing titles I think might contribute to a discussion of action research. I thumb through my file cabinets for articles that might be useful. I spend some time in the library hunting for new material. I surf the World Wide Web to see what I can find on teacher research. I set up a class library, compile a bibliography of the materials I have located, and work on my opening letter to the teachers.

I also happen to be reading Hillerman's novel, *Sacred Clowns*. I read it quickly, enjoying the story and his further development of both Leaphorn and Chee. Reading a new novel by a particular author when you've read all eleven of his previous books is something akin to watching a television series. I find myself reading this one, not to find out *whodunit,* but for what I glean about the ongoing lives of Leaphorn and Chee. These two characters hold my interest. In particular, Leaphorn's explicit induction of the younger officer Chee into the techniques of detecting, of doing *action research,* grabs my attention. I finish the novel, then I immediately read it again.

> Leaphorn said...studying Chee "...when we're working on something, I want you to tell me everything. Everything. Don't leave out stuff you think is trivial, or doesn't seem to bear on what we're interested in. I want it all." (p. 25)

The difficult thing about *doing* action research is that you have to override most of what you've learned about research as an activity. In a traditional research culture you begin by framing a question, setting up a situation which might provide some information, collecting data which bears on the question, then writing up results.

Action research isn't like that at all. The research activity begins in the middle of whatever it is you're doing—something happens that you didn't expect—for Leaphorn and Chee it's a couple of apparently unrelated murders, one in their jurisdiction, the other outside it—and you begin wondering about what's going on.

The dilemma in an action research situation is you may not even realize something interesting has occurred that you ought to think about unless you're already in the habit of keeping a journal or reflective log. Because teaching, like other activities which occur in and around schools, is so complex, we're accustomed to coping with the many things demanding our attention at once without really thinking about them; we generally don't make a point of recording those moments which surprise or perplex us or stand out for some other reason during the course of the day. So, unless we follow Leaphorn's advice and create for ourselves regular reflective accounts of what's going on, we're not likely to get anywhere. As Leaphorn advises Chee, "I want you to tell me everything...don't leave out stuff you think is trivial." In fact, you won't know what is trivial until patterns begin to emerge, and even then what seems trivial may turn out to be significant later—you just can't tell.

The hardest part of beginning an action research project is developing the discipline to keep a written account of what's happening, particularly when you have no idea what you're looking for. For unlike traditional research, action research begins not with a research question but with the muddle of daily work, with the moments that stand out from the general flow, and unless we record those moments they vanish—unavailable as data for reflection, for discerning some larger pattern of experience. So it's necessary to keep fairly detailed notes. Whether it's a journal, a daily log, critical incidents (Newman, 1987, 1991) jotted on index cards, or more extensive field notes, without a written account the enterprise cannot proceed.*

"You look for connections," Leaphorn said....
"I can't see anything to connect them," Chee said....

---

* I have tried audiotaping notes, but who has the time to transcribe tapes? It's just more work. Written notes, even in point form, are definitely preferable.

> Leaphorn rubbed the back of his hand across his
> eyes. He looked glum. "I can't either, but I always
> look. It's an old habit....
>   "I don't like coincidences," Leaphorn said. Even if
> this isn't much of one....(p. 26, 27, 28)

We begin the action research course by reading *Sacred Clowns*. The teachers expect some instruction on how to do action research. This is the best account I've ever read! In addition, I juxtapose a variety of professional works with Hillerman's novel. During the first month the teachers also read a number of articles and book chapters either describing teacher research or showing teacher research in action: Virginia Richardson (1994) on conducting research on practice; Frederick Burton (1986) and Glenda Bissex (1988) on action research; Eleanor Kutz (1992) on myths and realities of teacher research; Cathy Fleischer (1994) on researching teacher research; Eleanor Duckworth (1987) on teaching as research.

I mentioned earlier that I prepare a class library. In that collection, which I bring to class each week, I have included a range of action research studies—masters' theses, doctoral dissertations, published articles, as well as several teacher research anthologies. The teachers choose individual selections to read in conjunction with our common reading material. It never ceases to surprise me that graduate students, by and large, have no idea how to look for connections; their predominant learning strategy is to read and memorize. So we spend a great deal of time looking for connections in articles, chapters, and books, learning how to think with the authors, using these accounts as mirrors for reflecting on our own experiences.

> I noticed last week in class during the small group discussions that
> you had some difficulty using the readings to reflect on your own
> writing, reading, learning/teaching. I suspect most of you are used
> to reading for the 'facts' a given article or chapter offers, or for
> 'tips,' but I'm attempting to help you read more interpretively/
> reflectively. That means using the professional writing as a MIRROR
> to see your own learning/teaching more clearly. The point of such
> reading is to use someone else's experiences/arguments as a
> jumping off point for an examination of your own. My friend and
> colleague Diane Stephens calls this THINKING WITH. She's referring to
> something Margaret Spencer describes—the text allowing us to
> read ourselves (Spencer, 1987). Seeing ourselves in new ways,
> taking a new perspective on our own life circumstances, is the real

> purpose of any reading. The heart of our enterprise is to become
> more reflective practitioners. I'm trying to help you examine your
> teaching in new and critical ways. I've done a number of things to
> set up potential contrasts which may lead you to see yourself
> differently, to question your assumptions, but for these
> experiences to have that affect you have to make a contribution—
> you have to turn your gaze back toward yourself. It means not
> treating what you read as some isolated object but using it to help
> you generate questions about your teaching, about your
> assumptions. (Judith Newman, Reflection: 10/6/94)*

In addition to using published accounts to explore connections, I encourage teachers to begin collecting and recording critical incidents (Newman, 1987, 1991). Critical incidents are what I call those moments which have allowed me to stand back and examine my beliefs and my teaching critically. They are stories used as tools for conducting research on ourselves. A critical incident can be triggered in the midst of teaching, but I have also suddenly found myself contemplating my teaching while I'm reading something. Or I have overheard a comment that has made me wonder. Noticing how someone else is doing something I've always taken for granted or suddenly seeing my own learning differently has helped me learn more about teaching. Latent critical incidents are everywhere, not just in the classroom, and they offer important opportunities for learning about our professional practice.

Because I find it so difficult to keep extensive field notes while I'm teaching, I have evolved, with the help of many teachers, a technique of jotting a phrase, or a sentence or two, on one side of a three by five index card at the end of the class—just enough so I am able to reconstruct a situation or event later—using a different card for each potential story. Then I use the other side of the card to reflect on what happened. I have learned to ask myself "What makes this moment surprising?" "What questions does it raise for me?" "How does this change how I think about my teaching?" Later, when I have time, I develop stories based on incidents

---

* These reflective excerpts are taken from my unpublished journals. This particular reflection was written October 6, 1994. I have also used excerpts from teacher's written reflections. They are identified in a similar manner— with a teacher's name and the date the reflection was written. **Note:** I have used fictitious names for the teachers and schools. Fictitious names have been given to all students mentioned, as well.

recorded on the cards. The following account of my experience with Cindy, a third grader, is an example of such a critical incident narrative.

It was my last visit to Elmdale School before Christmas. Several children in the third grade class were setting off to read to their grade one reading buddies and Cindy, especially, wanted me to accompany them. Cindy had rehearsed some book or other to read to her first grade partner; however, the class took a quick trip to the library just before the children were to read to their buddies. While in the library, Cindy came across Ezra Jack Keats' book *The Snowy Day* and decided that was the book she wanted to read instead. As far as I, and the other teachers knew, this was an unfamiliar book. We suggested she postpone reading it, but Cindy would have none of that—she was insistent, *The Snowy Day* was the book she was going to read.

I should have heeded her body language, but I was too busy being concerned about her having taken on more than she could handle that I didn't notice the way she held herself, her confident stride.

Cindy settled herself comfortably on the floor against the wall, her buddy by her side. I sat close, ready to help out if needed but willing to sit back and watch. Cindy positioned the book so Tamara could see. She read the cover and the title page, then she began reading the story as fluently as any other third grader—no hint of the difficulty she'd demonstrated all fall. She came to the page ...*He climbed a heaping mountain of snow*, ...paused ever so slightly, turned to me and said ...*I'll just say 'humungus'*...then read ...*He climbed a humungus mountain of snow*...without waiting for any confirmation from me.

I was both surprised and delighted. Here was a solid demonstration of fluent reading in action. Cindy was monitoring the sense of the story, the flow of the language, picture cues, and graphophonic cues, and orchestrating the whole in such a way that meaning was maintained. That was the moment when I registered her posture—leaning against the wall comfortably, head high, book loosely held in her lap—the very picture of a confident reader. It was clear that in this situation Cindy believed she could read—the first time I had witnessed her confidence. I knew she was on her way.

Afterward I asked Cindy how she had been able to read so well. She couldn't explain—I hadn't really expected she could, most kids do as she did, they shrug when they've got it together, "It's really nothing," they imply nonchalantly. I was wondering whether she was familiar with the story, but she said she wasn't when I probed. It was clear to me, as I watched her handle the book, that I wasn't witnessing a memorized reading—Cindy was REALLY reading. The lesson for me was a powerful one. I had been helping her teachers build supports for Cindy. We'd done considerable shared reading with her and a small group of other students. We'd written stories and helped her transcribe hers, helped her prepare for reading to her grade one buddy. So concerned about building a supportive environment, we'd forgotten we had to leave room for challenge. Fortunately for us, Cindy herself knew when it was time to stretch—in hindsight I could recognize the signals. The incident was a clear indication from Cindy that she didn't need quite so much support any longer. We pulled back. (Judith Newman, Reflection: 3/27/1995)

I encourage the teachers to begin collecting their own critical incidents, to look for the unexpected, to notice surprises, and to record them. We discuss their incidents in class using them as a basis for thinking with whomever we happen to be reading.

Over the last decade, as people have moved in new directions, from quantitative research methodologies towards naturalistic inquiry, many new and interesting forms of research have emerged. Variously identified as teacher research (Cochran-Smith and Lytle, 1993), action research (Winter, 1987; Carr, 1989), reflective practice (Schön, 1983), at the heart of all of these investigative enterprises has been a common focus on practice-as-inquiry. There are as many variants of practice-as-inquiry as there are people exploring its possibilities. There is no one "right" way of doing action research, of being a teacher researcher, of engaging in critical reflection. Practitioners engaging in these more open, reflective ways are inventing methodology as they go along.

There are huge differences of opinion about what actually constitutes practice-as-inquiry; I encourage the teachers to explore the research literature widely in order to acquaint themselves with the range of possibilities. Stephen North (1987), for example, contends that practice becomes inquiry only when practitioners identify a problem, search for possible causes and solutions, test those solutions in practice, validate their observations and then disseminate their findings. For North, the making of new knowledge requires some distanced systematic investigation, done primarily as an end in itself. The researcher/practitioner is essentially detached from practice. In North's opinion, inquiry isn't research unless it follows the rules of traditional quantitative methodologies.

Donald Schön (1983, 1987), on the other hand, sees practice-as-inquiry conducted principally to inform and change ongoing practice. For Schön, inquiry occurs when the practitioner reflects while engaged in action and subsequently on the action itself.

Surprise, says Schön (1987), is at the heart of any reflective activity.

> Surprise leads to reflection within an action-present. Reflection is at least in some measure conscious, although it need not occur in the medium of words. We consider both the unexpected event and the knowing-in-action that led up to it, asking ourselves, as it were, "What is this?" and, at the same time, "How have I been thinking about it?" Our thought turns back on the surprising phenomenon and, at the same time, back on itself. (p. 28)

The most difficult thing about being an observer is recognizing the unexpected; it's much easier to record the expected. Yet we really learn most from the unexpected—it's when something didn't go as we thought it should, or someone's response was different than we thought it would be, or they do something we wouldn't have done, or we would have done it in a different way, that we can begin to see what our expectations/ assumptions are.

As action researchers we're trying to examine our assumptions. But, obviously, before we can examine assumptions, we need to discover what they are. By exploring both familiar and unfamiliar situations, we position ourselves to be able to interrogate our professional practice.

Schön's comments might lead you to think that surprise and reflection yield immediate insight. However, Frank Conroy (1991), in a delightful critical incident, makes it clear that understanding indeed may not occur at once; it may, in fact, elude us for quite some time.

> ...The light bulb may appear over your head, is what I'm saying, but it may be a while before it actually goes on. Early in my attempts to learn jazz piano, I used to listen to recordings of a fine player named Red Garland, whose music I admired. I couldn't quite figure out what he was doing with his left hand, however; the chords eluded me. I went uptown to an obscure club where he was playing with his trio, caught him on his break, and simply asked him. "Sixths," he said cheerfully. And then he went away. I didn't know what to make of it....A couple of years later, when I began playing with a bass player, I discovered

more or less by accident that if the bass played the root and I
played a sixth based on the fifth note of the scale, a very
interesting chord involving both instruments emerged.
Ordinarily, I suppose I would have skipped over the matter and
not paid much attention, but I remembered Garland's remark
and so I stopped and spent a week or two working out the
voicings, and greatly strengthening my foundations as a player.
I had remembered what I hadn't understood, you might say,
until my life caught up with the information and the light bulb
went on (p. 68-69). ...you [just] never know when you're going
to understand something you hadn't understood before. (p. 70)

You can sometimes speed up the understanding process by keeping
an anecdotal account of what you can't quite figure out.

"I know you don't believe in coincidences," Streib said.
"But they do happen....And this looks like another
one. Unless you can see some possible link."
        "I can't," Leaphorn said.... (p. 53)

I want the teachers to understand that, in action research, methodology
evolves from the situation itself. You don't begin by deciding to use narrative
inquiry (Connelly and Clandinin, 1988) or dilemma analysis (Winter, 1986).
The methodological specifics emerge from the inquiry. However, common
to all forms of action research is the search for patterns that connect
(Bateson, 1978).

The trouble with connections is that they're not always immediately
apparent. A large part of identifying connections is being able to name the
issues emerging from an inquiry. One of the ways I go about this is by
taking the critical incidents I have collected and sifting through them for
stories that seem to have something in common. Then I attempt to describe
the connection.*

---

* I evolved this strategy for myself. Later I encountered a description of it in one
of Sue Grafton's novels. [*"I" is for Innocent* 1992 New York: Fawcett Crest: 271-
273]. Kinsey Milgone, her detective, records clues on index cards which she
pins to a cork board on a wall in her apartment. When she's trying to make
sense of an investigation she takes the cards down and sifts through them in
the same way I do.

My efforts to articulate my sense of what the incidents are about is helped by reading. One of the reasons I encourage graduate students to read widely is that, as they become more adept at thinking with published authors, they discover new ways of perceiving their own work. They discover ways of naming their experiences which are grounded in the on-going work of the research community. A crucial facet of action research, then, consists of connecting our personal experiences to the wider world of scholarship, of situating reflective moments within the broader research discourse.

> He sat in a well-worn recliner ...relaxing, comfortable,
> ...Leaphorn found his mind settling into an old, old
> groove. This was when he did his best thinking—just
> before sleep. He would review whatever puzzle was
> bothering him, turn the facts over and over, look at all
> sides of them, knock them together, and then explain
> it all to Emma—as much to organize it in his own mind
> as to ask her opinion.... (p. 82)

Leaphorn continually thinks about the evidence and he discusses his emerging interpretations and his questions with Chee and with any other officers who might be around. The reason for talking out his thoughts is, he reflects, as much to organize them in his own mind as to ask someone else's opinion.

An important aspect of doing action research, then, involves meeting regularly with other folks to talk aloud what's going on in your head. It's very easy to avoid periodically organizing your conjectures into some kind of coherent account of what could be going on. In the context of a course, our regularly scheduled classes and my constantly nudging the teachers to reflect provide frequent opportunities for them to hear themselves speculate about their interpretations. It's more difficult if you're doing research on your own. I have made a point of developing a corps of readers—people who are good at helping me think out loud—with whom I share my speculative thoughts and my writing in progress. I need that kind of constant feedback in order to shape my ideas. I structure the graduate class so that the teachers can hear themselves talk on a regular basis.

> "...He told you that Kanitewa thought the man who
> killed Dorsey would be after him?
> "Right," Chee said.
> "And the man was a Navajo?"
> "Oh," Chee said, embarrassed. "...He said
> Kanitewa said this man was medium-sized and kind
> of old. I think we just took for granted we were
> talking about a Navajo because he didn't say 'white,'
> or 'Chinese,' or 'Hispanic.'" (p. 101)

Action research is as much about uncovering our assumptions as it is about seeing new connections. Our interpretations of experience are shaped by our assumptions, by our biases, by what Frank Smith (1975) refers to as 'the theory of the world in our heads' (p. 11). We operate in our professional capacity as teacher, principal, program assistant, resource teacher, psychologist, curriculum consultant, or superintendent on a set of beliefs which are largely tacit. We operate generally from an intuitive sense of things without actively articulating what our assumptions might be. As Chee admits, he and Blizzard had assumed the person Kanitewa was afraid of was Navajo simply because the boy hadn't specified non-Navajo in his description; their assumption precluded them even asking the question. Chee's disclosing this assumption opened for Leaphorn new possibilities in the investigation.

The same is true of an action research inquiry. We start with our unexamined assumptions, but slowly we come to see how our assumptions shape our decisions and our responses and we become able to contemplate alternate ways of acting. An action research report therefore is, or should be, an account of uncovered assumptions, a record of the researcher's learning journey.

> Leaphorn shook his head, laughed. "... I used to think
> I was logical. Usually I am." ...He walked around
> behind the desk, rummaged in the drawer, and took
> out a box of pins. "Ever have that happen to you?
> Your brain tells you one thing. Your instinct another."
> (p. 102)

Intuition plays a big part in any action research enterprise. An important aspect of being able to step outside of situations is learning to attend to the *feel* of things, of trying to understand what it is we're reacting to when responding or making decisions. It's all very subtle—learning to register how something is said, the tone of voice, what is left unsaid, facial expressions, accompanying gestures, motivations and how they are expressed—what we refer to as body language or nonverbal communication.

Engaging in action research requires learning to recognize your hunches and recording them. Most are likely to be wrong; following them will lead you down false trails, but from time to time that gut feeling contradicting what your brain is telling you will prove important for seeing something from a new perspective.

> "You remember what I was saying the other day about putting in the details? Your report reads: 'When Bluehorse came out Kanitewa was sitting in his pickup.' But was he crouched down out of sight, or sitting up? That's an example. If we knew that it would tell us something about how scared the boy was at that point." (p. 105)

Back to the details. At first the teachers had a horrendous time keeping a written record.

> I resisted writing for a long time. After all, I was being reflective in the classroom, making mental notes of what was going on with the children. I have a good memory, why did I have to record my observations? I quickly learned through this action research project, however, that mental notes have a way of getting lost among the millions of thoughts crossing my mind. As much as I hate to admit it, I finally had to resort to a journal, I had to make written notes in order to remember what happened. (Joanna Ballam, Reflection: 4/20/95)

I suspect there are two reasons why teachers avoid writing about their experiences. First, it's hard to know what to record when you have no idea what you want to focus on. Second, there is anxiety about what they might discover about themselves and their professional competence. There is a definite reluctance to commit themselves to paper even though no one else is reading what they write unless they specifically ask someone to respond to what they've written.

I haven't found a sure-fire way of overcoming this resistance. I share some of my own research journals, I provide critical incidents and reflections from other sources, in an effort to free up the teachers' writing. But it's still an up-hill effort to get the teachers to record events with enough detail for them to have comprehensive data from which to build their own narratives. I keep returning to Hillerman and reading aloud excerpts from the novel; ultimately, however, it's their own unfolding inquiries that allow the teachers to tune in to detail.

Writing has a larger role to play, however, than simply recording observations, reflections, questions, and connections. Writing is crucial for making sense of experiences. Gordon Wells (1994) explains:

> Solitary reflection certainly leads to a growth in understanding, but writing one's thoughts down makes it possible to revisit them and review them over time….When writing is undertaken to communicate one's understanding to others,…even more benefit accrues. For, with the requirement to make one's meaning clear and explicit to a real or imagined reader, one is forced to reexamine one's ideas and assumptions in a much more rigorous way than when writing for oneself alone. As a result, one is often pushed into radical rethinking and revision. (p. 31)

Writing isn't a mopping-up operation, an onerous add-on. It is an integral aspect of the inquiry process. As such, it's a critical vehicle for creating meaning; it's at the very heart of any action research enterprise.

I enjoyed reading the short stories for this week again. Although I've read them many times before, I found this reading different— affected by Robert MacNeil's *Burden of Desire*[1] in surprising ways. I was, for example, a lot more aware of the various authors' descriptions and wondered about their experiences and how they were reflected in the detail attributed to the characters' lives. I found myself using the writing to see my own world differently.

The large flakes were soft and new then and almost generous and the earth to which they fell was still warm and

---

[1] MacNeil, Robert. (1992). *Burden of Desire*. New York: Doubleday.

as yet unfrozen. They fell in silence into the puddles and into the sea where they disappeared at the moment of contact....[2]

Alistair MacLeod's passage has made me aware of the trees yesterday weighed down by the wet snow on their unshed leaves. I was also aware of the warmth of the day and my surprise at it building up even though it felt too warm for the snow to last. I noticed the postman in his yellow slicker and the cold drips on his visor and the edges of his sleeves.

...she kept the shop open late even when her ankles felt swollen and tired....[3]

writes Sara Maitland and I think about how my legs felt on Sunday after delivering "Yes" campaign flyers for two hours in the wonderful cool autumn sunshine. The tightness in both calves pulling with each step and sapping my energy until I slumped on the curb unable to take another step.

There's something sneaky about Pa, maybe it is the way he walks kind of sideways, with his eyes always darting all over the place.[4]

Anna Marie mentioned a conversation she eavesdropped on a week ago in which she noticed one of the women who kept looking around, not engaged with what her friend was saying. I found myself watching the intent faces of the folks listening to Bob Rae, the Ontario Premier, at a gathering Saturday evening. I noticed one gentleman who was off by himself, arms folded, legs crossed and wondering what was going through his mind.

She got a rag in the kitchen and retraced her chipping progress, enjoying the texture of the flaking plaster as she went.[5]

---

[2] MacLeod, Alistair. (1986). To Everything There is a Season. In *As Birds Bring forth the Sun*. Toronto: McLelland and Stewart Ltd.

[3] Maitland, Sara. (1987). Miss Manning's Angelic Moment. In *The Book of Spells*. London: Methuen.

[4] Kinsella, W.P. (1983). The Bottle Queen. In *The Moccasin Telegraph*. Harmondsworth: Penguin.

[5] Engel, Marian. (1985). The Last Wife. In *The Tattooed Woman*. Harmondsworth: Penguin.

> I could feel the rough texture of the carpet last evening as I scrubbed at the spots where I'd sprayed too much cleaning fluid and become frustrated with the foaming suds I couldn't get rid of even with dilute vinegar.
>
> What our collective reading of *Burden of Desire* and our writing has done for me is make me much more sensitive to the words on the page and the associations they evoke. Although I don't have a story into which to fit these fragments of my life, I find myself storing them away for some future writing. Anna Marie said my comment that writers must be observers, must be watchers, had stuck with her. I can feel myself becoming a much more conscious watcher than I've ever been before (Judith Newman, Reflection: 11/20/92).

Not only are writers observers and watchers, action researchers must be too.

> Streib maintained his position, leaning against the doorjamb. "If you ask Lieutenant Leaphorn..., he'll tell you to look for clues. Then you ask him how you know it's a clue, and he'll give you a wise look."
>
> "I'm in favor of just looking," Leaphorn said. "You never know what you'll find."
>
> "That's Joe's theory," Streib said. "You don't look for anything in particular. You just look...." (p. 50)

Traditional research paradigms are so deeply ingrained that it's difficult to persuade people to just start in. "What am I looking for?" I can't answer that for you, I say. "Couldn't you just give me some topics to research?" But those would be my questions, they wouldn't be yours.

The teachers lack experiences with self-directed learning. Their academic backgrounds have consisted largely of memorizing texts and regurgitating information on assignments and exams; they have had little or no opportunity for defining and following through on self-initiated projects. While they actually know how to be self-directed in their practical everyday lives, they're dependent learners academically—they expect me to lay out everything for them in advance.

The feature of action research, therefore, which poses the biggest obstacle for people is dealing with the uncertainty inherent in the process.

You don't usually begin this kind of inquiry with a focused question. You don't know what matters, what to notice, or what to ignore. You don't know what information to collect, who to interview, where to look.

In the beginning, you just have to do a great deal of messing around. That makes teachers very uncomfortable. At first they think I don't know what I'm doing; they distrust me and are skeptical that anything worthwhile will ever come from what a number consider a useless exercise. I continue to be supportive, yet non-directive, because I know this is likely the first time in their academic experience that they have been asked to identify and pursue a problem for themselves. Their floundering used to make me uncomfortable, and I'd rush in with suggestions in an effort to help them over their discomfort. What I learned, however, was that I just made them more dependent on me. Now I wait out this period which, for some people, can take most of a term. However, I don't just sit back, arms folded, during this time; I ask questions, I respond to theirs, I suggest things to read, I set up opportunities for people to talk to one another about their inquiries, but I leave the identifying and shaping of an inquiry to each individual. Eventually, an interesting thing happens. Vaguely discernible patterns begin to emerge for a couple of the teachers; then others begin to catch on. The teachers find themselves asking more focused questions, having ideas about what to look for, seeing connections they haven't seen before. Their inquiries take form, and the teachers lose their sense of being at sea.

> He had found nothing that provoked interest except some shavings from a wood much heavier and darker than the oak, fir, and pine that almost everyone seemed to be using. Nor did it match the various half-finished tables, benches, table-lamp bases, rolling pins, and kitchen shelves racked in the workshop storeroom. Leaphorn put a sample of it in an envelope and into his pocket. Later he would find someone to explain it. Or perhaps he would simply forget it. It had more relevance to his personal curiosity than to this homicide investigation. (p. 152)

There can be all kinds of evidence accumulated during an action research inquiry—artifacts like school and class handouts, descriptions of assignments, worksheets, students' work samples, memos, school announcements, notes to parents, class publications, photographs, audiotaped interviews, videotaped sessions, transcriptions of the tapes, journals, portfolios, correspondence with and among students and teachers, curriculum guidelines and other policy documents, government announcements, newspaper clippings, and on and on. Like Leaphorn, action researchers are curious, constantly alert for anomalies. They collect evidence even though they may have no idea at the time what insights any particular artifact may afford. The trick here is to make the familiar and routine, which are largely invisible, visible. I repeatedly say to the graduate students, "Our object in the beginning is to make our professional practice problematic." We do that, in part, by looking at what's commonplace within our working environment and attempting to see it with new eyes.

However, in and of themselves the artifacts we accumulate are merely supporting data. The focal evidence consists of our written reflections, our questions, our interpretations of the artifacts, our musings about what's going on, our correspondence with ourselves which tracks our changing understanding of our practice-in-action.

> "You know Streib already searched this place," Toddy said. "I don't think he found anything interesting."
> "He didn't know what to look for," Leaphorn said.
> Toddy suppressed a grin and restored his expression almost to neutral. "That's supposed to be better, isn't it? Didn't I hear somebody saying that just a little while back? 'If you know what you're looking for, then you look for something specific and you don't see something that might be important.' Somebody was saying that."
> "Well," Leaphorn said, grinning himself.... "But this time we're a little wiser. We know that Dorsey made an ebony cane....Let's forget that stuff somebody told you and look for anything that would tell us who he made that cane for." (p. 221)

As an inquiry unfolds you become more focused about what you're noticing and recording. You begin having specific questions which drive the inquiry; it becomes necessary to revisit situations, this time with a more discerning eye. A tension starts developing between the evidence you've accumulated and what's still puzzling.

❖

Reading in the professional literature and thinking with the authors now takes on a new purpose. As Gordon Wells (1994) explains:

> There comes a point…when the teacher-researcher needs to read about other people's research and about the theories they have used to interpret their data.…Now, those books and articles, that before seemed so remote and irrelevant, suddenly take on a completely different significance. No longer on the receiving end of a transmission line, the teacher-researcher is able to engage with the text with a purpose that makes the reading into a dialogue between fellow researchers. (p. 31)

This is often the point when the tensions of teaching emerge. The teachers begin to see beyond the narrow frame of the specifics of teaching to a wider political landscape. They begin to wonder about issues of power and control, about gender, class, and race, about censorship, systemic constraints, resistance—students' resistance as well as their own—the impact of conflicting theoretical orientations, and accountability. They start to examine the attacks from outside, from other teachers, administration, parents, business, government, the media, and wonder what these attacks have to do with them personally. They start to develop an awareness of the complexities of teaching and learning.

The teachers' inquiries shift focus. I help them revisit their worksite, I encourage them to re-examine what they've collected and written, I suggest authors they might want to think with, and we talk with one another. It's at this juncture that people begin examining their assumptions.

How testing damages students is an issue of great concern to me. I wrote yesterday about how Chip refused to go along with the reading tests. I recognize that to a great extent I spent the last school year trying to "correct" his "deficits" rather than supporting him by building on his strengths. Why did I persist with practices I could see weren't helping him? More important, I need to focus on what I should do in the future. (Marlene Chase, Reflection: 7/18/91)

"You know," Blizzard said. "I think maybe all three of us are in the same boat I was in at that *Cheyenne Autumn* movie the other night. I couldn't understand

why all the Navajos were hooting and blowing their
car horns. Different culture. Different perceptions....
Different value systems, you know. Hard for us
outsiders to comprehend." (p. 263)

The politics of schools and schooling emerges. The teachers begin
asking a new kind of question. It's as if they discover themselves really to
be outsiders with a different culture, different perceptions and values.
They struggle to comprehend schools in a completely new way.

> Why are the dominating sides of literacy, teaching, and
> schooling more often practiced than the liberating
> sides?
> Why is it that despite the rhetoric that education is the
> backbone of democracy that participants in schooling
> have so little voice in matters of consequence in the
> classroom?
> Why are they so unfree?
> Who is really served by the current organization and
> practice of schools?
> How can the liberating sides of literacy, teaching, and
> schooling be realized? (Shannon, 1992: p. 2-3)

I encourage the teachers to situate their own experiences within a
broader analysis of institutional structures and change. I nudge them to
look and listen beyond the pervasive staffroom complaining to attempt to
understand the anxiety and anger rampant among teachers. I ask questions
that I hope will lead people to think about their own feelings of being
threatened, intimidated, confused, and powerless.

> It's hard to change when the people around you expect you to
> believe as they do. We all need to think about our personal
> alienation—the kind that Harman and Edelsky (1989) raise—when
> we do anything that's the least bit different from the others on
> staff. We don't have to say anything critical—the very fact that
> we've done something different draws attention to us and implicitly
> acts as a challenge to everyone else. Here's where personal beliefs
> come in, here's where an understanding of the politics of change
> helps. We have to understand that the moment we act rather than
> comply we separate ourselves from the group. So making changes,
> operating from a different theoretical perspective, is not something

to be undertaken lightly. We have to realize there will be consequences—with students, with parents, with colleagues, perhaps even with family, as many people have experienced. In what ways have you encountered the alienating affects of attempting to change? (Judith Newman, Reflection: 11/14/94).

The teachers start to identify the tensions of teaching as political. They examine existing power relationships and begin challenging them. They begin contemplating a different kind of classroom—one in which teachers share power with students. They challenge the labeling and categorizing of students with learning problems. They examine accountability issues and ask who is served by the drive for standardized testing. They wonder about fiscal constraints and the climate of attack in which they work. This is the beginning of an overt political analysis of teaching and schooling. Slowly the teachers build an understanding of the issues and a language for making political arguments.

> Leaphorn was saying something about linkages.
> "Hey," Chee said, loudly. He got down from the tail-gate and stood facing Leaphorn....
> Leaphorn looked at him waiting.
> "Just a second," Chee said, thinking it through. "I'm beginning to see why you want all those details in your reports." (p. 290)
> Leaphorn was smiling slightly now. ..."but we still have problems."
> "I know it," Chee said. "...I didn't put anything about Applebee in my report."
> "Well, there was no reason to do that," Leaphorn said. "...Now we see it matters. Can you think of anything else that might matter, knowing what we know now?" (p. 291)

In contrast with quantitative methodologies where you collect data and then write up findings, in action research writing is at the core of the research enterprise. It's through writing that the stories and the connections which link them begin to emerge. Often the tensions of teaching only take shape during writing. Consequently there's no advantage to postponing writing until you think you have all the data you need. That's what many budding teacher researchers attempt to do, but because writing is the principle research tool, it's advisable to begin writing as quickly as possible.

If you think getting the teachers to keep a detailed running record is difficult, try getting them to start writing! All of their misconceptions about writing kick in and avoidance is rampant. "How can I begin if I don't know the outcome?" Just start by fleshing out one story, I say. "Which story should I begin with?" Whichever one feels right; whichever calls to you. "But I have no beginning." Don't worry about that, just start.

I point out parallels with detecting—"I didn't put in anything about Applebee in my report," Chee says, to which Leaphorn replies, "Now we see it matters." The same is true of understanding and writing up action research. You begin drafting with the stories you have. It's the writing itself that raises more questions and sends you back again and again to the worksite and to the professional research literature. The writing and the inquiry are in continual conversation. You discover through writing why "you want all those details in your reports." Your observing, recording, and reflecting become more refined, more focused; your writing expands; the interpretations become more articulate, more comprehensive. "Can we think of anything else that might matter, knowing what we now know?"

> Joe Leaphorn sat in the chair...and considered....As he was thinking... Leaphorn's lifelong Navajo conditioning to look for harmony in all things bore fruit. Abruptly, he saw the connections, how it had happened, and why it had happened. (p. 295)

If only the insights from an action research project could fall into place so readily! Unfortunately an inquiry doesn't usually deal with a single circumscribed event in the way a homicide investigation does. Leaphorn's successful investigation will lead to the identification of a murderer. Rarely does an explanation for action research stories pop into mind this neatly; although I have had the experience of sudden insight into some aspect of my teaching while I'm reading in the professional literature (even sometimes while reading a mystery). Other teachers have, too.

> The first of Cuban's (1984) reasons why schools have remained virtually unchanged really touched home. I could see myself caught up in the first reason: school is a means of social control and sorting. I was supervised by my VP this term, and what he was most concerned about was students' obedience and my control or, in his eyes, my lack of it. He wrote in the supervision report that I should never proceed to give directions unless I

have the attention of all the students. What he was referring to was a split-second decision I happened to make while he was present in the class. I had decided to take the risk and just be myself during that supervision rather than orchestrating the kind of performance I thought he might want to see. I had done a math patterning mini-lesson where I had the complete attention of the class. The kids were now off to do some independent follow-up on their own when I thought of something else to tell them. I realized, however, when I tried getting their attention and didn't succeed, that they were now engrossed with what they were doing. I could have insisted on their attention and made them listen to me, but in a successful moment of being a reflective practitioner I decided to let go, realizing that it was something they would probably figure out on their own if I gave them the chance. And where did that decision get me? A written demerit. All over such a momentary interval of time. It made me see clearly why schools are so slow to change. Although I had the self-confidence not to be crushed by this administrator's lack of understanding of, or appreciation for, what I was trying to do, my gut feeling is to play it safe next time—to orchestrate what he wants to see: the teacher in uncontested control. Sadly, I can now see where a lot of teacher conformity comes from (from Newman, 1991: p. 235).

He had no evidence and no way he could think of to get any. Maybe it would surface, maybe it wouldn't. But Leaphorn wanted to understand it. So he sat in Dorsey's chair…and worked out how it had probably happened. (p. 298)

With his understanding of the crime, Leaphorn is able to find evidence to bring the case to closure. The same obtains for the action researcher. As the tensions of teaching become more fully understood and articulated, the inquiry comes to a close. The teachers are changed by the experience. They have become more astute about the political forces which act on them. They discover they have a choice—to comply with the status quo of schools or to challenge the constraints which impact on them and their students.

The point of engaging in action research, in my estimation, is to help me uncover my assumptions and to examine my instructional practices. It's this reflection, this turning the gaze on myself, that characterizes practice-as-inquiry. As Schön argues (1983):

> When a practitioner becomes a researcher into his own practice, he engages in a continuing process of self-education....When she functions as a researcher-in-practice, the practice itself is a source of renewal. (p. 299)

The outcome of such self-education is recognizing the tensions, conflicts, and contradictions operating within my practice as well as in schools and school systems. But recognizing inconsistency isn't the end of practice-as-inquiry. As I learn to detect disparities between my practice and theory, I need to take action; I need to change what I do.

Engaging in action research, in practice-as-inquiry, is uncomfortable and sometimes dangerous. It forces me to confront myself. It makes me vulnerable to colleagues and administrators who don't see inquiry into practice as having any value— "You call that research?"—who feel attacked by the implications of what I learn about learning and teaching, who are threatened by my questions which challenge the status quo.

Action research allows us to pose some important questions, it invites us to see contradictions in our own beliefs and practices, it affords insight into the large political issues and, most important, it challenges us to change.

❖

Bateson, Gregory. (1978). The Pattern which Connects. *The CoEvolution Quarterly*, Summer, 5-17.

Bissex, Glenda. (1988). On Learning and Not Learning from Teaching. *Language Arts*, 65: 771-775.

Burton, Frederick R. (1986). A Teacher's Conception of the Action Research Process. *Language Arts*, 63(7): 718-723.

Carr, W. (1989). Action Research: Ten Years On. *Journal of Curriculum Studies*, 21(1): 85-90.

Cochran-Smith, Marilyn and Susan Lytle. (1993). *Inside/Outside: Teacher Research and Knowledge*. New York: Teachers College Press.

Connelly, Michael and D. Jean Clandinin. (1988). *Teachers as Curriculum Planners: Narratives of Experience.* New York: Teachers College Press.

Conroy, Frank. (1991). Think About It: Ways We Know, and Don't. *Harper's Magazine,* November: 68-70.

Cuban, Larry. (1984). *How Teachers Taught: Constancy and Change in American Classrooms, 1890-1980.* New York, Longman.

Duckworth, Eleanor. (1987). Teaching as Research. In *The Having of Wonderful Ideas.* New York: Teachers College Press: 122-145.

Fleischer, Cathy. (1994). Researching Teacher-Research: A Practitioner's Retrospective. *English Education,* 26(2): 86-124.

Harman, Susan and Carole Edelsky. (1989). The Risks of Whole Language Literacy: Alienation and Connection. *Language Arts,* 66(4): 392-406.

Kutz, Eleanor. (1992). Teacher Research: Myths and Realities. *Language Arts,* 69: 193-197.

Newman, Judith M. (1987). Learning to Teach by Uncovering Our Assumptions. *Language Arts,* 64(7): 727-737.

Newman, Judith M. (1991). *Interwoven Conversations: Learning and Teaching Through Critical Reflection.* Toronto: OISE Press.

North, Stephen. (1987). *The Making of Knowledge in Composition.* Portsmouth, NH: Boynton/Cook.

Richardson, Virginia. (1994). Conducting Research on Practice. *Educational Researcher,* 23 (June-July): 5-10.

Ruddock, J. and Hopkins, D. (1985). *Research as a Basis of Teaching: Readings from the Work of Lawrence Stenhouse.* Oxford: Heinemann Educational Books.

Schön, Donald. (1983). *The Reflective Practitioner.* New York: Basic Books.

Schön, Donald. (1987). *Educating the Reflective Practitioner.* San Francisco: Jossey-Bass Publishers.

Shannon, Patrick. (1992). Why become Political? In Patrick Shannon (Ed.), *Becoming Political:* 1-11. Portsmouth, NH: Heinemann Educational Books.

Smith, Frank. (1975). *Comprehension and Learning.* New York: Holt Rinehart & Winston.

Spencer, Margaret. (1987). Text in Hand: Explorations in the Networking of Literacy and Literature or New Literacies, New Texts, Old Teachers. Paper presented at the 5th Invitation Riverina Literacy Centre Conference, Wagga Wagga, NSW, 20-22 August, 1987.

Wells, Gordon. (1994). *Changing Schools from Within.* Toronto: OISE Press.

Winter, Richard. (1986). Fictional-Critical Writing: An Approach to Case Study Research by Practitioners. *Cambridge Journal of Education,* 16: 175-182.

Winter, Richard. (1987). *Action Research and the Nature of Social Inquiry: Professional Innovation and Educational Work.* Averbury, England: Aldershot.

PART ONE

RESEARCHING
SELF

Teacher/action research is about
discovering ourselves, about
uncovering our assumptions—
assumptions about learning, about
teaching, about values and beliefs.

An important first step, therefore, in
becoming a teacher/action researcher
is to enter into an exploration of how
we compose our own practice. What
beliefs underlie what we choose to
do in the classroom? What internal
and external constraints affect the
decisions we make? What counts as
"data"? What might we do differently?

Wendy Peters in THROUGH THE LOOKING-
GLASS attempts to reveal her beliefs
about learning by looking at herself as
a graduate student. Her purpose is to
understand more fully what drives
what she does as a music teacher.

Janie McTavish in JOURNAL WRITING
AND ALIENATION uses collaborative
journal writing with a colleague
to uncover concerns and questions
about her teaching.

Susan Wastie in REFLECTION, PAIN AND WONDERFUL IDEAS examines what happens when she decides to learn how to roller-blade and uses this experience to reflect on her work as a speech pathologist.

Finally, in EXPERIENCE, Patty Kimpton, a B.Ed. student, offers a fictionalized account in which she juxtaposes a couple of experiences, one in school and one at home, which help her think about learning in new ways.

Through the Looking-Glass

Wendy Peters

This Side of the Looking-glass: Commonsense

In the fall of 1994 I took a leap of faith and enrolled in my first graduate courses in Education. Why a leap of faith? Two reasons, really. The first grew out of my undergraduate experience—full-time studies and full-time career as a music teacher provided a rich palette of enterprises to keep in motion. When the academic work was meaningful, when I was finding connections to my reality as a musician and music educator, keeping all of the balls in the air was somehow manageable. When the work lacked meaning, however, as was increasingly the case as I moved out of elective and into compulsory coursework, preventing the routine from dissolving into chaos became an exercise in endurance of both mind and spirit.

Although my original intent had been to complete an integrated B.Mus./B.Ed. degree, my disillusionment with the program became such that I decided to complete only the B.Mus. and make a beeline for what I hoped would be the greener pastures of graduate study. It was my fervent hope that the graduate experience would facilitate a move beyond the superficial, allowing me to delve into ideas which would have the power to inform my practice—deep, guiding principles which would transcend educational fads and fancies.

The second reason that my enrollment in graduate study seemed so much a leap of faith involved my concern that my background, both as a B.Mus. student and as a private music educator, might not prove sufficient for the rigors of the M.Ed. program. I suspected that most if not all of my classmates would have teaching certificates and considerable public school experience, and I couldn't help but wonder if, beside them, I would be found lacking in some fundamental way. And so it was with both hope and trepidation that I forged ahead.

Of the courses in which I enrolled, it was Action Research: Educating as Inquiry which initially intrigued me most. I knew nothing about Judith Newman personally or professionally, and even less about action research, but the course had been suggested to me by someone I respect a great deal. I understood from this person that Judith had a reputation as an excellent educator who possessed a unique perspective and whose approach was often judged unusual by conventional standards. That was enough recommendation for me—a Mennonite by accident of birth, I had had just about enough of conventional thinking.

The experience of the first class quieted my fears and lent credence to my hopes. I went home feeling exhilarated. Anxious to not let any aspect of the experience escape, I opened my course journal that very evening by recording those ideas introduced in class which I found most striking. In brackets after each I recorded my own initial reaction. Reading through these reactions now, several months after the fact, I recognize those which are embarrassingly misguided, those which ultimately proved prophetic, and at least one which hints at the stance with which I entered the course:

> Point 2. Teaching is inquiry. [Isn't this the foundation upon which the evolution of Piano Plus* is based?] (Wendy Peters, Reflection: 9/15/97)

My reaction to the statement "teaching is inquiry," as brief as it is, conveys a wealth of meaning to me now that was not apparent when I so earnestly penned it. It reveals something of my assumptions concerning the nature of teaching and, indirectly, my assumptions concerning the nature of learning. And these assumptions placed me squarely on the commonsense side of the looking-glass. But with that I'm getting ahead of myself.

The fall of 1994 marked my entrance to graduate studies and ushered in my ninth year of teaching. I had devoted the previous eight of those years to the business of developing the ultimate approach to the teaching of music. While this approach relied to some extent on the philosophy of what I call sound before symbol, or in other words and very broadly, musical experience preceding and facilitating musical literacy, it relied most heavily

---

* *Piano Plus* is the name of the private music education enterprise created and directed by a colleague and me which seeks a synthesis between piano study and the philosophy associated with the Orff-Schulwerk approach to music.

on what John Mayher (1990) would surely describe as an optimum skill sequence:

> ...in the commonsense view...complex processes and abilities are to be understood as consisting of a set of simple skills which can be separately mastered. This idea in turn gives rise to the notion that some skills are basic, and to the belief that the way to acquire the complex wholes is to master the simpler parts and then put the whole thing together.
>
> It seems so completely commonsensical to proceed in this bottom-up direction when learning to read or write or play the piano...that the normal patterns of schooling have consistently been organized to reflect such sequences. Indeed, the only major debates that have tended to occur about how to do this most effectively have been about what the optimum skill sequence is and when it should be begun, and not about whether or not such a sequence is the best characterization of the learning processes involved. (Mayher 1990: 50-51)

My original journal reference to the "evolution" of Piano Plus seems false and misleading now as I reflect upon how this so-called "evolution" manifested itself, namely, in changes and modifications to the sequence and therefore the curriculum, as a result of my relentless pursuit of the optimization of both. That's not to say that those eight years did not see changes in my philosophy as well; it's just that in the absence of any explicit learning theory, these changes represented blind endeavors whose effectiveness were limited at best. All good intentions aside, the nature of my pursuit confirms that I was, as Mayher would say, a commonsense teacher, believing, at least implicitly, that students learn what teachers teach.

Further proof that my stance was firmly rooted on the commonsense side of the looking-glass was that I had little argument with the commonsense metaphors for learning:

> ...[the] learner as empty vessel to be filled with the content of education, the learner as maze runner who needs to master the basics of complex processes by learning them separately and in an appropriate sequence, the learner as sponge who absorbs information and squeezes it back out when appropriate, and the learner who practices through drills to develop good habits and avoid bad ones. (Mayher 1990: 50)

My quest in search of the ultimate curriculum was beset by the usual aggravations, but none as persistent as the issue of congruence between the prescribed sequence of skills as laid out in the Piano Plus curriculum and the piano materials available on the market to support this curriculum. The further refined the sequence became, the less useful these externally produced materials were. I often complained that the authors of these materials lacked the insight I had developed about sequencing. And no wonder; their books frequently placed concepts in an incorrect order. This meant a great deal of flipping around—very messy! It would have been so much more satisfying to assign pages in the order in which they appeared in the book.

Especially irritating was that some concepts were presented poorly and others omitted altogether. Finally, exasperated with how poorly these materials conformed to my optimum skill sequence (I used say, "How poorly they met the students' needs"), and with my trusty curriculum as guide, I began to develop my own piano repertoire and auxiliary exercises. I settled happily into my task, secure in the knowledge that the full realization of this venture was surely destined to be one of the key achievements of my career. My plan was simple, I would create compositions and exercises, assign them, then rate their success and make modifications based on student performance and comments.

I was knee-deep in this labour of love when I attended that first class with Judith. When I heard her speak of teacher research and action inquiry, my every experience in developing, first the curriculum and then the repertoire of pieces, quivered in response. "Yes!" I thought exuberantly, "teaching is research!" When Judith spoke of gathering data, my thoughts leapt to the notes I had been keeping on the effectiveness of the compositions, and when she spoke of questions arising from the data, I was reminded of the myriad of questions my notes had produced. I had literally hundreds of questions. It seemed to me that I was already ahead of the game. It seemed to me that I was already a teacher researcher. This should have made me suspicious, I know.

A few weeks later Judith opened class with an invitation to talk to her about the direction we each saw ourselves heading in terms of defining an inquiry. I recall speaking about the process of creating the ultimate repertoire series. I don't remember the exact words I used to describe my venture, nor do I remember Judith's exact response. I do know, however, that in the conversation which ensued, "yes, but" played a prominent role. Judith mentions this subtle form of resistance in her book *Interwoven Conversations* (Newman, 1991). I came across this passage quite by accident some time after this conversation had taken place and was immediately assaulted by a keen sense of *déjà vu*. As I read, the memory of that conversation sprang unbidden to mind, and I knew without a doubt that my every response to Judith that day had been made in the spirit of "yes, but...". Imbedded in Judith's questions to me was a challenge to several firmly held beliefs, and I responded by defending my curriculum and repertoire project. In doing so, however, I became aware of a tension between the language I used to describe my inquiry and the language the other members of the class used to describe theirs. While they wrestled with the articulation of the seemingly weighty questions which were emerging from their data, I piled my questions effortlessly in great heaps. I began to sense that my questions were common and shallow beside the mystery and depth of theirs.

And then it hit me: my questions were all comfortably within reach of answers. Where the other members of the class were expressing concern that they might not be able to resolve their questions satisfactorily, I felt equal to the task of answering every single one of my own. With this realization, dissatisfaction replaced my former exuberance. There was something fundamentally wrong with my questions, but what?

And so began the quest for questions of a different hue. I wasn't entirely without a clue about where to start looking; I sensed that these new questions could be drawn, perhaps even had to be drawn, from the same data as the first—the same notes, the same teaching experiences. My position on the commonsense side of the looking-glass had not changed, but the search for a different vantage point from which to view my data was a step in the right direction—a step closer to the one which would carry me through the looking-glass.

Through the Looking-glass

The looking-glass represents whatever assumptions we hold that prevent us from framing a problem differently, from viewing the same situation from a different perspective. The shift in focus which allows us to see our assumptions with new eyes is the very act that facilitates our ability to see past the assumptions, our ability to step through the glass, as it were. Ultimately I did this with as little fanfare as did Alice in her adventure. Just as she leaned into the reflection and felt its give, so did I relax into my assumptions, admitting for the first time the possibility that every last one of them could be open to revision. This new openness to possibility is what I think carried me through to the other side.

The place I stepped into was not so unlike the one I had left. The differences were there, but they were subtle. And when I cast my eyes upon my data from this new vantage point, I began to make out the shadowy outlines of questions which seemed at once new and yet familiar. I suspected that in that familiarity lay an awareness of the existence of questions which had been with me all along, but on a level far enough removed from conscious thought as not to disturb my comfortable stance on the commonsense side of the looking-glass.

Making out the questions was not unlike trying to see in the dark. When the lights first go out, you're blind as a bat. Gradually, however, as your eyes become accustomed to the new level of light, you begin to make out more until you can see quite clearly. At first the questions were tentative, but as I became accustomed to my new surroundings they emerged faster and surer: Why do some students seem to instinctively know what it means to "add expression" to a piece, and can do it, while others do not and can not? Why do students approach the study of a piece from a technical standpoint rather than a musical standpoint? How does the environment I create contribute to this? Do students entering the Piano Plus program see the "big picture" of being a musician? How does the student's perception or lack thereof of the big picture, or "whole building" as Peter Elbow (1976) would say, affect what and how they will learn? And in a similar vein, what do students entering the program expect to be able to do, and how does this affect what and how they will learn?

As I pondered these new questions, I was struck by a feeling of helplessness—I felt unequal to the task of answering them. These were the kinds of questions world-renowned experts in my field might tackle, but not me. It was easier to imagine that the ability to resolve these questions resided somewhere else. I felt daunted, but I rejoiced in this feeling, knowing that it was proof that I had stepped through the looking-glass. When the first flush of success faded, however, I was left with the realization that while I had accomplished what I had initially set out to do, there were more challenges ahead of me; in particular was the problem of naming the two sides of the glass. The fundamental difference between them and, therefore, the two sets of questions remained a mystery to me, and as long as this were to remain so, I suspected I would not be able to pass through the glass at will.

The Other Side of the Looking-glass: Uncommon Sense

John Mayher (1990) has a name for the other side of the looking-glass, the side opposite commonsense—he calls it *uncommon sense*. He believes that uncommon sense represents a different perspective to the one prevalently held by educators today, and lists the keystones of this view as

> ...learners going beyond the information given; language being learned in use; the power of narrative in learning, in memory, and in development; the normally creative use of language; and a focus on learning not teaching. (Mayher 1990: 3)

I believe it is the educational communities' tendency to focus on teaching rather than learning that is largely responsible for trapping so many on the commonsense side of the looking-glass. The way through to the uncommonsense side lies in a shift in focus away from teaching to learning. My experience suggests that such a shift requires not only a re-examination of assumptions but also considerable reflection upon the very nature of learning. For me, that meant having to explore my own stories as a learner.

From the outset of the course I was engaged, as were the other members of the class, in a program of reading drawn largely from literature exploring action research; specifically the theoretical and philosophical foundations upon which it rests. A vital component of this exploration included a written exploration of reaction and reflection—in short, a journal. The first article that the class was asked to read and respond to was Judith's own *Learning to Teach by Uncovering Our Assumptions* (Newman, 1987). I understood some of what the article tries to convey, but really struggled with the theoretical models of transmission and interpretation which Judith lays out mid-way through the piece. Actually, I understood the transmission model all too well—it was the interpretive model which I just couldn't seem to wrap my head around.

My attention was quickly diverted away from this first article and its challenges, however, by the second, from Herbert Kohl's *I Won't Learn from You* (Kohl, 1994). In it, Kohl discusses the phenomenon he calls "not learning" or "willed refusal to learn" (Kohl, 1994: p.2) and how it is so often mistaken for failure or inability to learn. The ideas advanced in this article resonated with my own learning experiences with an intensity that took me by surprise and nudged me into awareness of that curiously empty space where it had always seemed my school memories should have been. The paucity of high school memories seemed especially conspicuous. Reading Kohl's text solved the riddle of this space, revealing it for the first time. It wasn't really empty after all, it just had seemed so for want of a name. For the first time since I began my course journal, my pen moved across the page in steady, unceasing rhythm, the only struggle that of keeping up with the impressions tumbling out of memory:

> I could feel a certain resonance when Kohl described "not-learning" students as those who "had consciously placed themselves outside the entire system that was trying to coerce or seduce them into learning..." and who "were engaged in a struggle of wills with authority..." (Kohl, 1994: 7). While reading, I began to drift back in memory to high school. I was that student who had placed herself outside of the system and defied authority. I too had not believed that I was a failure or inferior to the students who were conforming and doing well. (Wendy Peters, Reflection: 11/12/94)

This realization focused my attention for the first time squarely on myself in the role of learner. This sudden shift in gaze helped me to think differently about the learners in my classroom, and, in doing so, I became suddenly aware of the contradiction between my own experiences as a learner and the experiences I was initiating for them. It came as quite a shock to realize that my actions were little or no different from those of the teachers who unwittingly contributed to my experiences of "not learning," and I was jolted into an awareness of a whole set of assumptions implicit in my actions as a teacher, the majority of which lay unexamined. It was clear in that instant that I needed to determine what these were and examine them closely. This seemed an overwhelming task—I hardly knew where to start.

As it turned out, however, it wasn't really a matter of starting but of continuing—continuing to read, respond, look for connections, reflect, and above all, sustain momentum. And so, with no particular plan in mind, and left unfettered, my writing eventually began to find its own meaning, its own focus: me the learner instead of me the teacher.

Initially I responded to this turn of events with an uneasy feeling of guilt. Everyone else in the course was engaged in the serious and disciplined business of conducting a classroom-based inquiry while I was indulging in a love affair with myself. How embarrassing to be so obviously self-absorbed. I apologized for it, intended to change it, even tried to change it, but ultimately proved unable to do so. Instead, I gave in. I abandoned myself to myself, and with this act felt as though I could not have taken up a position any further from my classroom and my practice.

As the love affair progressed, I became particularly fascinated by the process I went through in order to be able to truly own an idea, discover its "shape." For weeks I felt adrift in a sea of only quasi-related bits of information and ideas, struggling to wrest a "shape," any shape, from the chaos of my thoughts. When these thoughts did finally coalesce, allowing the first connection between my learning stories and my search for a different perspective which sparked that step through the looking-glass, I was thrilled. Plunging headlong into the next challenge, that of naming the two sides, catapulted me back into chaotic thought patterns, but with an interesting result:

> Last week's response felt good, perhaps because it represented a culmination of sorts, the making sense of seemingly random bits of thought, essentially a shape revealed.... This week, however, as I look under different rocks, collect new thoughts, and begin to wrestle with them in the attempt to find connections and, therefore, shape, I am again in a state of dissonance, of tension, with nothing whole to offer. I note with interest that this does not feel as frustrating as it has in the past, and I wonder if perhaps I am coming to understand, and perhaps trust, the process by which I learn. (Wendy Peters, Reflection: 1/18/95)

In rereading this passage in my journal I was struck by the implications of this last statement. The idea that I might not have to remain a mystery to myself was a powerful one. This statement also caught Judith's attention. To it she responded with the comment, "Sounds like you are," and then the question, "Why is that?" This question proved critical to my ability to step back and assume a more global view of the situation, to ask, "What's going on here?" What conditions were responsible for the unique, intense learning experience in which I was engaged? Initially I settled on risk-taking as my answer, and from there it was only a hop, skip, and jump to reflection on the nature of learning itself:

> ...as I contemplated Judith's question yet once again, it began to dawn on me that the discoveries I was making concerning my personal learning style were made as a result of having taken

certain risks—risks that I wouldn't normally have taken in my approach to thinking/writing/reading in relationship to a course. These risks in turn yielded (and continue to yield) discoveries and insights on a scale and of a quality that I had (have) not previously experienced.... This beginning of an answer [referring to risk] has lead me to reflect upon the very nature of learning. It seems to me that learning, like music, cannot be experienced in any concrete form. Its essence cannot be captured on the printed page or expressed by a number. Like music, learning consists of a series of events which unfold (possessed of movement) over time—a process. (Wendy Peters, Reflection: 1/25/95)

With these thoughts fresh in my mind, I turned to my reading for the week, a chapter from Garth Boomer's *Negotiating the Curriculum* (Boomer, 1982), ready for the first time to hear a message that had surely been embedded in most, if not all, of the reading in which I had thus far been engaged. Early in the chapter, Boomer contemplates the extent to which Australian teachers and departmental curriculum statements address themselves to aspects of learning theory:

> Few departmental statements addressed learning theory. Certainly teaching theory abounded, either implicitly or explicitly, and it was possible to argue that, however tenuously, teaching theory must be based on some notion of how people learn. However, our team in South Australia concluded, on the basis of widespread inquiry, that few teachers could articulate what they assumed about learning. By having a learning theory... I mean being able to state one's own best-educated understanding as to how people come to internalize new information or to perform new operations.... Imagine education-department curriculum guides, with no explicit learning theory, being taken by teachers with no explicit learning theory and turned into lessons for children who are not told the learning theory. Some of the best of these children then graduate to become teachers. And so on. Isn't it about time that we all tried to articulate what is surely there behind every curriculum unit, every assignment, every examination? (Boomer, 1992: 5)

As I read, it all seemed to just fall into place, and I knew that I had at long last arrived at a naming:

> I just read Garth Boomer's *Negotiating the Curriculum*. What he
> had to say concerning teaching versus learning theory really turned
> some lights on for me, particularly as concerned my problem with
> the two question sets. I realized suddenly that the first set, the
> one with which I feel most comfortable, represents aspects of
> teaching theory, while the other set, the one with which I feel the
> least secure, represents aspects of learning theory. (Wendy Peters,
> Reflection: 2/7/95)

I had done it! In naming the fundamental difference between the two
sets of questions I had come to understand that the two sides of the looking-
glass represent teaching and learning, commonsense and uncommon sense.
At last I felt that I understood: learning and teaching may well be two sides
of the same coin, or the looking-glass, but the teaching stance assumes that
most if not all of the energy and impetus originates from the teaching, and
that is the fatal error. If it is as Frank Smith suggests, that "learning is what
the brain does naturally, continually," and that it is "only in artificially
contrived experimental settings or instructional situations that the brain
usually finds itself not learning..." (Smith, 1983, p. 101), then it is clear on
which side the energy and impetus reside. The implications in Smith's
statements are also clear: where there is life, there is, by definition, learners
and learning. Teachers, of the type implicit in the notion of institutionalized
learning, on the other hand, are a relatively new phenomenon in the history
of the world. It is not ours to lead, but to follow. Understanding this, I felt it
possible that I would be able to step through the glass at will. Not always
easy, but possible.

A fitting conclusion to this story, bringing it, in a sense, full-circle, is
an excerpt drawn from the interim reflection I wrote just days later to mark
the half-way point of the course:

> This morning I turned to the first article I was asked to read for
> this course, Judith's *Learning to Teach by Uncovering Our
> Assumptions*, and my original reflections on it....Well, the "click" was
> almost audible when I realized that the section I had so wrestled
> with initially carried the subtitle, *A Learner-Centered Classroom*. I
> saw, in that split second, that all of my most profound struggles
> this term had really been with different shades of the same idea—
> coming to grips with the implications of teaching versus learning
> theory, with the transmission versus the interpretive models of
> teaching, with common versus uncommon sense. (Wendy Peters,
> Reflection: 3/1/95)

All roads, it seems, lead back to the two sides of the looking-glass and what separates them.

So What?

But there is a larger circle in which my story is situated—the one which begins and ends in the classroom—my classroom. The question which is most likely to set our feet on that path is "So what?" "So what?" asks what implications my newfound focus on learning will have. How will this shift in perspective change the way in which I interact with my students? How will it change the way in which I interact with my colleagues? With some surprise I realize that instead of "How will?" I must ask "How has?"

Even though throughout my quest to make sense of my own stories of learning I had felt at times that I had turned my back on my teaching, I realize that my students had not been as excluded as I initially assumed. In retrospect, I see that every change in my stance, however slight, effected a change in my teaching even though my gaze was focused elsewhere.

Accompanying the realization that I would have to make explicit the assumptions underlying my practice and lay them open to scrutiny was the realization that from this point on, everything associated with the Piano Plus curriculum was suspect. And so, rather early in the course and in the year, my pampered and fussed-over curriculum began to lose its power to shape the events in my classroom. My suspicion that it was largely ineffective was reinforced early in November when David, one of the most intensely engaged and obviously gifted students in my level 5 class, interrupted my lesson on advanced meters to ask a question. His question, addressing a concept which I considered to have been covered in level 1, stopped the lesson dead in its tracks. It showed me that David did not understand the basic underlying concept of simple meter necessary to reach an understanding of advanced meter. This incident does not represent an isolated or unique event my classroom. But rather than my usual commonsense response, the one which sought to fix David through judicious application of teaching theory, my burgeoning uncommon sense suggested that I seek to understand David and then let his learning guide the experience from there.

This incident proved critical in another way as well, it helped me think about the whole of my teaching in a new light. If David wasn't ready for this lesson, then who? If David didn't understand the basic underlying concepts of meter, then who? And more to the point, what were the students learning in my classroom? They clearly weren't learning the lessons I thought I had taught.

This bothered me considerably. Having to accept that the students weren't learning what I was teaching meant that I would have to admit that my optimum skill sequence was not doing the job I claimed it did, presumably never had. That I had been nursing and championing this approach for nine years, it is not easy to admit to being wrong. But it was too late to turn back—I had become sensitized to the phenomenon of students not learning what I was teaching, and the more I probed, the more evidence I found among my students that this was indeed the case. And yet, they were all functioning as musicians. The more I thought about this, the more bemused and out-of-control of the situation I felt. There must have been something in my instruction which they found useful, or they couldn't function as musicians. I was stumped—how did my students decide what to keep and what to throw away? Eventually my confusion and panic settled into a shape—an answer with meaning at its core. John Mayher writes about the role meaning plays in learning: "The learning itself may be tacit or unconscious, but the motivation for performing the tasks which will lead to learning has to be a sense of personal meaningfulness for the learner" (Mayher, 1990: 104).

Of course! I myself am proof of this. How many times have I said that I never truly understood many of the theoretical concepts underlying musical composition until I had to teach them to others. Where was my mind when I uttered these words? If only I had really listened to what I was saying, which was essentially that a vast portion of what I was laboring to teach my students was as useless to me in practice (still is, for the most part) as it clearly was for them.

This realization wiped out what was left of my curriculum as surely as if it had never existed. But it wiped out more than that; it wiped out most of everything I thought I knew about what it means to be a musician or to be a music teacher. This, in some ways, has paralyzed me as a teacher. Until I discover those skills which do have meaning, what can I "teach" in my classroom? In my efforts to find this out, I give each concept the litmus test of student meaningfulness. If it doesn't pass, out it goes. I've been ruthless—there hasn't been much I've felt justified in keeping. Which brings me to something else that has been largely wiped out for me— inclusion and acceptance by my colleagues. The practice of testing all concepts for learner meaningfulness has placed me well outside the boundaries of even my most liberal-minded colleagues. I understand. With what I have thrown out this year, I would have wiped out most of their positions as they know them. I hasten to stress those last four words, however, and what they imply. It is not the ends we as music educators seek that need to be altered so much as the means by which we strive to achieve them.

My paralysis extends beyond the "what" and "why" to include even the "how." How do I present those skills and concepts I have decided to include this year? Just as my curriculum became suspect, so too have the behaviors that constitute my teaching rituals. Here is where my experience as a learner in Judith's course comes into play in the larger context. By focusing not on my experience, but on the ways in which Judith supported and sustained my learning, I begin to imagine how I might do the same for my students. This inevitably leads me back to risk and the role I believe it plays in learning, but it also leads me to dig even deeper: What conditions made it possible for me to assume such risks? I believe the answer lies in the beliefs upon which enterprises are based. Judith discusses these early in *Interwoven Conversations*: "...learning is collaborative, universal, and incidental... Frank Smith (1988) describes learning situations based on these beliefs as enterprises" (Newman, 1991: 15).

Frank Smith identifies the four main criteria that characterize an enterprise as no grades, no restrictions, no coercion, and no status. Judith expands on the nature of enterprises when she describes what she attempts to do in each teaching/learning venture which she heads up:

> ...teach a group of teachers in exactly the same way as I'd teach five-year-olds—in a collaborative learning classroom, where the motivation for learning comes from the learners, where students take risks and are able to build on their existing strategies, where learning is largely incidental (the result of doing something that really interests the students; in a situation where there is no fear of being graded, constrained by a minimum of restrictions, where no one is being coerced into complying with teacher demands but encouraged to find her own way, where everyone is a learner and everyone is a teacher. (Newman, 1991: 17)

Yes! This is exactly what Judith accomplished in the action research course in which I was a participant, and once again I can cite my own learning experience as proof. The conditions Judith sets out are exactly those which facilitated what I consider to be the most extraordinary learning experience of my life.

So, how will this experience change the way in which I will interact with my students? I will strive in every learning/teaching that I am involved in to initiate, support, and sustain the conditions which Judith outlines above, and in doing so, strive to lead from behind, allowing the learner to shape the experience. And how will it change the way in which I interact with my colleagues? This question represents even more of a challenge, for as John Mayher points out,

> To accomplish the changing of minds is a formidable thing to attempt. It is hardest of all with adults who have developed a repertoire of more or less successful strategies for interpreting the world and coping with its problems and don't want to be bothered reexamining them, much less changing them. I'm further handicapped by the fact that one of the cornerstones of my uncommonsense is that I know I can't tell, transmit, or teach anything about this directly, because my uncommon sense of learning denies the worth of such a procedure. (Mayher, 1990: 4)

Boomer, Garth. (1982). Negotiating the Curriculum. In Garth Boomer (Ed.), *Negotiating the Curriculum*. 123-132. Sydney: Ashton Scholastic.

Elbow, Peter. (1976). *Writing Without Teachers*. London: Oxford University Press.

Kohl, Herbert. (1994). *I Won't Learn From You*. New York: The New Press.

Mayher, John. (1990). *Uncommon Sense: Theoretical Practice in Language Education*. Portsmouth, NH: Boynton/Cook.

Newman, Judith M. (1987). Learning to Teach by Uncovering Our Assumptions. *Language Arts*, 64(7): 727-737.

Newman, Judith M. (1991). *Interwoven Conversations: Learning and Teaching Through Critical Reflection*. Toronto: OISE press.

Smith, Frank. (1983). Demonstrations, Engagement, and Sensitivity. In *Essays into Literacy*. Portsmouth, NH: Heinemann Educational Books: 85-106.

Smith, Frank. (1988). Collaboration in the Classroom. In *Joining the Literacy Club*. Portsmouth, NH: Heinemann Educational Books: 64-79.

JOURNAL WRITING AND ALIENATION

Janie McTavish

"...trust me. You'll know what to do with the data after you collect it." (Newman, 1994)

Whenever one of us asked Judith what to do with the information we were gathering about the students in our classrooms for some, as yet, unknown purpose, her answer always reminded me of Kinsella's line from *Shoeless Joe*, "If you build it, they will come."

"If you collect it, an idea will come," was perhaps more appropriate in our case, though I often felt that building the whole baseball diamond would have been easier. And so, I collected data. And yes, an idea did come.

I met Barry at a conference. He lived in a nearby town, and we were both language arts consultants in our respective school divisions. As we discussed the similarities, the thing we felt we had in common was our sense of isolation. As consultants, we were not connected to any particular group—we were not part of a school staff, nor were we administrators. Teachers and principals were wary of our presence in their schools, and we generally felt left out. We had both had many opportunities for professional development, attending workshops and conferences, and we felt it was time to step back and look at what we had learned during the past two years.

Barry suggested we collaborate on a journal project. We agreed to identify some topics that interested us and record them in a journal which we would mail back and forth.

The project began slowly, neither of us wanting to risk appearing less intelligent or knowledgeable than the other, so it was June before we finally began. This reluctance was obvious in our writing as well, and although we talked about taking risks, we began tentatively.

Our language was formal and carefully chosen, Barry writing with a computer and transcribing it into the journal, while I used pen and white-out to cover any mistakes I made. In addition to mutually agreed upon topics, we had our own personal objectives for professional development.

June 17, Barry:

> Since this is the first entry in our journal experiment, we should take time to define the project's purpose and scope. I have questions about response journals, the writing process, portfolios, and reading. It has been at least seven years since I taught a high school English course, and seven years away from rapidly evolving language arts philosophy and practice is a long time. I often feel a little like Rip Van Winkle when working with language arts teachers. In exchange for the language arts expertise you provide, I offer ideas related to curriculum integration, restructuring, and curriculum development which you may find of value. My purpose is to share information that will create mutual professional growth in our respective school divisions and hopefully generate new ideas as result of our dialogue.
>
> Our journal should be a place for intellectual risk-taking. Adult learners need to trust before they take risks. In our case, prior conversations, our professional backgrounds, similar life experiences, and a common desire to learn provide that trust framework. Because clear thinking is often reflected in clear writing, the journal is a place where our writing can be improved. My writing, like all writing, is never really finished. I hope to understand as well as be understood. Therefore, I encourage your critical analysis of my writing.

July 19, Janie:

> Our first disagreement. I do not want to criticize your journal writing. I worry that this will hold back your thinking, as it would with our students. I see the journal as a place to clarify our thinking, rather than our writing.

Barry was working with a teacher, Marcie, piloting a locally developed environmental studies course. She wanted to introduce journals in the form of a field book. For the next few entries, we dealt with issues concerning implementing and evaluating the journal, which led to a discussion of evaluation in general.

August 30, Janie:

I'd like to stay with evaluation for a bit and attempt to summarize what we've talked about. Does this sound something like where we're going with this?

1. establish criteria (determine what we value) with students;
2. measure personal growth and learning against criteria;
3. include opportunities for self-evaluation;
4. describe the learning—anecdotal comment—negotiate with students;
5. report—translate learning to a grade. How?

I have great difficulty making the quantum leap from number 4 to number 5 and have never reconciled this in my own teaching and learning. However, given our current reporting systems, especially at high school, we need to find a way to do this without compromising ourselves too much. Could we negotiate with the students to establish what would constitute an A, a B, etc.? Or would we look at the overall picture and say, "There's A amount or B amount of growth here? How can we put a grade on thinking? I think it's time to change the rules.

September 12, Barry:

I should mention that this is my first "free" write in this journal. I have left the computer out of this completely. I hope you can forgive my grammatical indiscretions. After eight years in the clutches of university profs; I am very nervous about unedited work.

The questions you pose about assigning grades are really a microcosm of a much larger educational issue. Your analysis reveals two sides of the evaluation issue. On the one side you have the grade reporters—managers-technicians—"quants"—experts who view education as a technical process. Opposite to that are those interested in learning—the "qualitatives"—generalists-observers. They are the minority, therefore they are required to conform to the quants because the quants run the system. This rather simplistic analysis of evaluation means that reporting is not for students or teachers at the present time. It is for the technicians who like to keep score.

What is really happening here is that a group of people led by
language arts types like you are restructuring the evaluation
process inside an education system that is not restructuring. A
central variable of any restructuring effort is evaluation and
assessment. Do you think the kind of evaluation you outline would
be enough in a world after restructuring? Before we ask, "What
grade would you like?" we should say, "Do you want a grade?"
    I am beginning to think that assigning a grade is really irrelevant.
It is very important to the students, but I will try to wean them
away from grades as the course goes on. Is this part of their
learning? I don't really know. I know this sounds a bit fuzzy at this
point, but the students and I will sit down and work this out
together.

September 14, Janie:

Yes, I think being weaned away from marks is an important part of
our students' learning. If we can be successful in communicating
the real purpose of formative assessment, then for many students
a grade becomes unnecessary, but this does not always apply when
reporting to parents and administrators, the "quants in sheep's
clothing"...

We had an opportunity to meet in mid-September. The conversation
turned to our journal project. Barry and I had been corresponding madly,
staying up late and rising early so we could get the journal in the mail. We
began to courier it: the more quickly we responded, the sooner we received
a response in return. We were hooked, and I began to wonder if this would
be possible with my students.

September 19, Barry:

I was interested in your comments about "non-threatening"
environments on Saturday night. Do we really want non-threatening
environments for students? If non-threatening means no challenge,
no stress, no external pushing, how are students to be motivated?
We learn best when we are a little bit uncomfortable. A non-
threatening environment is like the '60s—tuned out, laid back,
straight line. It is often discomfort that pushes us on. For example,
your questions threaten my thinking. They make me uncomfortable,
which leads to thinking, which leads to change. Change is good. Am
I making any sense here?

September 24, Janie:

When we talked on Saturday night about non-threatening environments being conducive to learning (how did we get onto that topic?), I thought later that you and I needed to define what it is that "learning" means. But after reading your comments, I think it's the non-threatening part that needs to be clarified. You suggest that I threaten your thinking with mine. I think what I do is challenge you, push you to think harder, to take some risks, just as you do to me. And I think we allow ourselves to be pushed in this way, in fact, embrace it, precisely because we do not feel threatened, because we trust we can both learn from and contribute to each other's ideas. I hope you were able to take that giant step away from your computer because you knew that it was safe to do so. This is a non-threatening environment.

Surely this isn't a return to the classroom of the '60s? Think of all that we've learned since then—about reading, writing, process, response theory, learning styles, assessment, instructional strategies—would teachers like you and I, for instance, have bothered to engage in this kind of professional dialogue so we could become better at helping our students learn? Sounds very much like a rhetorical question—I rest my case!

Can you accept this definition of "non-threatening"? You know best how you learn—perhaps you do need to feel threatened. I know that I don't, and I probably operate on the assumption that my students don't either. I need to do some more thinking about this. Are we really saying the same thing?

As we continued to correspond, our responses got longer and messier. Barry incorporated much of the thinking we had done into the environmental studies course and, more specifically, into the field book. In my classroom I continued to struggle to get to know my students. They were such a diverse group in age, grade, ability, language, background, and literacy. The only thing they had in common, I thought, was substance abuse. The primary, quite separate, focus of their program was treatment for their drug dependency; their education was secondary.

These students were hard to read. I knew nothing of their backgrounds, and they were reluctant to let me in. They were pulled out of class throughout the day for such things as medical appointments, anger management programs, and parenting classes.

As a teacher I was given little information about what happened outside the classroom. It occurred to me that I couldn't get to know the students because I was not working with the "whole" of them. There were so many things going on that influenced their classroom behavior and attitudes about school and learning that I didn't know about. I also realized that they had far more in common than just an abuse problem.

September 28, Barry:

Tomorrow will be the second hand-in day for the field book. Their books should have lots of info related to their three-day stay at the lake. I anticipate interesting discussions. I have some concerns with the field book and the class evaluation in general. Some students have not completed an entry yet. We have twenty-three students and about fifteen have completed a response. I don't want to force them to write and I don't want to attach a grade to their writing. After their first writing I sat down with each student and asked them to think about where they saw themselves on the scale of criteria we had developed. They are thinking about this and will discuss their ideas at the next conference.

October 7, Janie:

I've done some thinking about your concern with field book entries not being completed. In one of our earlier conversations we talked about the importance of using a journal "actively." Students have to write in it regularly, read from it, share it, talk about it, teacher needs to take his or her cues from student responses, and so on. Could part of the reason that only fifteen of your students have completed an entry be attributed to the "non-active" use of the journal? I think you're right about not wanting to force your students to write. However, what were the original criteria for success in this course? Are you setting the kids up for failure if you don't start to make some demands? How will you negotiate a grade if there is little to build on? Do you consider the field book an integral component of the course—if yes, then maybe you need to give some more thought to its use—if no, then is there a need for the students to use one?

You're in a difficult spot with the field book—uncharted waters. Lots of good sense about where you want to go, but no way of knowing for certain how to get there. Evaluation is always tough as we struggle to make it fit where it doesn't belong, and then we get caught between wanting to get on with what's really important and having to chase kids down to complete assignments. And then we further complicate it with negotiation and self-evaluation, which is where we really want to be. If you decide to persevere (don't give

up!) then you'll get closer next term and then next year. What was
the purpose of that field book, anyway...?

I was beginning to feel uncomfortable giving Barry advice about using a journal in his environmental studies course since I had not figured out how to make it successful in my own practice. What had happened with our journal that made it so important to us? Why had we become so passionate about it?

During our journal conversation, Barry was completing his thesis on restructuring high schools, which led to a journal conversation about curriculum, instruction, assessment, and leadership. Because I had many questions, using the journal to explore them helped Barry to reconsider and solidify his thinking about restructuring.

October 14, Janie:

The whole concept of restructuring is certainly not new—why has it
recently become such a buzzword? We have such a way of
complicating things. Isn't providing climates for improving student
learning what we are all about? If we focus on instruction,
curriculum, and assessment, shouldn't the rest just follow? Aren't
we really just talking about good teaching? About doing our jobs?
Why are we continually looking for ways to stall? What will force us
to get on with doing what we should be doing? The kind of
leadership you refer to that is so critical in order for change to
occur, is not likely to happen for a very long time. How can we
influence, for example, the hiring practices that currently result in
the kinds of administrators that are running amuck, or principals
that are hired and judged on their abilities to manage the plant?
This has further implications for schools and teachers. Evaluation
of teacher performance is directly linked to the kind of leadership
that is present—what are these principals evaluating?—what do
they know! Are they asked in an interview, I wonder, what their plans
are for improving student learning? And if they do have a plan,
what kind of support will they receive for implementing it? Even at a
school like ours, where the staff is making real efforts to
restructure based on a middle school philosophy, which to me is
very much like what you are describing when you define
restructuring, where the teachers are empowered and the principal
shares the same vision and is providing the necessary support and
leadership, they have still been successful in affecting only two of
the three central variables. When I asked about evaluation, they

were less enthusiastic, for although they had restructured with respect to instruction (teaming and integration) and curriculum (dramatic arts focus and options), they felt they could do little about evaluation at present because they were tied to a divisional reporting system. Now, does this make sense?

I agree that as consultants we are limited in influencing what's happening with respect to existing leadership unless we are prepared to seek out administrative positions. And I don't believe I have the character, though I don't suggest that this is a weakness. Perhaps it's our vantage.

I received a call from one of the principals yesterday. He insisted that I had to go to his next parent council meeting to present the department's side of the argument in the destreaming issue. I declined—didn't see that as my responsibility. He continued to tell me that he was going to offer an honors English course next year to get the top kids out of the regular classes. That way, the teachers will have to deal with only the middle and bottom kids. I was speechless, partly because I couldn't believe he said it, but also because I knew there was nothing I could say that he was prepared to hear. I realized how pointless my efforts had been to get administrators to think differently about this. But as I am writing about it, I realize that it is easy for me to spew out what the research says about streaming, but could we be wrong about this?

October 26, Barry:

I shared part of our journal in a workshop I did at a recent conference. The participants were interested in our views on evaluation. I think a few thought I was insane. Some of the teachers in the session stayed afterwards to find out more about the journal—it seems that they are feeling the same way we did. Hold on a minute! I just realized that I said "did"! What do you think about this revelation? I hadn't thought much about it until now—does this mean it's working? Let's talk more about this!

The course is going on (sounds like a letter from the front—the war drags on). The field books have taken off with some of the kids. I've exchanged mine with them, and they wrote some pretty impressive stuff. A few are still not writing. We will put the hammer down tomorrow! Demands! None of this '60s stuff.

October 27, Barry:

My partner, Marcie, gave them twenty minutes to write in class this morning—she forced them. I don't know if the class liked this. Maybe it's time to stop journals.

We are still wrestling with evaluation. I keep turning the
responsibility for evaluation back to them. "What criteria could we
use?" and "Why?" are common questions I ask. They carry a great
deal of baggage with them concerning evaluation. However, I don't
hear, "Is this worth marks?" much anymore. Marcie is a little fried, I
think. She is getting weary of my "too liberal" (her words) approach
to the students. Maybe she's right. If you were a parent, how would
you deal with a 1960s-raised teacher who no longer felt marks were
the most important thing?

As we continued mailing our journal back and forth, the tone of our
writing changed. We became less concerned with telling each other what
we knew about the topics we had originally identified. Instead, as we
began to trust each other more, our journal became a place to play out our
thinking. We started to wonder more, and the entries were filled with
questions, some of which had no answers and some which required none.
We scribbled in the margins, crossed out, drew arrows, wrote hastily, and
took great liberties with grammar, trying frantically to keep up with our
thinking.

November 8, Janie:

As I thought about your revelation, it struck me that what's
happening here, with our journal, is just what we believe (hope?) will
happen with our students. We've moved from writing and thinking
that is ordered, cautious, question and answer (were we feeling
threatened?) to thinking that is more reflective and open-ended. We
are using our writing for a different purpose (hence the different
voice). Should this kind of reflecting on our learning be part of our
journal entries? Will this kind of reflection help us understand our
students' learning?

November 17, Barry:

Marcie and I did the progress reports for the class yesterday.
Some positives—attendance is up and the evaluations the
students wrote indicate they like what's going on here. We looked at
all the grades we had collected. As we tried to figure out what to do
with them, Marcie said, quite out of character, that she felt no real
need to prove our students' place in the course, that calculating all
the scores, weighting them, and giving a value seemed irrelevant. We
agreed that in the next term we need to be more rigorous about
establishing criteria with the class and having the students use
the journals to think about how they are doing in relation to the

criteria. Marcie's reaction has really surprised me—maybe I'm getting through. Although we get more from this group than any other teacher in the school, Marcie is still unhappy with their lack of effort . I can understand her feelings at times. She wants the students to be good writers and readers, but their past is a litany of failure. I say we just need to go with what we've got! Wish I had more answers for her—she doesn't take much comfort in my admission that I'm learning as I go!

November 26, Janie:

While you may feel that you don't have many answers, it sounds like there are some great things happening, both with Marcie and with the students. A grade is perhaps not irrelevant, but rather, secondary? Your students must feel good about themselves, some maybe for the first time they can remember. It must be confusing for them—you're involving them in their learning, asking them to take some control, expecting them to do some thinking, but this only happens for one period a day. Quite a lop-sided tug-of-war! If change has not occurred as quickly or dramatically as both you and Marcie had hoped, maybe it's understandable. What do you think? I also have to admit that I'm kind of making this up as I go. Is that the same thing as learning?

I'm not sure what happened next, whether it was reading a thesis that Judith had recommended or whether it was time for one of the students to leave, but before Barry could respond to my last entry, I had introduced my class to journal writing.

In our teacher research class, Judith had given us an article to "think with." In my response I had written about our journal project. Judith suggested I read a thesis that had been co-authored by two women living in different provinces who shared something in their teaching practices that drew them together (Buley and Vasquez, 1994). They named it "alienation." As I read through their correspondence, I realized this is what Barry and I had been struggling with. And in that same moment I understood that this is what my students were feeling as well. It was this critical incident that convinced me to try, one more time, to give my students an opportunity to experience the same excitement that was driving Barry and I.

The following morning, with the students' desks pulled all around me, I handed each one a notebook and said, "It's time for you to tell me your stories." And they did, looking almost relieved at being given a chance to talk about things that were such a part of them. It was one of those times when, as teachers, we get the big pay-off. As excited as I was, I was also angry with myself, annoyed that I hadn't taken my cues from our own journal and acted earlier.

With some nudging and prompting, the students started to write in their journals often and for many reasons. Some wrote letters that needed to be written but not necessarily mailed. Others found poems that they liked or wanted to remember and recorded them in their journals. A few resolved daily conflicts. Many of them wrote about life at home or about how scared they had been when they were arrested, how crazy they got when they drank too much, or how much smarter they used to be before they started sniffing. For some, writing helped them deal with their confusion about simultaneously feeling homesick and being afraid to go home.

December 6, Barry:

> It's time to take stock. What have we learned these past months? About the journal? About ourselves? About our students? Here's my list:
>
> 1. This has been the most valuable P. D. that has happened in a long time. Maybe ever.
> 2. Establishing trust was critical.
> 3. This kind of writing has let me clarify my thinking about restructuring which will in turn affect my thesis in a positive way.
> 4. We were motivated to write because of our similar backgrounds and interests.
> 5. Going through this process has given me valuable insight into my students' learning. Our journal kept me from giving up the field book idea and helped me to help the students.
> 6. I have changed my thinking about evaluation, and I will continue to put the ideas that we discussed into practice. Keeping a record of these changes has helped me to understand evaluation more. I have a great deal to learn, especially about setting up criteria and including my students in the process. Unfortunately I have more questions than answers.
> 7. I have learned some things about myself. I know that I like being pushed and challenged by your questions. I also know that I do not need to feel threatened in order for learning to take place.

What are your thoughts about this? I invite your comments, additions, deletions, etc.

December 15, Janie:

I agree. It has really made a difference being able to talk about things with you. You're right about having a written record. Doing this over the phone wouldn't have been nearly as effective. Being able to read, think with, re-read, and then write is important. I love reading back through the journal to see how our thinking has changed and to look at the connections we have made. I think what has motivated us to write has been more than our mutual interests and backgrounds, though that may have been what it was at the start. I think that it's because we are talking about things that are important to each of us. It's good to know that this works. I mean, are you going to ask your students to do a piece of narrative writing about something they really care about or about what life would be like if they were a pair of socks in a laundromat? Knowing the stages we have gone through should help us to be more sensitive about our students' learning. The real test is what happens in our classrooms, but I feel much better equipped to help them. I wish we could articulate what happens that allows us to trust and take risks. Let's work on this.

I'm happy to report that the kids are writing madly in their journals (does this sound familiar?). Those who were reluctant at first are being influenced by the others—their responses are short and cautious, but they seem to be interested. The rest of them have really taken off, except William Bear. Makes me wish I'd done this in September. Unlike us, they are not concerned about the appearance of their journals, and have jumped right in to the messy stage. The angrier they are, the harder they scribble. They are asking if they can read each other's—did this happen with your students? We have agreed that this is a personal decision and that we will respect each other's desire for privacy, but many of them have volunteered to share. I am worried about William. I will have to be careful here as he becomes very agitated if I press him to write. It's almost Christmas and the kids don't seem to be excited about it. The closer it gets, the grumpier some of them are becoming. I have decided to start doing some research for my course. It feels good to finally have a focus. I have no idea where I'm headed with this, but Judith assures me that I'll know when I get there. I have decided to trust her on this one.

January 6, Janie:

> I have missed these conversations. Glad to be back at it. Some of
> my students did not return after the holiday. Apparently, this is
> not unusual. They may turn up later. Unfortunately two of them are
> my research subjects, so I am a little concerned. Dana was
> discharged over Christmas since she had come back drunk, and
> William has been placed in a foster home. Judith suggests that I
> continue to collect data from Henry. With my secondment starting
> on February 1, I don't know how far I'll get with this. However, I'm
> convinced that writing in their journals has made a difference for
> these kids, as it has done for you and me. They have all been busy
> writing about their holidays and their Christmas presents and what
> kind of trouble they got themselves into. I have noticed something I
> find a little unsettling. When someone is discharged, or has gone
> AWOL, or has graduated from the program, or simply goes for a
> home visit and doesn't come back, the others hardly acknowledge it.
> They don't seem to miss their buds, and when I tell them that I do,
> they look at me like I'm kind of unusual. Do you think they have been
> shipped around so often that they don't let themselves care? Have
> they accepted that important people in their lives will eventually
> leave them? Does this alienate them? I don't normally give them
> writing topics for their journals, but I'm thinking that I may ask
> them to write about this. Is it any of my business? Let me know
> what you think.

Henry enjoyed writing in his journal, as long as he could keep it short. Because of his limited vocabulary, he asked anyone who might be listening how to spell almost every word, and if we ignored him, he asked louder. I noticed that no one wanted to sit beside him. What he wrote about was often determined by what he could spell, and I was concerned about this. I encouraged him to just give it a try, but he was too insecure and stubborn to do this. It was my hope to teach Henry to read through his own writing. He thought this was a great idea and worked hard at it. It was slow going, however. There was something going on that was making Henry nervous, and he began to disappear after coffee and spend the rest of the day in his room.

January 16, Janie:

> I apologize for keeping the journal so long, but I wanted to talk
> about how things are going with Henry. He's been keeping his
> distance from the classroom and seems frightened by something. I

tried to talk to him about it, but he just clams up. He came to see me this morning. He told me that if I would write things down for him in his journal, he would tell me what was bothering him. When I asked him why he didn't want to write it himself, he replied that it would take too long! I agreed, and could hardly keep up. There are a couple of older boys who have been scaring him. A few days ago, they hung him by the ankles out a third-storey window. He was terrified—thought he was going to die. They have also been touching him and have threatened to hurt him if he rats on them.

The boys know that this kind of behavior isn't tolerated here and will get them discharged. He hadn't slept for days, and the only way Henry knew how to deal with it was to run, which he planned to do tonight. Putting it down on paper and then reading it with him seemed to be a great relief. I suggested that he take his journal to his social worker, which he agreed to do, but only if I would go with him. It was almost as if letting his worker read about it, rather than talking to him about what had happened, was like he wasn't "telling on" the boys. After the boys had been discharged, which was as soon as their social workers could pick them up, Henry came back to class. He didn't want to write, but he read and re-read what I had written. This really got to me. Am I making too much out of this? I am going to the post office right now, as I really need to hear from you.

January 22, Barry:

I got this in the mail as soon as I could, so I hope you are able to read it. It sounds like things have been a little crazy there. I don't think you're making too much out of Henry's scare. Maybe it just hurts to care? Maybe that's how your students feel? You sound like you want to pull away from them. That's understandable. Only a few more days to go....

What are you going to do about Henry? Do you have enough data to put something together? An interesting question. Do we ever stop collecting? My students have handed in their field books for a final grade. I'm really impressed. Marcie and I are much happier with how things went after the mid-term. Seems that we were able to learn from our mistakes. I will definitely use the field books with the next group of students. Most of the students have asked that we return them after we grade them—maybe they want a record of their thinking as well. I hope so.

January 31, Janie:

This will be quick. I want to get it in the post before I pack it and it disappears forever into my basement. I met with the new teacher and filled her in about what we do here. I told her about Henry, and she agreed to keep his journal for me when he leaves. She doesn't know if she'll continue, as she hasn't had much success with journals in the past....

I waited until yesterday to tell the kids that I'm leaving. I think they've been hearing rumors for a week or so, but nobody mentioned it. They obviously know that I've been packing, but this hasn't piqued their curiosity in the least. No one responded, asked me why, in fact, some of the students didn't even bother to look up from their books. I don't know what I expected. I've seen them react this way a dozen times. I do know that it doesn't feel very good. Ah, alienation....

February 14, Barry:

We have run out of pages in the journal, which is why I'm writing from back to front. How is the job? Do they know what to do with you yet? Do you miss your students? Have you met the other consultants on your team? A new semester has started. Word spread, and Marcie and I have more students than we can handle. We introduced the field book idea and asked them to do an initial entry about why they chose this course, what they are hoping to get out of it, and so on. Only about half the class handed it in. No problem. I know what to do about it.

February 22, Janie:

It was great to get the journal in the mail. My office is on the third floor, in the far corner, and I don't have a window. I haven't met very many people yet. No one seems to go for coffee, at least not to the staff lounge. The same with lunch. I'm feeling kind of isolated, you know, alienated.

I will buy a new journal tomorrow....

Buley Jan and Vivian Vasquez. (1994). *Written Conversation as Inquiry: A Team Thesis*. Unpublished M.A. Thesis. Halifax, N.S.: Mount Saint Vincent University.

Newman, Judith M. (1994). In-class communication.

REFLECTION, PAIN, AND WONDERFUL IDEAS

Susan Wastie

"Part of real inquiry is being pushed
into the discomfort zone" *

*I couldn't tell my story...
that day.*

Tell me your stories
Says Judith
What happened?
My classmates tell theirs
Trish's is about the water skiing
Laughter from the class
I try
I really try to laugh from deep down
But can't
Tension
I wait for a chance to tell my story
Jan tells her story
Death by computer
The class laughs
I try
I really try to laugh from deep down
But only
Tension

---

* Watson, Harste, and Burke, 1987.

Emily, Thoko, and Ed tell their stories
Getting lost
Reading maps
Backseat driving
The class laughs
I try
I really try to laugh from deep down
But only more tension
Christine mimics a game show
And pushes her hand on an imaginary buzzer
To get her turn
(Now why couldn't I think of something funny like that?)
The class laughs
I try
I really try to laugh from deep down
But tension is in my hands
Now my neck
Judith asks for more
The class is silent
I try to explain
Tension
I want to tell
My story
But can't
The words stick in my throat
Tears fill my eyes
I couldn't tell them my story
That day
Because
My
story
was
sad.

Let me begin by saying that I was not a teacher when I came to the Simon Fraser 1994 Summer Institute in Teacher Education. I was a speech language pathologist, different from the others. "What does a speech pathologist do anyway?" asked Jenny, a classmate, on the first day. I was used to having this question fired at me and I came up with the usual answers.

Why was I in this course—Teacher Research: Literacy in the Community? I was absolutely certain I knew the answer when I registered. I was sure I would learn about literacy and about action research. Being interested in family issues and second language learning, I thought the course would afford me an opportunity to go into the community with supportive "others" and collect data that, perhaps, would be useful in my research: family, preschool children, literacy, home language, language loss, culture loss, family loss, and peer influence in the absence of family. Yes, I told myself, this was definitely why I was here.

That "here" for me was not only about to turn into a very loud WHERE? but also loud WHAT, WHYS AND HOWS. "What does a speech pathologist do?" Jenny's question would haunt me.

Beginning to "Think With"

Julian, now seven, had received speech therapy because people couldn't understand what he was saying. At the age of three he feared socializing with his peers; increasingly he allowed adults to speak for him so that even at that young age he was already being viewed, and was viewing himself, as a failure. However, with some speech therapy he subsequently blossomed into a child who talked a great deal more freely. Although pleased with his progress, his parents and I felt that Julian could still use some help. But more than being concerned about his articulation, we were worried about impending learning difficulties—a "waiting for something more to go wrong" with his handling of written language. After all isn't that what we keep reading about? All those children with early speech and oral language problems now having difficulty processing text (Kamhi and Catts, 1991)?

In an effort to understand what Julian might be facing, I read Wells (1993) and I talked to Marie, a resource teacher also taking the course. I was beginning to wonder about reading problems, particularly after Judith commented one day that most reading problems are "caused by instruction, not remediated by it." Her comment really threw me. I realized that for the next few weeks I would be undertaking a journey.

Keeping a journal helped me map my journey as I revisited Vygotsky's social view of learning—learning is the internalization of social patterns and structures (Vygotsky, 1978); Halliday's functional-systemic view— that the form of language evolves from its social function and is thus a social invitation (Halliday, 1975); and Piaget's psychogenetic view—that learning is the *active* means by which organisms accommodate or assimilate to their environment (Piaget, 1967). I remembered my discomfort with behaviorist and innatist views of learners as passive beings to "whom things happen and to whom things are done" (Goodman, 1993: 79). I needed to see learning with new eyes. I wondered how could I learn about how Julian learns so that my teaching could "fit into life in progress" as Herb Kohl had urged us during his institute noon-hour lecture.

So my "thinking with" continued; but as I read, talked, and listened more, my sense of unease grew.

Moving into the Discomfort Zone

The "move" started on the Friday night of the first week of the institute. I was having dinner at an Italian restaurant with some friends. I was not being very sociable because I was preoccupied with the course, the different projects we had started, and the four books I had optimistically borrowed from our class library. Could I possibly read them all over the weekend? Overwhelmed? Yes! As if this weren't enough, by the end of the evening I found myself taking on yet another assignment: learning to roller-blade! I justified my rash decision by thinking that I could use the opportunity to observe my approach to new skill learning and relate the experience to learning in general.

What does Fleischer (1994) tell us? "Make the familiar unfamiliar" (p. 97). Challenging myself athletically has never been a problem (except when I was younger and suffered from asthma) so that part of the undertaking was familiar to me. However, this new physical skill was rendered unfamiliar by two things: first, the donning of some strange pieces of equipment; and second, having to deal with my fear of doing serious damage to my body. How could my attempting to learn to roller-blade relate to literacy learning? Maybe I could see some parallels between my own experience and the students' fear of reading and writing.

My friend Sherrie and I went to English Bay and rented some skates, elbow pads, and knee pads. We sat on the grass by the seawall and put on our blades. I was amazed to find I could stand on the things but then found myself clinging tightly to the wire fence. I didn't have a picture in my head of what I should be doing, though. Sherrie gave me some tips on stopping but I found I only wanted to stand and watch how the boys, playing hockey in the car park behind us, were doing it. I needed an expert. So I watched the boys for a while. These kids looked as if they had been born with skates on their feet. They glided, stopped at will, turned effortlessly and could look ahead for obstacles. All this while they chased a ball with a hockey stick in their hands.

Too much to think about. Let me concentrate on one foot at a time. OK. Push with my right, watch how they do it, out to the side a little, not straight. Oh, oh! Too fast! Where's the brake? Too late! Grab the fence again. Phew, I survived. Move behind Sherrie and practice going up and down the little path next to the fence for a while. Sherrie is telling me I'm doing well. She has become the expert. But then she is better at it than I am because she has ice-skated. My fear increases. She has just told me we are ready for the seawall. All those people and hills! No, not today. I am sure I will fall. Everyone told me I would fall. I told me I would fall. Too old? I'll show them though. Just do it. Skate! Good. Avoid dog on leash. Go down small slope. Concentrate. Obstacle: a huge slope that will take us towards the water. Cling to post. If we go down here I will not only generate speed but if I don't make the turn I could be in the drink! Wait. Watch two young women ahead of us. They bend their knees and put their right skate out to apply consistent braking action all the way down to the bottom. No, too risky for a rookie like me, but Sherrie... OK, Sherrie you try. Sherrie takes a nose-dive down the hill. I ask if she's all right. She laughs and tells me she'll live. Nope. No way I'm going down. Two more women breeze around the corner. How do you go down here, I hear Sherrie asking them. Sherrie, let's just walk...please! I don't say this out loud...yet. "You just point your skates down the hill and go-o-o-o!" one women's voice fades into the distance. "Coming thro-o-o-ugh!" they shout as they round the corner at the bottom, thereby avoiding the watery grave I have envisioned for myself. The next instant, Sherrie, a blur of blades and pads, whizzes by and disappears around the corner. "These things should be banned," I think, silently envying her bravado. I look around for an escape route. Someone has thoughtfully built some steps with a handy little banister alongside. So gingerly, not knowing if skates do stairs, I creep down the steps. Well, so far so good. I have made it down this immense hill with all my bones intact. So I cheated a little. Let me try a smaller hill before the big one. On the level surface I try a turn. Left is easier than right. It's all getting easier. A new obstacle—a curb. I panic a little but try the things I know I can do. Am I having fun yet? Yes,

> kind of. It is fun being with Sherrie, but I want to be good at this, not just have fun. The seawall straightens for a stretch. No people! I can go faster. I am going faster. (Susan Wastie, Reflection: 7/8/94)

It was at this point something magical happened. I found a rhythm to my skating. I didn't need to watch each foot. I could look up and see where we were going. I felt the warm wind in my face. I saw Science World in the distance. I could see Granville Island and people sitting enjoying the sun. But the greatest feeling was the effortless speed with which I was moving over the ground. Me going fast! I pushed harder. I swung my arms from side to side. I was going up and down (little) hills. I caught up with Sherrie who had her skates off.

> Her feet ache. So do mine, but if I take my skates off now I might never get that feeling back. I am getting confident. I am going to skate off on my own...just a little way. OK, here's another small hill. (Susan Wastie, Reflection: 7/8/94)

Yes, but I hadn't learned how to go downhill while turning! My life flashed before me. Time stood still. My skates were in the air. I was down. On my backside and in pain. So much pain I thought I was going to be sick. Sue, why didn't you listen to your friends and your own inner voice. They told you. My worst fear is now a reality. In pain, on the concrete. Then the other pain began to set in...humiliation. I wanted to cry, but all my years of being a competitor served me well and I forced a smile to reassure Sherrie as she looked down at me anxiously and asked, "Are you OK?" I tell her yes, sort of, but perhaps we've had enough for one day.

Skating back to the car I was not at all confident. I still felt like crying. I couldn't reflect on anything until later. Much later. On the way home I hobbled in to Mark's Work Warehouse to buy some shorts and a shirt. Suddenly, at a nearby sporting goods store, I find myself staring at shiny new skates comparing prices. "What are the best kind for beginners?" I hear myself asking the salesperson.

What made my experience so fearful? It wasn't the activity itself because I had chosen it. Was it fear of pain, humiliation, fear of failure— the invisible barrier? Did I want to try it again even though it was difficult and painful? You bet! Otherwise why would I be looking at buying my own equipment? What happened that made me revalue myself as a roller-blader and not label myself a failed skater? What did my experience say about other fearful learners and how they approach activities in the classroom? What do we know about our learners and their fears and what can we do to make sure learning activities are user-friendly?

I had some insights about learning that day:

- Learners need to be curious and willing to try.
- They need to trust themselves and whoever is teaching.
- Learners need friends with whom to compare notes about the experience.
- Encouragement and patience are crucial (Sherrie kept saying, "Great!, You're doing fine," and, "That's it." She did not chastise me for coming down the stairs instead of following her down the hill. She just smiled and accepted my way of getting to where she was).
- There has to be some initial success (I can stand on these things!).
- Lots of models to imitate (surrounded by learners of all different levels and abilities mixed together, each going at their own pace).
- Choices—lots of different ways of approaching the task (This way, that way, fast, slow, up, down, walk, skate, take off skates, leave skates on etc.)
- Opportunities to apply what the learner already knows about his or her own learning to the new situation.
- Major focus on process but some sense of direction (it didn't matter whether we got anywhere in particular but we knew the path we were taking went somewhere we wanted to go).
- A sense that there's always tomorrow: we need only to focus on what we can do today.
- Experiencing the joy and magic of mastering the whole beyond the parts (for me it was experiencing effortless speed).

*Beyond Discomfort and into "The Having of Some Wonderful Ideas"**

Armed with insights about my own learning, I approached the planning and implementation of Julian's therapy sessions differently. The

---

* With thanks to Eleanor Duckworth (1987).

first week that I began to think of my therapy-as-teaching I introduced my new laptop computer to Julian. I wanted to consciously nurture learning rather than control it. I wanted to create "a milieu that enables a social collaborative venture" (Newman, 1991). Like Newman I began "by establishing a physical setting with materials that I (thought) might be engaging" (p. 21).

The problem, I realized afterwards, was that I had forgotten the collaborative part. It was already my agenda. I had already set up a disk so Julian could write messages to Miles, another student (I would be visiting Miles and I thought we could ask him some questions on the word processor and then read his replies the next time Julian and I met). I'd already created a disk for each of them with their names on neat printed labels. This, I believed, was going to be a different kind of learning experience for the boys. We would talk through writing. I already knew that Julian loved anything mechanical or electrical so I let him plug everything in and I switched on the computer. However, I had forgotten in my haste that little fingers take time to learn new skills. I had not even considered the difficulty that maneuvering the cursor around the screen would give him. I let him experiment, for a short time, with the tiny little button that served as a mouse. Not only did it have to be pressed down with varying pressure but with the slightest push to left or right the cursor whizzed across the screen at lightening speed. Julian pushed the button repeatedly like a person frustrated at a crosswalk because the lights won't change. Finally I had to take control or by the time he got his "mouse finger" he was going to destroy the computer. "This way Julian. Go up here. Click on here. See? OK?" He flopped back in his chair to let me do my thing. He read my first message to him, "Hi this is Sue speaking...." It began this way because I wanted both Miles and Julian to see that writing was just another way to talk. "Let's talk to Miles now." I wanted him to try to type something, but he just said, "You do it Sue." A critical moment then, which has since turned into a critical incident in my understanding of learners.

He had not accepted my "opening invitation" (Newman, 1991). What should I do? Insist? Shut off the computer even though I really believed he would be interested once he got going? What would get him going, though? I had failed. My focus turned back to Julian. I needed to go back to the social need of the learner, and so I asked him what he wanted to say to Miles and he said it. After all isn't that what I had told him we would be doing. Is that how children's trust is subtly eroded? I wasn't tricking Julian into writing or was I? This is what he said and what I typed: "Hi Miles. What movies have you seen? I have seen *Mrs. Doubtfire*. It was very good, but there was something not very nice in it. I have seen *Beethoven 2* and *Aladdin*. I have seen *Turtles 3*, but it was kind of stupid. Bye for now. Julian."

I then showed him how we could change the type and size of the letters. At this point Julian said something that touched the now different observer/listener in me: "Sue, you know what? Sometimes computers can be boring!" What he was really saying was my agenda is boring. I agreed with him, "You're right Julian. So let's do something different with it." I clicked on to the solitaire game and we spent the next twenty minutes having a great time watching the cards whiz this way and that. Why hadn't I started with the game? It would have given him a chance to gain control of the cursor without me breathing down his neck. He was thrilled when he actually completed it and the deck of cards cascaded down the screen. He shouted to his mom to come and look, which reminded me that I must talk to his parents about the direction his therapy was taking and the reasons for the change. Their support was paramount in all of this. Later, as I reflected upon the mistakes I had made, I tried to think about what to do differently.

The following week my only agenda was to take the computer, some of Julian's favorite toys and games, and give him choices—real choices. As I walked into the house he excitedly grabbed the computer and didn't ask what other toys I had in my bag as he usually did. He opened it. He switched it on. He asked to play solitaire. "Don't you want to see what Miles has said?" I asked, testing the waters. He agreed, but mostly to please me. First he re-read what he had written the week before, then he read Miles's response: "Hi Julian. I have seen the *Little Big League*. What tv shows do you like best? From Miles."

At that moment, just as he had his fingers poised over the keys to type, he quickly withdrew them. I saw a look of apprehension on his face. What was it? I did a quick flashback to the times I have seen him reading or attempting to write anything with his mother. I saw her asking him to sound-out the words. A painful task for Julian. He is at the stage of invented spelling, and his mom sees this as a sign that confirms her worst fears about his literacy potential. I rapidly returned my focus to Julian and asked him what he wanted to say. He replied, "I like *Baywatch* and *Batman*." I hypothesized that if Julian was fearful of failing, then I needed to give him a way out without losing face, a way that would build trust and lead him to accept my invitation to learning. So I showed him the spell checker. I explained that even grown-ups don't know how to spell things properly all the time and this was a helping hand. He could just type what he wanted and then go back and check the spelling. His eyes lit up. I asked him then if I could show him how it worked and he replied, "Yes!" enthusiastically. What we needed now was a word to spell wrong. Wrong? We were going to spell a word wrong on purpose? He chose the word "like" and decided he was going to leave the "e" off the end. He went through the selection process and clicked on the correct spelling. Then his first "having of a wonderful idea" happened. I don't mean by this it was his first wonderful idea, I was sure he'd had these before. I mean that this was the first time it had happened when I was fully cognizant, like Eleanor Duckworth, of what having these moments really signifies. She considers the "having of wonderful ideas the essence of intellectual development"(p. 1). When Julian saw how the spelling had been changed he looked puzzled and said: "You know, I thought what would happen would be that we closed up the computer and left it for a while and when we came back and opened it again all the words would be right." A wonderful, wishful, original thought of his that revealed so much.

I told him what a great idea that was and explained that I didn't think a computer such as the one he had described had been invented yet! He then just settled himself in his chair fingers poised once more. He reached out and positioned the hard copy of his conversation with Miles that I had printed out for him and searched for words to copy. And so he typed. Slowly, but this time he was typing for himself: "Hi Miles. I like *Baywatch* and *Batman*. What TV shows do you like best?"

Then I heard him quietly rehearsing the next sequence of letters to remember from the text to the keyboard: "From...F...O...R...M—from Julian" (back to keyboard). Next he said "F...O.," but he doesn't type it (looks back at paper). Then, "F...R...O...M" (emphasizing R). Then, "F...O...R...M." And again, "F...O...R...M"(back to keyboard).

I could only guess that Julian was rehearsing because he knew something wasn't quite as it should be. He backspaced to delete the "o" just as I whispered, "Check again" before he resumed typing. As soon as I said it I questioned why I had done it. Julian was doing just fine. On reflection, I think it was because I sensed his body tense. I just needed to be a calming voice that implied he definitely could do it. I was trying to lead from behind.

We played solitaire again and Julian told me how his mother had taught him to play with real cards, and he explained some of the differences between the computer version and the card version. Discourse. "Learners shape situations by engaging in conversation with them; both the situation and the learner change as a result of the transaction" (Newman, 1991: 20).

As I reflected on the positive turn this activity had taken, I still felt that we were not into real engagement yet, that this whole experience was based on my assumption that Julian wanted to talk to Miles. The boys had spent some time together at a computer camp last year, so they at least knew one another. I was sure there must be some questions that Julian had. If so, perhaps we could use e-mail to create a written discourse. I asked him if there was anything he wanted to know about. Anything he was interested in. "No" he told me, "Nothing." I pressed on because without real questions evolving in a social milieu, authentic written discourse was impossible to create. I wondered if Julian's difficulty coming up with an answer was because this kind of question was unfamiliar to our usual conversation. So I pulled out some memories and reminded him of the fun we'd had finding out about pirates and making treasure maps. Or what about the construction playmobile he'd loved so much? He thought again. "No. Nothing," he said.

I began to pack up my computer ready to leave and then another wonderful idea happened.

"Sue, let me tell you something. I've always wondered how people become construction workers. Do you just walk in or what?" Then another idea. "You know who I could ask? My Uncle John. He's a construction worker and I've never thought about asking him." Wonderful ideas—the essence of intellectual development.

I walked out of the house with Julian's mom who was off to a meeting in a bit of a rush. Not the best time to tell her of the new things we were trying. I gave her the good news first: Julian had taken the first steps towards writing for himself, and with a purpose that was more than just for the sake of practicing spelling! Then the bad news—I had revealed the magic of the spell checker to him. I explained that this seemed to be the turning point and how he had approached the experience subsequently. She looked at me with just a hint of shock in her eyes. "That's exciting," she said, not altogether convincingly, but obviously willing to reflect my feelings about the event. The following week I had an opportunity to explain to both parents my observations about Julian's learning; I even described my own struggle. I told them of their son's wonderful ideas and their significance.

His dad listened with interest. I described how Julian seemed to approach writing with a fear of failure, and we discussed how we could all engage with Julian.

So back to the beginning. My story made me feel sad. Sad, not because I was alienated from the teachers by my profession, or because I couldn't tell my story that day, but because I was so troubled by self-doubts about my practice. I was attempting to meld theories from education and theories about language-learning within a medical model of service delivery. However, everything I had ever learned from the children and their drive to make meaning through language, their families, and the communities in which they live screamed at me to try not to fit them into a deficit model, but a model that upheld the principles of learning that I was discovering. My story is sad no longer because in order for me to get to the bigger story I needed to examine myself critically, both as a learner and a speech language pathologist, and to begin to think of therapy as teaching—something I have always really known it to be. I can now face my vocation believing that I am, in truth, a teacher. The process was painful, but as Wells (1993) tells us:

> teachers, like learners in general, start with different reasons for engaging in the topic; they also differ in the nature and extent of the knowledge they can bring to the inquiry...the routes they take and the staging points they pass through in the course of their journey will inevitably be personal and individual. (p. 29)

Now my real journey can begin.

Duckworth, E. (1987). *The Having of Wonderful Ideas*. New York: Teachers College Press.

Fleischer, C. (1994). Researching Teacher Research: A Practitioner's Perspective. *English Education*, 26(2): 86-124.

Goodman, K.S. (1986). *What's Whole in Whole Language*. Toronto: Scholastic.

Goodman, K.S. (1993). *Phonics Phacts*. Portsmouth, NH: Heinemann Educational Books.

Halliday, M.A.K. (1975). *Learning How to Mean: Explorations in the Development of Language*. London: Edward Arnold.

Hillerman, T. (1994). *Sacred Clowns.* New York: Harper Collins.

Kamhi, A. and Catts, H. (1991). *Reading Disabilities: A Developmental Perspective.* Boston: Allyn & Bacon.

Newman, J. (1992). *Interwoven Conversations: Learning and Teaching through Critical Reflection.* Toronto: OISE Press.

Piaget, J. (1967). *Six Psychological Studies.* D. Elkind (Ed.). New York: Random House.

Stephens, D. (Ed.). (1990). *What Matters: A Primer for Teaching Reading.* Portsmouth, NH: Heinemann Educational Books.

Vygotsky, L.S. (1978). *Mind in Society: The Development of Higher Psychological Processes.* Cambridge, MA: Harvard University Press.

Watson, D., Burke, C., and Harste, J. (1989). *Whole Language: Inquiring Voices.* Toronto: Scholastic.

Wells, G. (1993). *Changing Schools from Within.* Toronto: OISE Press.

EXPERIENCES*

Patty Kimpton

Students literally erupted from the room. Jostling and bumping each other in their haste to escape to a safe place where they could talk and vent their pent-up frustration they made a disorganized, chaotic stream to the cafeteria. Emma breathlessly made her way to a group of familiar faces exclaiming as she drew nearer, "I'm gonna die in there, I just know it!"

Mark, Carole (with an 'e'), and Jag made room for her in their circle as she drew closer.

"I think that was one of the most painful experiences I've had to date," commiserated Carole. "Can you believe he took two whole hours to read that study, word for word yet!"

"It's not that bad," responded Mark. "Just give him what he wants."

"Hmmm, I wonder what that is?" said Jag.

"You mean we have to just sit there for two hours while he listens to himself talk?" retorted Carole somewhat acidly. "I've paid three hundred dollars for this class, I resent being talked at. Jeez, I read that thing in ten minutes, even I could find some way of making it interesting. Why couldn't he just ask us to read it and then maybe we could talk about it?"

Carole suddenly became aware that Jag was trying to get her attention. He looked at her and then beyond her while nudging Mark who was nearest to him. Taking his cue Carole and Emma looked behind them and spied their prof coming through the door. Carole was tempted to continue her tirade regardless of his overhearing, but decided against it, the last

---

* Not all teacher/action research needs to be reported as a first-person account of experience. Fiction can also serve as a mirror for readers. Patti Kimpton's story "Experiences" is an example of how fiction can be used to research self.

thing she needed was to get on the bad side of the prof so early in the semester.

They retreated a safe distance away, out of earshot.

"Do you think it's going to be like that all semester?," asked Jag.

"So what if it is," retorted Mark. "It doesn't matter anyway. These are our last courses in school. This time next year we'll be certified teachers. I'm going to do what he wants, get my mark, and get the hell out of here."

"Maybe we should say something to him. I mean we could be diplomatic and all, it might make a difference you know," suggested Emma.

"Yeah right," said Mark scornfully. "Then we'll all be on his shit-list. He'll think we're just a bunch of rabble-rousers and will write us off."

"But if we don't say something we'll end up hating every minute we're in that class," wailed Emma.

" I already do," said Carole. "Matter of fact I'm already thinking of skipping every other class. I mean participation is only ten percent of the mark."

"I like participating," said Jag. "Doesn't look like we'll be doing much of that here though."

"Well at least we only have two assignments to do," contributed Mark. "What a laugh hey, one's worth forty percent and the other fifty percent. I could probably have them done in the next month and then it'll be clear sailing."

"You know what I did while he was reading? I read some stuff for my other class and made some notes," laughed Carole.

"Now there's an idea," responded Emma. "We can use it for a study period for something else."

"Yeah, something useful," Carole retorted.

"Whew, what a day," Ted Pilate sighed as he lowered himself into his chair at the kitchen table. He liked his chair, it was large and solid, made of durable oak. It had been passed down to him from his father, whom he remembered sitting in it while reading the paper and waiting for supper to be ready. He liked the feeling of familiarity he got as he settled into his chair. Times may change , he thought, but a good chair like a good idea can resist the erosion of fads and trends. He liked to compare his chair to his work. Like his chair, his work never succumbed to the fashions of the day.

Both were grounded in solid, dependable craftsmanship—something which he feared was sadly amiss in today's world. No way would he trade his chair for the latest Lazy-Boy Recliner or Ikea patent leather rocker. He knew the value of what he had, and he knew the value of what he passed on. Take his class today for instance. He had spent a lot of time writing up the study he presented to his students. It was a fascinating topic and had occupied his time for the better part of a year. He had researched it in meticulous detail, conducted surveys, ran statistical analyses, and bounced it off a few of his colleagues; ones he knew would understand his motives. They had contributed to the final product by offering some valuable insights and by proofreading and editing prior to publication.

It was obvious those kids today couldn't understand the article. That's the problem with this program, he thought, I'm getting students in third-year undergrad classes who have no grounding in methodology. They wouldn't understand the methodology of a research-based study if it stood up and slapped them in the face. Well by the end of the year they would, or they would be repeating it again next year. He was not about to be another *laissez-faire* instructor who catered to and pampered his students.

Pulling out paper and pen he began to make notes for his next class. They would begin by reading the first two chapters in his book on research-based study. Following that he would assign topics for a research paper due in a month's time. In a couple of weeks they should be well acquainted with the model they'll be using, he thought, by then they'll be ready to begin writing.

"Whadja get, whadja get?" Emma asked excitedly. They had met again in the cafeteria after their class, it had become their place to hang out and swap stories. Carole, Jag, and Mark were scanning and flipping through their returned assignments.

"What did *you* get?" returned Carole, looking up from her paper.

Emma smiled, "Ninety six percent, yahoo! I was so worried about this paper. I must have read his directions a hundred times."

"Let's see," said Jag extending his hand for her paper. As he leafed through it he read aloud some of the comments, "Nice thesis statement, well-developed body, logical procession of three-point argument, excellent use of supporting quotes. "

"Let's see that thing," said Mark as he snatched it away from Jag.

"Hey, take it easy Mark," Jag responded with some annoyance.

"Well no wonder he liked yours, you quoted from his book...and look at this statement, I remember him using this in class. Maybe if I'd brown-nosed I'd have got an 'A' too." Mark's eyes sparkled with anger as he flicked the paper down on the table.

"I didn't brown-nose," Emma retorted, her voice beginning to rise with anger. "We've all been saying, give him what he wants, so I did. What's wrong with that?"

"What's wrong with that is there isn't a single creative thought in there, at least I tried to be creative," rejoined Mark.

"Ha, and where did that get you, let's see your paper," and before he had time to react Carole had grabbed his paper and was reading aloud, " Wow, no wonder you're so pissed. Listen to this guy: "Where's your evidence? Where's your evidence? You have attempted a philosophical discourse using overly general claims, with essential components of the requirements for the paper missing!"

"Take a look at what he did to my end notes and bibliography, he ripped them apart. See!" Mark took his paper flipping to the last few pages, jabbing at all of the pen slashes, question marks and commentary. "You haven't cited the ibid's correctly, underline, italicize, look, he corrected everyone of them. Shit! I spent hours on this paper, I thought I had presented a good case and he just went ahead and shredded it. Can you believe it, he gave me a 'C'." Mark slumped in his chair dejectedly. "I hate this class," he muttered.

"Maybe for our final assignment we should work together, we could proof each other's work and share our information. What do you think?" Jag asked.

"I dunno," said Carole. "We can't all submit the same stuff, we'll really be up the creek then!"

"Yeah, we'll get turfed for plagiarism, or we'll all end up failing," returned Mark despondently.

"Well, I'm going to work with Emma, she seems to have his system figured out," laughed Jag.

It had been a long, exhausting day. It was with some relief that Carole lowered her backpack to the floor. It overflowed with her recent acquisitions from the university library. Giving it a little kick, she pushed it off to the side of the hall and made her way to the kitchen. She rounded the corner and came upon Lexie who was industriously chopping and cutting various vegetables in what was obvious preparation for supper.

Lexie looked up and smiled, "Hiya Carole, how was your day today?"

"Exhausting! I'm sweating like a pig and I just spent three hours at the library getting resources for an assignment due next week. Thank goodness it's the last one. Ummm that smells good, are you making borscht?" asked Carole lifting the lid off a pot and seeing beets swimming in water.

"What's borscht?" asked Lexie.

"It's beet soup, my mom makes it all the time."

"Oh, I like soup. Is it hard to make? I saw these beets at the market today and they looked so good, but I've never cooked them before, am I doing it right?"

"Yes, you just boil them. That's why I thought you were making borscht."

"Can I make it with this?" Lexie asked, motioning towards the vegetables she had cut up. "I was thinking of a stir fry since I have to use up these vegetables before they go bad, but soup sounds better."

Carole surveyed the food Lexie had prepared: onion, carrots, rice, tofu, tomatoes. "Yeah sure. You can use a chicken stock to lend flavor to the base and then you add veggies. My mom uses lentils, chickpeas, beans, whatever is at hand. Fridge stew you know."

Lexie looked delighted, "Oh, Wow! I'm going to make borscht. Do you think I should add more beets?"

Carole thought a moment, "It's up to you. If you like it thick put lots in. I use garlic and a flour and water paste to thicken it. Sometimes I add sour cream, but that's the way we eat it."

"Hmmm," Lexie looked into the pot, "do you think I should cut them up?" she asked, referring to the beets.

"Well probably a bit, they're pretty big. I've seen some borscht made where the beets are cooked and then shredded or grated into the soup, others where they are sliced or chopped. I think it's a matter of individual taste."

"What about the leaves?" questioned Lexie.

"Sure, we put them in all the time."

"Wow, look at the color. Actually the green makes a good contrast on the red," and Lexie proceeded to rip the leaves and toss them into the pot.

Carole watched Lexie's treatment of the leaves. She was on the verge of telling her how to chop the leaves, but deciding against it left Lexie to experiment with her soup and headed upstairs to shower.

An hour later the fragrant smell of borscht wafted up to her room. She couldn't resist following her nose downstairs where she found Lexie and her boyfriend eating borscht.

"Ummm, that smells god, can I have some?" asked Carole.

"Sure, help yourself, there's some fresh rolls in the basket here too." smiled Lexie.

Carole already had her spoon in the pot so as to have a taste before filling her bowl. "Ummm, it's good hey!"

"Yeah, but it's missing something. Maybe it needs sour cream. Oh I know! I forgot to put the chicken bullion in. Wait a sec Carole," Lexie proceeded to dissolve a cube of chicken concentrate in hot water. She added it to the soup, gave it a quick stir, and proceeded to taste it. A wide smile lit her face. "Oh yeah, that's much better. Now you can have some. Have seconds Jong, this is much better!"

Carole proceeded to fill her bowl and seated herself at the table. Jong took Lexie up on her invitation and filled his bow l a second time. Conversation slowed to a halt as everyone busied themselves with their food.

"Oh, that was great Lexie. Thanks a lot."

"Thank you Carole!" said Lexie, "Oh wow, now I know how to make borscht. Another thing I know how to cook. I'm so happy."

"Me too," said Carole, reclining back in her chair. "Not only did I have a great supper, but I didn't have to cook it."

"I think it's my turn to make a contribution, who wants tea?" Jong asked.

Both women nodded their assent, and while Jong proceeded to set the kettle to boil the conversation turned from food for the body to food for the mind.

"Are you working on your assignment tonight Carole?" said Lexie.

"Ugh, don't remind me. I just finished eating," Carole replied.

A feeling of camaraderie enveloped them and they laughed in mutual understanding.

Carole settled herself at her desk. Her books lay open around her. She picked up John Dewey's *Education and Experience*. It was a small, slim book that one of her profs had recommended when she asked what experience meant in the context of the classroom. Everyone kept saying that teachers need to give students learning experiences. Carole was having some difficulty figuring out what that meant. Was she supposed to entertain them? How could she offer them learning experiences? When she looked at her own learning experiences, especially the research class she was in, she was even more at a loss. She certainly wasn't being entertained there, and it was not the learning experiences she wanted to have with her students.

While she found Dewey's book helpful, she still didn't have a clear picture of what experience looked like in reality. With a mental shrug she put the book down. Her eyes wandered over the other books before her. I should be doing something, she thought, and at random picked out Newman's *Interwoven Conversations*. I'll just skim this, she thought, and beginning with the foreword and preface she quickly worked her way into chapter one. She was pleasantly surprised by the format of the book. It wasn't the dry text she had been anticipating. It was more of a narrative of the author's experiences of teaching, both the how and the why.

Carole became aware that she was very interested in what the author was saying. One line in particular leapt out at her, "...learning is collaborative, universal, and incidental" (p. 15). The author went on to elaborate Frank Smith's discussion of learning as enterprises, and the four criteria of an enterprise based activity: no grades, no coercion, no restrictions, no status. Almost unbidden, a quote of Dewey's crossed her mind, "An experience is always what it is because of a transaction taking place between an individual and what, at the time constitutes his environment...The environment is whatever conditions interact with personal needs, desires, purposes, and capacities to create the experience which is had " (Dewey, 1938: 142-143).

Carole laughed to herself, that reminds me of Lexie and me making borscht tonight, she thought. All of a sudden something seemed to click. That is exactly what happened tonight. Lexie's learning occurred through the interaction of, and transaction between, her needs, desires, purposes, and capacities, and her immediate environment. She needed to eat and she needed to use up the veggies in the fridge. I happened to come in and look in her soup pot, made an assumption, and began discussing her meal preparation. Her desire to make borscht involved her in an enterprise. The enterprise was not graded, it was non-coercive, there were no restrictions; I had removed myself so as not to define or regulate what she did, and there was no status between the two of us and who had experience cooking borscht. Lexie, in Newman's words, "took a risk and built on her existing strategies"—in this case those of cooking (Newman, 1991: 17). When I left the room she was encouraged, empowered to find her own way.

Hey, thought Carole, like Newman's description Lexie's learning was collaborative; it was between the two of us, it was universal; cooking and eating; and it was incidental; I just happened by and made a borscht comment which led to a discussion. Wow, thought Carole, I think I'm beginning to understand what experience means. It was with a great deal of satisfaction that she returned to the Newman book.

Dewey, John. (1938). *Experience and Education.* New York: The MacMillan Company.

Newman, Judith M. (1991). *Interwoven Conversations: Learning and Teaching Through Critical Reflection.* Toronto: OISE Press.

Part Two

Learning From Students

At the heart of teacher/action research is the struggle to learn from our students. What sense are they making of what's going on? Are they engaged or are they turned off by the experiences we offer them? How are they perceiving the classroom world?

Most teachers find becoming a "kid-watcher" a difficult undertaking. Learning to observe students and to see the world from their perspective is not easy because it means allowing ourselves to become vulnerable. Given the realities of classrooms it's a certainty that whatever activity we try, whatever invitation we extend, it will be wrong for some students. Consequently becoming a better observer means discovering what's not going right. It requires an act of bravery to engage in this kind of inquiry.

In Listening to Children's Voices, Kim Crass examines the lessons her students teach her about how to teach them. She examines how the

public dialog about education
affects her teaching.

Rosemary Manning, in REAL LIFE
AS CURRICULUM, explores how two
students in particular have taught
her the importance of "real-life"
experiences for helping students
become readers and writers.

Veronica Yeung, a classroom
paraprofessional, recounts her inquiry
into the role of "real books" in the
literacy development of several at-risk
young students. Through her work
with these students she discovers how
to follow the children's lead. She also
discusses how educators can overcome
isolation in their efforts to uncover
their assumptions.

LISTENING TO THE CHILDREN'S VOICES

Kimberley Crass

I was standing at the back of the meeting area watching my Grade One children engage in an activity that was completely their own. What I observed caught me by surprise.

I giggled to myself as Janel and Tonia dragged a brightly painted red and yellow box to the front of our class. The box was nearly as tall as the girls and it had the word mailbox on the top flap. They settled themselves on a small wooden bench with the mailbox towering between them. Their very actions and movements drew immediate attention from the rest of the children, as they knew it would. After all, who better understands the interests and loves of a child's world than children themselves? With every pair of eyes glued to the front of the room, the two girls began to speak. "This is our mailbox and we want everyone in the class to write letters to each other and mail them in our mailbox. We'd like to have a letter writing day every Tuesday and we'll be the mailmen who deliver the letters." A hand shot up from the crowd, fingers tense, begging to be recognized. "I know how to make envelopes," John said. "So do I," echoed Melanie from across the meeting area, and before long the two envelope experts were explaining to the rest of the class how to make paper envelopes.

"I think we need a stamp for those envelopes too," said Geesha from the crowd. "Why don't we use the Canada flag stamp from our writing center to put on the envelope." There was general agreement and excitement evidenced by the nodding heads and the whispers. You could tell the entire class was already imagining themselves involved in letter writing. Janel and Tonia wasted no further time. They began handing out writing paper and sending the others back to their desks to become involved in the activity.

The children brushed by me on the way to their tables with not so much as a word. It was as if I were not there. They did not need my direction at this particular moment. They were in control of what they were doing and loving it. The only time I became part of the conversation was when one of the children just happened to say, "Aren't you going to write a letter Ms Crass?" I took a piece of paper and sat at a table with a group of children who were eagerly writing and constructing envelopes. I picked up my pen and started to put a message on paper, but I did not get very far. My thoughts drifted back to the meeting area in wonderment of what had just transpired. I could not believe what I had just witnessed. The children were so involved with the activity that there was not a single discipline problem. There was not even a necessity to remind anyone to pay attention or to listen to the person talking. Thirty minutes earlier I had conducted a science lesson, which might have captured seventy percent of the children's interest. The rest of the class had to be pulled into the conversation. These two situations were like night and day!

Why such a difference?

I looked around one more time. There was an energy in the room that I had not felt for a long time. I could feel a sense of power that was not apparent when I am in control. These Grade One children were alive with ideas, questions, and possibilities, and all they wanted was a chance to be heard. Their voices sang out loud and clear and beckoned for everyone to join in.

It had been a long time since I had experienced this kind of excitement about learning. It had been a long time since I had heard those children's voices. In fact, it has been three long and silent years. I laid my pen down on the table, leaned back in my chair and remembered my favorite year of teaching.

It was 1991. I was in my seventh year of teaching and I was leaning towards trying something a little different in my classroom. I had been reading *Creating Curriculum: Teachers and Students as a Community of Learners* (Short and Burke, 1991) and felt that providing children with an opportunity to plan, organize, and think about a unit of study together was an avenue worth exploring. I felt confined by the organization of the traditional curriculum which was, and still is, developed by experts outside the school, implemented by teachers, and received by students. I wanted to involve the children in actively thinking about curriculum so that they might learn more from the experience and that I might learn more about the children. So began the most memorable year of my teaching career.

My class that year consisted of twenty-eight Grade Two students, none of whom I really knew because I had just begun teaching at the school the year before. I began the year with a number of activities which helped us get to know one another and allowed us an opportunity to share our lives. The children brought in pictures of their families and other things that were meaningful to their lives. They listened intently to the stories of classmates that were similar to theirs, as well as those which were different. The stories that were different made everyone a unique and special individual in our classroom. I brought in pictures of my ninety-seven-year-old grandmother, my dad, my cat, and my earring collection for "show and tell." As I told stories about my life the children began to see me as a person in the classroom and not just as a teacher. It did not take long before a sense of closeness and caring developed within our entire group. I will never forget my reaction when I received a get-well package of flowers, cards, and magazines at my home after I had been absent from school for a little more than a week. The parent who delivered it also carried a message from the children: "The flowers are to make you feel better, the cards are to make you feel better, and the magazines are for you to read so that you do not get bored." This feeling of bonding with students was one that I had never experienced before. The conversations and a sharing of our lives built a climate of caring, respect, and need for one another.

Taking the time to learn about each other as people paved the way for the effective cooperative and collaborative work that followed. Our study of animals was one of the many themes that we explored together as a class. Although I had developed many animal themes on my own, I had never before explored the potential of developing a theme with twenty-eight other individuals. By allowing this to happen, I witnessed, and engaged in, collaborative learning first hand. I remember being extremely nervous. Allowing children to have as much voice in the classroom as myself was unnerving to say the least. What if their ideas were silly? What if they did not have any ideas to offer? What if they were not at all interested in being involved? My doubts were quickly answered by an overwhelming response from everyone in the class. I respected their ideas, their choices, and their voices. They responded to my sincerity and interest in what they wanted to do with a counter-reaction of commitment and active engagement in the weeks ahead.

The children offered varying perspectives on the development of the animal theme, ones that I had never considered before. My teacher agenda, which I let the children know ahead of time, was to look at the animal categories and to do some animal research. How we were going to accomplish this, together with what we were going to do, were curriculum decisions that were negotiated between the children and me. The children's ability to have a high level of involvement in the choices and decisions for what and how they were learning brought about an overwhelming sense of empowerment that heightened the children's motivation and their ability to learn for themselves.

One of the most amazing and powerful discoveries for me as a teacher became evident when the children took charge of their own learning. After we had planned the kinds of things we wanted to do, the responsibility for accomplishing these objectives was placed in the children's hands. For example, if the children wanted to have a zoo keeper visit the classroom, the responsibility for contacting the person, arranging a time, double-checking with the rest of the class, and organizing the event was no longer solely mine. That sense of power and responsibility was in the hands of the ones who wanted to make things happen, the children. I assisted in whatever way I could through consultations. I made suggestions and offered advice, as well as proposed other alternatives to consider in problem-solving situations. But the responsibility for carrying out the action belonged to an individual or group of children.

It was through this transfer of power that I observed children starting to "wake up" in my classroom. It was as if a switch that had lain dormant had finally been turned on, and with it came the ability to think for themselves. Each and every child realized, in small but meaningful ways, that he or she had a voice and an ability to effect change. The children were motivated to learn because they were able to connect their own experiences and interests to what was happening in the classroom. I watched the children organize guest speakers for the classroom, plan an animal day, teach animal crafts, design bird feeders, record information about which bird feeders worked better than others, design and create an animal journal, plan animal writing activities, and organize a schedule for animal visits. I was amazed that the children actually possessed the ability to successfully do all these things. Nothing was impossible for them to accomplish when given the power and support to act. For the first time in my teaching career I witnessed young children becoming aware of the their own ability to solve problems by thinking for themselves, not just relying on someone with ready-made answers or a predetermined curriculum. I had never realized that children had the potential to do this, at least not at the ripe old age of seven.

Through the course of this unit of study, as with many other topics throughout the year, the children and I shared the responsibility for planning, organizing, and developing a curriculum that empowered and energized us all. Together we turned the classroom into an enterprise which survived on team work, dialog, and an underlying sense of respect and caring for the people involved in this venture.

It was a year that the children, the parents, and I have never forgotten. It does not take long to rekindle those memories when I run into my former students who fondly reminisce about the year. I also hear comments from their teachers now who say, "Those children still keep talking about their year in Grade Two." And I suppose the comments that really hit home are the ones made by parents:

> I loved the way you taught reading and writing and let the kids think about what stories they had to tell and let them choose what books they wanted to read. (Marilou Sampson, Conversation: 6/15/94)

> I liked the way you let the kids think for themselves not just be told what to think like in that community study they did. The kids decided what they wanted to ask, how they were going to gather information, and finally went out to collect that information from the community. Already I can see a difference between my ten-year-old daughter and my twenty-year-old daughter because of the two types of schooling they went through. My ten-year-old has no difficulty standing in front of a class and talking about what she knows or planning out how she is going to do something. Grade Two gave her the confidence to do that. (Pauline Thiebault, Written note: 6/20/94)

Those comments really solidify and justify that year of teaching for me. How could I possibly teach any differently knowing the potential that this type of learning environment had for those children in grade two as well as for the children I have yet to come in contact with?

❖

It has been three years now since I worked with the children in that class. For the last three years I have not come close to creating the same kind of learning environment that generated such excitement. I have often wondered what made the difference. It is only now that I have forced myself to consider what caused the change in my teaching.

The year after I taught Grade Two I moved to a Grade One classroom. In my first year in Grade One I assumed that the children would not be ready to take charge of their own learning. After all, they were only five or six years old, too young to handle such an undertaking. They had just left kindergarten and were much too young to be given responsibility for shaping their own learning. They first needed, I believed, to be shown how to do something before they would know how to do it themselves. Therefore, I pampered them by planning out our units of study on my own for the first half of the year. I suppose I was trying to show them what could be done and how to do it. By the second half of the year, I allowed them more freedom and responsibility, but by that time they had already bought in to the idea that I had all the answers and I was definitely in control. My second year in Grade One was much the same.

Now, teaching Grade One for a third time, I was frustrated by my inability to recreate the energetic learning environment that had been so successful three years earlier. In trying to dismiss the problem, I used the excuse that the change in grades was the reason for the difference. In some ways this may have been true. But after witnessing the development of the mailbox activity, I questioned whether or not this was the crux of the problem. The power that I felt in the children's voices during this activity caused me to think more deeply about what had occurred. The more I thought about it, the more uneasy and uncomfortable I became in dealing with next question that surfaced.

If these Grade One children possessed the ability to be responsible for what and how they could learn, then why had I not allowed myself to create an environment where this could happen? What had caused me to change?

My principal, Ms Martell, approached me just before Christmas. "I had a long conversation this morning with one of your student's parents on the phone," she said. I immediately became defensive and could feel my body tense. "What have I done wrong now?" I asked. She quickly put me at ease by saying, "Don't worry. It was a good conversation not a bad conversation. Mrs. Busoni wanted to talk about whole language. She wanted to be reassured that Emilio was receiving the best education possible. I talked with her for a while and suggested that I would ask you to call her back to help clarify any other concerns she may have."

I dreaded that phone call for the rest of the day.

My immediate concern was why was this happening now? We had just finished parent-teacher interviews two weeks earlier and Mrs. Busoni seemed satisfied with what Emilio was learning in Grade One. When I eventually contacted her and asked her to come back to the classroom to talk further about her child's progress, she didn't think that was necessary. She was satisfied with the last interview, she indicated. It was not far into the conversation, however, when I discovered the reason for her anxiety. She had had a conversation with one of the more vocal members of our community. This particular person believed in the "old way of teaching" and the importance of returning "to the basics." Mrs. Busoni was confused and wanted to know, "What is the difference between the old way of teaching and how you teach now? I know you do not teach 1+1=2 and 1+2=3 anymore. So how is it different?" I went on to explain that the symbolic number sentences which she just described are expected in Grade One but not without some basis for understanding of what it means first. Children work with concrete materials and manipulatives in order to secure a solid understanding of mathematical principles. They also work with pictorial representations of number followed by symbolic forms such as 1+1=2. She seemed to understand my explanation and commented that when she had been in school she hadn't understood math.

After we discussed several other concerns, the conversation ended politely and I encouraged her to call again when she felt a need. It was important for her to be interested in Emilio's educational development and the doorways to communication must be open at all time, I assured her.

I have had many conversations like this over the past few years. I have realized I need to inform parents through workshops, informal conversations, information letters, and articles about what I'm doing if I am to teach the way I want to. If I do not provide information the doors start to close and the voices of anxious parents become louder. Sometimes they don't hear what they want to hear and they become insistent. Increasingly, I've found parents challenging my teaching.

I love what I do and the children that I work with, but there are people in my community who do not support my vision of education. Their voices have become public, and in some cases are laced with political and marketing agendas. The fuel for their fire comes from a surge of mistrust and concern from media and business regarding the current state of public education. Complaints about whole language teaching, the lack of standards, child centered education, declining skill levels, watered down curricula, and other educational issues are in the news. At first I tried to turn a deaf ear to these voices, but that did not solve the problem. The more I listened, the more I realized those complaints were in direct conflict with my beliefs about how children learn and with my classroom practices. How could that be? Maybe my standards for assessing students' successes were not high enough. Could what parents and others be saying have some validity?

The minute I started questioning myself about what was important about how children learn, I began to change. As a teacher I had always reflected upon my student's learning and the teaching practices I employed. This time was different, however. I became defensive and less receptive to my colleague's advice. In some cases my colleagues would agree with my concerns. This would further complicate matters by fueling my fears and feelings of guilt that I was doing something wrong. I became concerned about "covering the curriculum." When I had taught Grade Two I used the curriculum as a guideline. I would pick topics as areas of study to be negotiated with the children. The children would also choose topics they wanted to study either individually or as a class; these topics may or may not have been part of the official Grade Two curriculum. I considered the process of learning to be more valuable than the end product of what exactly was learned. The children chose the topic, pursued their own questions, arrived at answers, knowledge, and asked new questions along the way. I regarded this new knowledge as important as the knowledge suggested by the curriculum guide itself. Ultimately, it is by children "actively creating meaning from their experiences by exploring, asking questions, gathering information and making connections" (ECEC, 1995: 16) that knowledge is created.

Over the last few years, however, I've been having second thoughts about the validity of my stance. Our minister of education and select parent groups support the view that basic skills need to be taught in the core subject areas. They believe that the acquisition of specific knowledge is important to help children move smoothly from one grade level to the next. On one hand I see that acquiring a common base of knowledge is important. On the other I see the value of knowledge that the children construct, but which should be valued more?

To further complicate my uncertainty, I recently happened to hear a presentation given by Andrew Nikiforuk (author and freelance journalist). He claims that our current educational system has produced "curriculum disabled kids." He argues that over the last thirty years there has been a disappearance of content within our schools because "teachers have been told how to teach rather than what to teach." He believes teachers have come to believe that "the process of learning how to learn something is more important than learning something." He challenges the validity of this viewpoint. "Knowing how to retrieve something, does not mean that children will know what to retrieve," he contends.

As I listened to Nikiforuk talk I couldn't help but think, doesn't the same work in reverse? Just because children know some basic facts, doesn't mean they will know how to apply them or use them in different ways. I was confused and frustrated. Here was an influential person with a very powerful voice discrediting everything that I believed in and understood about children and learning. I slid deep into my seat, uncertain about what direction to pursue.

It is only by reflecting on my teaching experiences over the past few years and listening to those voices that challenge my authority that I have come to realize why I have changed as a teacher. The criticisms, questions, and concerns of the public have affected me. They have raised more questions for me than I have answers, and this has left me with a feeling of uncertainty about whether or not I am providing the best education possible for children. This uncertainty has led to guilt, and the pressures of that guilt have caused me to conform to a skewed public vision of education that I do not believe in.

It is no wonder the children's voices could no longer be heard in my Grade One class. I started controlling their voices and limiting their power because outside forces were doing the same thing to me. I started telling the children what they would learn and how they would learn it because I was being told what to teach and how to teach. Without realizing it I was appeasing my uncertainties by changing my classroom practices to meet the challenges confronting me.

Recognizing the pressures that have caused me to change my teaching practices, I have a choice to make. I can either conform to a belief that values a teacher-controlled learning environment or I can choose to value an environment where children are encouraged to construct their own knowledge.

My strength and conviction as a teacher come from what I believe about teaching, learning, and children. My ten years of experience as a teacher and years of graduate work have provided me with the knowledge necessary to understand my work with children. Now, in this time of uncertainty, I must find a way to respect myself as a professional. I need to do this in order to develop a sense of direction and to value what I know about how children learn. The decisions I make about my teaching practices must be informed decisions based on evidence supplied through my work with children. My reality may not hold true for everyone, but at least it resonates a sincere and honest conviction about how I believe children learn.

My greatest tension over the last few years comes from not having answers to so many questions about my program and the way that I teach. Should I be more concerned with content than process? Should I be focusing directly on and testing intended learning outcomes when I know that children learn many things from any given learning experience? Are those learning outcomes the most important knowledge children should have? These questions have controlled me, confused me, and have caused me many sleepless nights. The anxiety of answering them has been heightened by the public demand that teachers be accountable for the product we are producing and the threat that changes will be made that are out of my control.

Feeling panic I started to listen to and believe in those "expert" voices. I began to control my classroom in the same way that I felt controlled. In education, and in society in general, we rely upon the popular wisdom and assurances of others. We receive that wisdom as it is presented because it is natural, commonplace, and "socially sanctioned" (Mayher, 1990). As adults, our ways of thinking about the world are more or less intact. It is often too difficult to re-examine those beliefs or to contemplate changing them. Politicians, especially at election times, "reduce complex issues to suspicious simplicity to make voters feel confident that solutions are within easy grasp" (Goodman, 1993, p.2). It is easy to be lured into a popular way of thinking that is authority driven. But simple solutions do not come readily packaged with a bright red bow as the politicians seem to think. In order to really understand the issues involved, you need to take the time to construct that knowledge for yourself.

As a teacher I must make the effort to engage with my children, learn from my children, and construct that knowledge for myself. I need to constantly question the "wisdom" of others and see if it really makes sense in light of my experience with children. I need not be afraid of the questions to which I do not have immediate answers. If I had all the answers, I would not be as I am today, in a position of wanting to learn more. I need to let my learning direct my teaching. This does not mean abandoning objectives or working without a curricular framework. It means offering students an invitation to explore in some specific direction and then following closely behind (Newman, 1991). I will discover those answers as I work with children. I need to use those questions to move forward in search of other ways of defining and understanding the world in which we live. Not every question or issue has an easy answer.

As I sit now and realize how I was consumed by uncertainty, guilt, and the pressure of needing to know all the answers, I can finally lift my head above the confusion and see that the most important issue for me is needing to hear those children's voices again. That last year that I spent in Grade Two was a year that not only made an impact on my life but touched the lives of the students and their parents as well. I look upon that year as an incredible year of learning for myself. The parents of those children that I occasionally meet still speak of that year as a terrific year of learning. But the most important message of success comes from the children themselves who pass by my classroom door every so often. Their stories and fond memories of a time not too long ago are worth their weight in gold. I cannot help thinking that there must be something of true educational value worth holding onto that is stronger than any words of wisdom from outside authorities. Our curriculum was based on respect, getting to know one another, and learning about the world around us. It was a curriculum that constantly called on children to apply what they knew in order to solve problems. The long-term evaluation of this process will be in how it affects their adult attitudes, abilities, and choices.

"It is teachers who, in the end, will change the world of the school by understanding it" (Fleischer, 1994: 90). In order for me to understand the world of the school, I need to hear those children's voices.

❖

Child-Centred Education: A Policy Statement. Early Childhood Educational Council. (ECEC). March 1995, Newsletter No. 3: 1-16.

Church, Susan. (1992). Rethinking Whole Language: The Politics of Educational Change. In Patrick Shannon (Ed.), *Becoming Political: Readings and Writings in the Politics of Literacy Education.* 238-249. Portsmouth, NH: Heinemann Educational Books.

Duckworth, Eleanor. (1986). Teaching as Research. *Harvard Educational Review,* 56(4): 481-495.

Fleischer, Cathy. (1994). Researching Teacher-research: A Practitioner's Retrospective. *English Education,* 26(2): 86-124.

Goodman, Ken. (1993). *Phonics Phacts.* Richmond Hill, ON: Scholastic Canada Ltd.

Hillerman, Tony. (1993). *Sacred Clowns.* Toronto: Harper Collins Publishers, Ltd.

Mayher, John S. (1990). *Uncommon Sense.* Portsmouth, NH: Heinemann Educational Books.

Newman, Judith M. (1991). *Interwoven Conversations: Learning and Teaching Through Critical Reflection.* Toronto: OISE Press.

Newman, Judith M. (Ed.). (1990). *Finding Our Own Way: Teachers Exploring Their Assumptions.* Portsmouth, NH: Heinemann Educational Books.

Shannon, Patrick. (Ed.). (1992). *Becoming Political: Readings and Writings in the Politics of Literacy Education.* Portsmouth, NH: Heinemann Educational Books.

Short, Kathy and Burke, Carolyn. (1991). *Creating Curriculum.* Portsmouth, NH: Heinemann Educational Books.

Wells, Gordon et al. (1993). *Changing Schools from Within: Creating Communities of Inquiry.* Toronto: OISE Press.

REAL LIFE AS CURRICULUM

Rosemary Manning

Ann Marie Adams, Karen Abbott, and Madonna Buckley sat in the row closest to the window. Ellen Thompson, Noleen Wadden, and Mary Lou Woodford were always in the row closest to the door. I had the good fortune of having a name in the M's so I was usually in the center row, near the back, best seats in the class. I could duck behind Janine MacNeil and sneak a quick conversation with Ann or Linda who sat to my left and right. My position allowed me to escape from the teacher's vantage point from the big brown desk at the front of the room.

Sometimes this seating arrangement was altered to accommodate differences in height. Each year Sheilagh Hanrahan would switch with Virginia Montoya who was too short to sit in the back. People who couldn't read the board would sit closer to the front and teachers would separate students who were caught talking to each other. I was able to maintain my strategic position through to the end of my high school days. Little did I know how much this school experience would influence what I would do in my own classroom when I began teaching.

My first teaching position was in a small fishing community about 200 miles from St. John's, Newfoundland. I was hired as the remedial math and language arts teacher, for a junior high school. On the first day I was shown my classroom, which was commonly called the "coat check" as this was it's purpose for community functions at the school. Inside this room there was a large teacher's desk at the front and a row of desks along each of the side walls, facing the black board. I was handed my schedule, a list of students who would come to me during their language or math class, a box of chalk, a large red plan book, and several pens, all of them red.

I thought my own school experience and my practice teaching had prepared me for the position. How difficult could it be to teach someone how to read? Any reader could teach someone else how to do it. Although I can't recall even thinking about what being literate meant, my assumptions about what counted as literacy were evident in the way I approached this group of students. I thought I had arrived. I'd crossed the threshold from practice teacher into the "real" world of teaching, and I was so pleased that my environment, small as it was, had been prepared. This environment was exactly the kind of setting I expected. What I'd learned as a teacher and student in such a situation was that in this setting the teacher is the conductor, the students are the orchestra. I was quick to meet the junior high teachers and discuss the students they would be sending to me for help. "David and Earl are twins. They won't give you any trouble. Darrin, on the other hand, is always looking for a way out of doing any work. You'll have to keep a close watch on him. Rodney is a lost cause. I don't think he can read, at least I've never heard him read." I was going to be well prepared for them. The teachers had shown me their plans for the coming weeks. "We'll start with the first story in their reader. I do that one first every year." I wanted to learn from these teachers and be prepared for the students. I spent endless nights planning lessons and getting to know the curriculum inside out.

Within a couple of weeks I had called Darrin's mother about his behavior and given Earl and David lines to write for not completing their work. I wasn't too worried about Rodney since he seemed to be keeping up with the rest. Monday morning of the third week, David and Earl came bouncing in, giggling something about the trouble Darrin was going to have if Mrs. Noseworthy sent him to the office.

"What happened to Darrin?" was my question.

"He said he's not coming here any more Miss," David said with a grin.

"Why not David?"

"He said he didn't need to come down here for help Miss, 'cause it's the same as being upstairs anyway."

What was I going to say to Mrs. Noseworthy about Darrin? Would her opinion of me as a teacher deteriorate because of a misbehaving student? What would I tell the principal when he asked what happened to Darrin? What would I tell Darrin's mother?

I felt I needed to prepare my defense for all of those people. I needed to find a way to convince them that I could work with Darrin and that being in my classroom was different from being upstairs. It occurred to me then that if what was happening with Darrin and the other boys wasn't working upstairs, it wasn't going to work for them downstairs either. I needed to change the downstairs "cloak room" into a classroom.

With new enthusiasm, motivated I admit more by my fear of loss of respect of fellow teachers than the needs of my students, I spoke to each of the boys' parents and we wiped our slates to begin again. My assumption about teaching at that time was that it was solitary. Teachers close their doors and do what they do independent of each other. I would never have thought of my fellow teachers as fellow learners. I was sure they had all the answers.

I contacted the coordinator for special needs with the school board who sent me order forms for reading resources. The principal agreed to spend some money on kits and workbooks that contained the skills the upstairs teachers had determined the boys needed to have. Spelling exercises, comprehension activity books, vocabulary building, word lists, and phonics worksheets were incorporated into my existing curriculum. My classroom became a very busy place with different activities going on at once.

The principal's proudest moment came in June when he announced that the pre- and post-test results of the remedial group had shown significant improvement. I knew there was something wrong with defining literacy by how students performed on standardized tests. My thoughts at that time were mixed. I was pleased that the principal had attributed my efforts to the boys' success, but these students were still failing courses and would have a very difficult time with the Grade Eight curriculum. I watered down their textbooks so they could understand the content. I had done a wonderful job keeping them abreast of the upstairs curriculum and preparing them for tests. But what had I taught them about reading? How much reading and writing did they actually do? I was so busy drilling and skilling, I never had had time to take them to the school library, which was adjacent to our room. I knew Darrin and the other boys saw themselves as failures in a system that reminded them of that fact every day.

My assumption at that time was that if these boys could only learn how to read, their problems in school would vanish. My definition of literacy, however, did as much to impede their learning as sitting in the upstairs classroom. No wonder Darrin didn't need my help.

In subsequent years I've met hundreds of students in gyms, malls, detention centers, and classrooms who have been failed by our school system. The number of students who either couldn't read or who were reading well below the grade requirement was astounding. Many of the students I met through my work with a stay in school program were at risk of leaving school before completing graduation requirements.

Fred was one of these students. He was a seventeen-year-old who had been in "special education" classes since Grade Four. He was referred to me by his classroom teacher because of his high absenteeism. When I met Fred for the first time, he talked about wanting to learn how to read. He said he didn't see the point in staying in school because even though everyone expected him to be able to read, no one was showing him how. I was determined not just to help Fred cope with the curriculum but to really show him how to read.

My assumption was Fred didn't know anything about reading. He told me his father couldn't read and his mother had only completed Grade Eight. I remember chanting to my colleagues over staff-room coffee: "He just needs to learn how to read, then he will succeed." Reading books was Fred's ticket to the literate world and future employment. My definition of literacy still meant mastering skills that would eventually lead to being able to read the printed word, but it had expanded to include the assumption that not until the Freds of the world could read would we stamp out such evils as crime and unemployment.

Frank Smith (1989) writes about the myth of literacy as the "'golden key' to everything from full employment and a reduced crime rate to the treasures of world literature and culture" (p. 354). He quite logically points out that "literacy doesn't make anyone a better person. Literacy doesn't generate finer feelings or higher values. Literacy won't guarantee anyone a job." (p. 354) What I didn't know then was that Fred was already very successful in negotiating his way in the printed world. For two months in a row he had received the "Employee of the Month" award from Pizza Hut. How could a guy who couldn't read survive in a restaurant? What was Fred able to do to cope with the orders written by rushed waiters? How did he know to put extra cheese, no olives, add mushrooms and green pepper? How did he apply for the job and conduct himself in an interview? Why didn't I learn those things about Fred while I was teaching him? I guess I was too busy teaching him, rather than letting him teach me what he already knew.

With Fred my limited definition of what literacy means and my transmission teaching methods did more to interfere with the learning process than to help it. What else could I have done? Paulo Freire (1985) suggests:

> Reading words, and writing them, must come from the dynamic movement of reading the world. The question is how to create a fluid continuity between on the one hand reading the world, of speaking about experience, of talking freely with spontaneity and on the other hand the moment of writing and then learning how to read, so that the words which become the starting point for learning to read and write come from the kids' ideas and not from the teachers reading book. (p.19)

Fred was already very successfully reading his world, but I didn't give him the opportunity to tell about it, write about it, or anything else he might have been interested in reading and writing.

Not that it is any consolation, but I know Fred's experience with me was not unlike his whole school experience. When he said no one was showing him how to read, he was really saying: "Show me how to read my world, not yours." Margaret Meek (1991) shared her experience working with adult beginning readers in this way:

> My mistake was to offer them my kind of literacy, to encourage them to be literate when they had no expectation of this as a state of being they could lay claim to. Only when I made reading and writing work for them, as a tool, as a means to an end, did I understand where they and I could begin....Working with older beginners taught me the lessons I had learned without being aware of them: that as we find different uses and purposes for literacy so our literate skills both increase and diversify. (p.71)

What I know now is that I didn't allow Fred or other students to tell their stories. Lucy Calkins (1991) writes: "Literacy is inseparable from living.... How can we expect students to write with vigor and voice if they are silenced throughout the rest of the day? How can we expect students to write from the particulars of their lives..." (p.13) if we don't let them bring the particulars into school? "How can we expect children to write well if we don't know their stories?" (p. 13) I thought I had all the answers for

Fred, but I didn't allow him to ask any questions. Fred challenged me on a daily basis to change what I was doing. He continued to skip school and he refused to do most of my prepared activities. He didn't return to school this year.

❖

Mike is another student I've met recently who challenges his teachers on a daily basis. On the day I visited his classroom, I began asking questions of two girls who were busy finishing off a piece of writing they'd been working on for some time. All the while I chatted with these students Mike wanted to get my attention. Since sauntering into the classroom after recess, he had finished eating a bag of chips, mumbled something rude or crude about teachers and school, checking with quick glances toward me to see my reaction. "It's your turn next," I assure him. He patiently waited for the next couple of minutes, allowing others around him to get on with their work without interruptions. When I asked what he'd been working on he headed towards a desk and handed me several books explaining, "I don't do what they do. It's stupid."

"So what do you do with these books?" Mike went on to explain he had only been in the school for two months since returning from the stay in school program. We chatted about that for a while since I was familiar with a similar program in Newfoundland. Mike was really impressed with that place, "'cause you could do whatever you wanted." We discussed "the problems with school" and the work teachers were making him do. Finally I asked for Mike's advice on what to do with the Mikes I would likely face in my classroom next year. "Just leave them alone," he said. I pointed out that when I came into the room the message he was giving me was anything but leave me alone. "So what do I do Mike? I've got ten of you in my class next year and you all want me to pay attention and leave you alone at the same time."

This conversation with Mike continued for a little while longer and I discovered some of his interests. I was really looking for something he could read or write about. I thought I had him when he said he wanted to be a fire fighter and he enjoyed reading *Fire House* magazine. "Why don't you bring some in?" I offered. "Yeah, that's what Mr. Albright said, but I don't want to write about anything. I know how to read. I don't need to know any more than I already do about reading or writing to be a fire fighter."

What to do with the Mikes in my classroom is a definite tension I have and will continue to face. Mike is not just saying, "Make me!" he's saying, "Who needs it?" Until students see a purpose for reading and writing in their lives they will resist just as Mike is doing. My job with Mike, as with all other students, is to give him an opportunity to see how fire fighters, mechanics, oceanographers, etc. use reading and writing in their work. Rather than me showing him what he doesn't know and why I think he should, Mike's life experience and aspirations must be the curriculum from which he will decide what he needs to learn. In a classroom where this happens, students like Mike don't fail. Margaret Meek (1991) talks about the Mikes, Freds and Darrins of our school system.

> ...I believe children fail when they lose confidence in their own
> ability to succeed. So my solution is to engage them in any way
> we can, in the process of *discovering* what reading is and not
> worrying about how to do it. (p.199)

What I need to do as a teacher is show my students, by example, how I use reading and writing in my daily life. They need an environment where they can use reading and writing to make sense of their worlds. In so doing they may begin to think of themselves as readers and writers.

In September 1992 I began what I intended to be a crusade towards mastering the "how tos" of teaching the growing number of "non readers" in Newfoundland schools. However, what began as a quest for teaching the masses has become a personal journey into the discovery of my own literacy, what being literate actually means, and "how to" create an environment that will challenge my future students to do the same. I know now, with the help of writers such as Calkins (1991), that

> The way to establish a school for children in each classroom is
> not to rush out filling a room with a variety of paper, bulletin
> boards, conference areas, editing checklists and an author's
> chair—those will all come in time—but instead, to fill the
> classroom with children's lives. (p. 11)

More importantly, I want the lives of my future students to teach me in the powerful ways my students of the past have done.

❖

Calkins, Lucy McCormick with Shelley Harwayne. (1991). *Living Between the Lines*. Portsmouth, New Hampshire: Heinemann Educational Books.

Freire, Paulo. (1985). Reading the World and Reading the Word, an Interview. *Language Arts*, 62,1: 15-21.

Meek, Margaret. (1991). *On Being Literate*. London, UK: The Bodley Head Children's Books.

Smith, Frank. (1989). Overselling Literacy. *Phi Delta Kappan*, January: 353-359.

For the Love of Books

Veronica Yeung

We were on our way back to the classroom when Jordan suddenly stopped, turned abruptly almost bumping into me.

"Let's go back," Jordan whispered.

"Why?" I asked in a low voice.

"They are doing writing," he answered, hardly audible, and there was a smile on his face.

Was that a smile of embarrassment or was it an apologetic smile? And why was he whispering? Was he afraid of letting the others know that he was there? It was true the class was unusually quiet since everyone was working on his or her writing folder. This was the second time something like this had happened. The first time, instead of explaining why he turned back, Jordan had just grinned sheepishly.

Jordan hated writing. There was only one sentence in his writing folder: "Batman is cool." The sentence was not his either—he had written it at my urging. He wanted to go back to the quiet corner where the two of us were reading. This individual tutoring time was something he looked forward to, apart from gym, of course. It was an escape from the classroom routine.

My only experience as a classroom teacher occurred when I taught history in a junior high school in Hong Kong after graduating with a B.A. At that time you did not have to have an education degree in order to be able to teach. A few years later I came to Manitoba, and upon completing a degree in Fine Arts I worked as a graphic artist. This let me stay home with my children while setting up my own business.

My interest in literacy began when my oldest daughter started nursery school. I decided she would have a head start if she could learn to read before entering kindergarten. Since I did not have a textbook to follow, I thought I would teach her to read English the same way I had learned to read Chinese. I reasoned that if I could learn Chinese ideograms, then she should be able to learn to read English that way—by looking at words as wholes. So I started reading to her frequently, took her to the library, helped her write messages and shopping lists, pointed out the environmental print, and so on, unwittingly doing all the "right" things, I discovered later. Megan was able to read before entering kindergarten. More than a decade later I discovered that my assumptions about learning to read were confirmed when I read an article by Smith (1973) in which he explained how we read words as a whole, not by looking at each letter. I used the same procedure with my two younger children when they in turn reached nursery school age. All three children were reading independently by the time they entered school. Being able to read opened up a whole new world for them. When I found my youngest daughter was spending two hours every day reading story books, I became so concerned that I tried every means to get her away from books without much success. I was worried that it would ruin her eyesight and that it was not normal for a four-and-one-half-year-old to read for so long. It was then that I saw the tremendous power of stories over the mind of the young.

A few years ago I decided to enter a master's program in educational psychology because I was interested in teaching students with so-called "learning disabilities" to read and write. I was intrigued by the media's portrayal of school children not being able to read. I wanted to find out what could be done. Not being a certified teacher, I had to work as a special needs teacher assistant.

Last November Jordan had been transferred to this school because his birth mother had succeeded in gaining custody of him and his three siblings. I had agreed to work with him in this new school in the mornings. Even though I could only observe him for half of the school day, I found his behavior in class quite different from the way he acted in our tutoring sessions. During group time, Jordan usually sat at the back and chewed on his sleeves or the top of his shirt. Sometimes he would tear off the top of his sneakers or color them with a marker or he would lean against the legs of the table or hide behind other students. Apart from his language deficit, the fidgeting and the hyperactivity was a result of fetal alcohol syndrome.

What was it that made Jordan look forward to our reading sessions? I was still operating with a prescribed basal reader curriculum. However, Jordan knew that after the basals he would have a chance to enjoy the library books which I brought along. Sometimes he would bring books which he had picked from the reading corner in the classroom. He seemed to sense that the basal reader was a necessary evil. Get it over and done with and then enjoy the library books. For Jordan, having someone read to him was a reward. The pleasure of being read to was not something he experienced at home. I was using the trade books as an incentive to get him to finish reading the basals and working in the workbooks. Letting him choose his own books gave him a sense of power and ownership in his learning and showed me how he wanted to learn, thus allowing me to follow his lead.

One day the resource teacher told me he wanted Jordan and Edwin to work together on their reading. He implied that Jordan's progress in the basal reader was too slow. He wanted me to hurry up and finish the unit so Edwin could join us. When I told him how Jordan could read several library books besides having finished the first level of the basal reader, his reply was, "I'll give you the next level." There was no excitement over the fact that Jordan could read those library book. Why was there such an emphasis on the basals? Was that the only "legitimate" way to show a student's progress? Shouldn't students' literacy development be gauged by their enjoyment of reading as well as the independent way in which they handle reading and writing in their everyday lives?

The worksheets had made Jordan adept at copying. Copying was the strategy he used to satisfy his teachers' demands for performance. This got to a point where he did not even take a moment to think for himself. When I asked him what a certain number was or how to write a certain number, he just looked up and copied from the number sheet on the wall. He often copied without understanding what he was doing. Sometimes when his mistakes were pointed out to him or when there were things that he did not comprehend, there was anger on Jordan's face. Was he angry at himself for not being able to understand? While working he would sometimes rip the eraser off the top of his pencil or deliberately break the lead.

> When children are judged deficient from the beginning of their school experience, the accumulation of failure can lead to acute feelings of powerlessness or anger. (Cameron, 1994: 277)

Before coming to this school, Jordan had been taken from his abusive father and placed in a number of foster families. One time he kept interrupting me when we were reading because he was worried about his younger sister being left home without an adult around. The children ended up being taken by Child and Family Services and later returned to their mother. The anger and destruction no doubt had to do with the turmoil in his young life.

> "Their devastating life stories affected the ways in which they learned to read and write" (Taylor, 1993: 143).

Jordan's classroom teacher said to me, "There's this bond between you. He's so used to you, we are the enemies." He read with expression in our reading sessions, but he held back when someone else worked with him. The resource teacher had also commented, "He seems to know more when you test him." His not knowing how to read the words when tested by another teacher reflected his self-consciousness and anxiety. I have come to see that emotions play a vital role in learning. We can only learn if we feel comfortable as learners. I think teachers, in their eagerness to have students learn to read, fail to take into account the individual needs of children. They are teaching words, not children.

Jordan showed me he could take control of his own learning. On St. Valentine's day the whole class had to make a card. After cutting and pasting, they had to write a message on the two hearts on the inside of the card. I asked Jordan what he wanted to write. He wrote, "Mom, I Love You Jordan" on one heart (all by himself without help). When I found out that the teacher had intended everyone to write (or copy from the board) "Happy Valentine's Day" on one of the hearts, I asked Jordan if he wanted to do that. His reply was, "No. That's too many words. I already did that" (pointing to his message).

Working with Gobii, another student, I had come to realize that it is important to see things from the students' perspective. So I would often ask Jordan, "How did you know that?" Most of the time he would shrug his shoulders. Occasionally he would smile and explain how he came upon his new knowledge. There were times when his face glowed as he realized he had made connections between what he had learned and what he was reading.

"I've just said that. Why do I have to read it again?" I explained to Jordan why he had to repeat the words. Yet how true was my assumption that by repeating he would remember? There was still the gap between belief and practice when I fell back on the strategy of focusing on word recognition. Sometimes when we walked past another study group and I saw the teacher using word cards, it would make me wonder if I ought to be doing the same thing.

My self-confidence grew not only in the way I taught but also in the way I reacted to the instructions given by other teachers. I was told to test Jordan with a list of words to find out how many words he could read and spell. I did the test, and even though he could only recognize a few of the sight words and could not spell a single one, I believed he and I were headed in the right direction because I could see his interest in reading grow.

Recently I was invited to watch how another teacher worked with Jordan and Edwin and was told I could use the same format for teaching the two of them to write. But as I watched, I knew it was not the way for Jordan. The sentences were patterned after the sentences in the basal. The emphasis was on writing conventions and how to spell correctly. What Jordan needs is an opportunity to find for himself a system that will work for him. My goal for Jordan is to help him discover and teach himself the writing system as a means of sharing what he wants to communicate. In Margaret Meek's words:

> They move from what they understand as a possible system to a principled grasp of the conventions, and in so doing discover the rules for the conventions that make them less dependent on the hazards of memory...they become better spellers because then, anyone will be able to read what they write. (Meek, 1991: 96)

Despite the fact that the basals are still the prescribed curriculum, I am now convinced that I must let students read stories which have relevance to their daily lives, help them use strategies and cues as they read, and let them find ways of expressing themselves in their writing. It is through reading trade books that they come to read the basals with fluency and comprehension; not the other way around as the other teachers would have me believe.

Today the resource teacher told me that after spring break he would like me to teach both Jordan and Edwin together for an hour each day. He laid out a lesson plan—write the sight words on a card, have the students trace the words with their fingers, let them make sentences with the words.

For writing, he would like me to pick out passages in the basal, have the students substitute words to make new sentences based on the sentence structure of the basal. There would also be workbooks. I asked him what the objective was—he said to emphasize sight vocabulary. Then I explained to him what I had been doing with Jordan—how we had been reading trade books and writing for real purposes. I pointed out that the structured approach which he wanted me to use would not encourage the use of invented spelling and it would only slow Jordan down. I went on to explain that focusing on the basals and emphasizing word identification skills might dampen Jordan's enthusiasm for reading, and I hoped his love of books would not die as a result. The resource teacher was beginning to get angry, "I know you have been taking courses, but this whole language approach does not work with students who have learning disabilities. They need to be taught the basics. I am taking my certification as a reading clinician, my professor was observing me teach Jordan the other day...." In short, he meant his way of teaching was an effective one and he advised me to follow it. My unspoken reaction to this was that it is precisely because these students have so-called "learning disabilities" that we cannot force them to fit into memorizing words in isolation. He used the term "sight word drill." It is the "drilling" bit that these students cannot accomplish because a few days later they are not be able to remember what has been taught.

Thinking back to my conversation with the resource teacher, it is not so much the methodology that I have problems with as the emphasis and the goals of teaching—the identification of sight words rather than the kindling of an interest in reading. This makes me all the more determined to nourish this love of books which Jordan has begun to develop. I am more convinced than ever of the power of stories.

> "Stories provide listeners with an increasing imaginative
> repertoire of ways of coming to terms with their emotions"
> (Meek, 1991 p.113).

After all, who knows if Jordan will not be apprehended tomorrow (he has been getting into trouble lately—smashing car windows, pulling the fire alarm and kicking in the glass door because his mother was not home, and as a result his family had been served eviction warnings)? I suspect one of these days I will arrive at school and be told that he is gone.

❖

Years ago, when I first started teaching history, I did it the same way I had been taught—transmitting what were supposedly indisputable facts, expecting students to memorize them and to reproduce correct answers on tests and exams.

> "Literacy must be appropriated by each individual as he or she strives to make meaning in the company of others" (Cameron, 1994: 271).

I can only watch as children develop their own personal understandings of literacy. I am learning to trust the children's innate ability to direct their own learning. I like what Meek has to say about not worrying about how to teach reading:

> I believe children fail when they lose confidence in their own ability to succeed. So my solution is to engage them, in any way we can, in the process of *discovering* what reading is and not in worrying about how to do it.... Sometimes I think they can't know what reading is, because everyone...is too busy telling them what to do. (Meek, 1991: 199)

Cameron, M. (1994). *Literacy Development Within the Curriculum: Narrative Accounts of Literacy Learning and Teaching in a Non-mainstream School.* Unpublished doctoral dissertation, University of Toronto.

Maher, A. (1994). An Inquiry into Reader Response. In G. Wells (Ed.), *Changing Schools from Within.* Portsmouth, NH: Heinemann Educational Books: 81-97.

Meek, M. (1991). *On Being Literate.* Portsmouth, NH: Heinemann Educational Books.

Smith, F. (1973). *Psycholinguistics and Reading.* New York: Holt, Rinehart & Winston.

Smith, F. (1983). *Essays into Literacy.* Portsmouth, NH: Heinemann Educational Books.

Stephens, D. (1990). *What Matters: A Primer for Teaching Reading.* Portsmouth, NH: Heinemann Educational Books.

Silverstein, S. (1974). *Where the Sidewalk Ends.* New York: Harper & Row.

Taylor, D. (1993). *From the Child's Point of View.* Portsmouth, NH: Heinemann Educational Books.

PART THREE

TAKING
NEW PATHS

An inevitable outcome of inquiry into
practice seems to be the realization that
the classroom calls for something new.
The evidence from our observations of
what's happening in our classrooms
makes it clear that if we want to really
engage students, we're going to have to
do things differently.

Sometimes inquiry begins because a
teacher has already identified tensions
and is now wondering where to go
next. Sometimes the impetus comes
from mandated curriculum changes
and a desire to understand what's
going on in the new situation. In either
case, the teacher/action research is
driven by a need to understand what's
involved in taking a new path.

James Beveridge, in ACTION RESEARCH:
AN ONGOING JOURNEY, walks us through
his work as a new principal of a rather
large secondary school. He describes
what he does, reflects on what it
means, and considers what he might
do differently.

Elizabeth Hughes, in CONTROLLING OR NURTURING? examines her teaching past and raises questions about "precision teaching" with Learning Disabled students in which she was engaged. Her recent return to the classroom, this time as a senior high school language development/resource teacher, provides her with an opportunity to take a new direction. She discusses the contradictions and tensions she faces in her classroom.

Jim Albright, in BACKING OUR OF THE ROOM, describes his journey with a reading/writing workshop. He outlines how he progressed from a "rote" implementation of "doing Atwell," as he calls it, to paying closer attention to what students had to say to one another.

ACTION RESEARCH: AN ONGOING JOURNEY

James Beveridge

We'd had a wonderful summer. During the first three weeks of July we visited with family and friends. Upon our return home the five of us, my wife Patti and I, our daughter Alexandria, and our sons Ian and Andrew, spent another two weeks relaxing at my parents' cottage. The memories of the chaotic end of the previous school year faded. Our time together as a family was exactly what I had needed. As the summer stretched on I found myself thinking more and more about my new appointment as principal. I felt rejuvenated and I was eager to assume my new challenge at the collegiate.

New to the school, I was very aware that I would be bringing my own set of beliefs, values, and understandings about educational leadership. Thomas Sergiovanni (1987) refers to this as one's mindscape—our mental picture of how the world works. Our mindscape provides a rationale for how we choose to act in our personal and professional lives. How would my mindscape, my beliefs and values, be received at the collegiate?

In the days and weeks before school began I found myself trying to clarify my own mindscape. I re-examined my beliefs and values about teaching and education as well as my views on leadership and the role of a principal. How was I going to begin the school year with a new staff? What impression did I want to create at our first meeting? How would the staff welcome me? Would my transition to the principalship be a smooth one? Newman (1991) refers to this process as one's "opening moves," and looking back now I can see that this was exactly what I was doing.

Seven months into my new position at the collegiate I still find myself asking questions and trying to learn more about the culture of the school. Terence Deal (1985) refers to the culture of a school as the patterns of thought, behavior, and artifacts that symbolize and give meaning to the school. I have spent considerable time talking and, more importantly, listening to what others have to say about the collegiate. Like all schools there are key players who are instrumental in creating and maintaining the culture of the school. I am only now beginning to understand some of the complexities involved in a fairly large high school. The past months here have been an exhausting but invaluable learning experience. I can now reflect on some of my past experiences at the school. Some of these situations might be referred to as critical incidents. I can also begin to examine my own leadership practice. Is what I say and what I do congruent? Do I "talk the talk" and "walk the walk" of educational leadership? In what ways are the students, staff, and the community responding to my style of leadership?

As I reflected on some of these incidents I gained some insight into my own practice as a teacher and principal. I found Smyth's (1989) questions about reflective practice helpful in framing my own understandings of my work as a principal. Part of a process that includes describing, informing, confronting, and restructuring, this framework fits with my own view of action research and the process involved in an inquiry of this kind.

Smyth's first question, "What do I do?", attempts to elicit a simple observational description of practice. His second question, "What does this mean?", seeks to discover the underlying principles that drive the practice. The third question, "How did I come to be this way?", looks at the political nature of teaching and educational practice. His final question, "How might I do things differently?", implies that action is an essential component of this process.

What Do I Do?

I am the principal of a collegiate located in a residential community of middle income families in Winnipeg. The community is predominantly blue collar. The school has been identified as an at-risk school and is eligible for funding from the province's at-risk grant proposals. I am responsible for the physical plant, supervision of all staff, professional and non-professional, all educational programs. I am the person the community holds responsible for the overall success of the school. A very tall order indeed for any individual. My role can be broken down into managerial, political, and educational functions. Larry Cuban (1988), in *The Managerial Imperative and the Practice of Leadership in Schools*, traces the history of the principalship. He suggests that much of the work of a principal today is centered on the managerial and political aspects of the job, often neglecting educational concerns.

My work is frequently dominated by managerial and political concerns rather than educational ones. To a certain extent this is the nature of the position as it is currently structured. Principals are part of the larger bureaucracy of the educational system. They have to deal with a multitude of concerns from the public, from senior administrators, and school trustees. If people don't attend to these concerns they may find their term as principal is relatively short-lived. There is a managerial imperative to the principal's role that one cannot ignore. The real challenge for me comes in trying to find ways of balancing the conflicting and time-consuming managerial and political aspects of the job with the equally demanding educational issues and concerns.

Our initial staff meeting proved to be an interesting start to the school year. After the usual opening-day procedures and details were completed, I took the opportunity to share with the staff my own philosophy of education, my views on leadership, and the role of principal. Being new to the school I felt that it was important for the staff to have a sense of what they could expect from their new principal. I realized that transmitting my beliefs in this manner was contrary to my usual preference of revealing my values through my actions. However, I felt I needed to establish a framework that would form the foundation for my relationship with the staff. Looking back now I can say that it was the right thing to do (I've had lots of positive feedback from staff on this point), but I realize I was taking a risk beginning this way.

Near the end of the meeting one staff member asked me how the school's plan to deduct marks from absent or late students fit with my philosophy of school as a place where the needs of students should prevail. The idea of systematically deducting marks from students for attendance seemed to be a rather simplistic reaction to this chronic high school problem. I knew from previous discussions with individual teachers that few supported this policy. However, there were some teachers who did support it and saw it as a way of removing students from their classrooms. It was obvious that there was going to be little consensus among the staff on this issue. I had spoken about how our structures and policies should reflect students' needs. Clearly this policy didn't fit. Sergiovanni (1992) speaks about leadership by outrage, where the core values of the organization are violated and the leader reacts accordingly. Deducting marks from students ended that morning. I wanted to give the staff a clear message that students and their needs must be our focus; policies and practices at the collegiate would attempt to reflect that.

Jeannie Oakes (1990) uses the term non-negotiable values. Part of this first meeting with the staff was exactly that. Meeting the needs of our students and developing strategies to deal with these needs was one of the non-negotiable values that our school would strive towards. As the principal I would not allow policies that violated these values.

Principals are often called out of the building to attend meetings and conferences. I make every attempt to be in school and to be visible. This affects the way I structure my time. I arrive just before eight in the morning to check my schedule for the day and, more importantly, to give staff an opportunity to meet with me and discuss whatever issues or concerns they might have. I also try to spend some time in the staffroom over the lunch hour. Although my time is often interrupted with school business, it still gives me an opportunity to sit down with staff members and chat informally. It seems to me that making oneself accessible to the staff is crucial to ensuring that lines of communication stay open.

I am surprised by how often teachers and other staff need to connect with the principal during the course of a day. Some of these contacts last only a few minutes while others are much longer. At times it seems everyone wants a piece of you and there isn't enough time to accommodate all the demands. I attempt to move around the school. Prior to class or during breaks I try to be in the hallways interacting with both students and staff. This gives me a chance to meet a number of students and chat with them about what's going on. High school students provide pretty straightforward feedback on what they think about their school experience.

I also try to visit each classroom once during the day. Sometimes I join in with the activity or lesson while other times I quietly observe. My presence in the classrooms was quite a surprise for teachers. Many of them were not accustomed to having the principal visiting. Initially some of them would actually stop whatever they were doing and ask if they could help me.

After seven months the staff are now quite aware of my classroom visits, and a number comment if I haven't visited their room lately.

Mark Enders, a social studies teacher, mentioned my presence in classrooms recently. He had been discussing Canada's global position with a class. He compared Canada's location with that of his classroom in the school. In previous years, he said, the room's distance from the office usually precluded any visits from administration. This year, however, it was clearly different.

I know Mark is neither uncomfortable with my visits nor does he see them as an interruption, but I wonder if some teachers do. Hargreaves (1994) has outlined the individualistic nature of the high school teacher and the culture of isolationism that exists both in teacher education and teacher practice at this level. One of my reasons for visiting the classrooms and the teachers daily is to breakdown some of this isolation.

One of my goals as principal of the collegiate was to begin building the necessary base for a collaborative school. Roland Barth (1990), in his book *Improving Schools from Within,* talks about a community of learners and a community of leaders. This community does not develop overnight, but it is something to work towards.

Early in the school year one staff member mentioned that she would like to see a code of conduct developed for the students. Another staff member commented that the code should extend to teachers as well. The discussion continued for some until Mary, one of our resource teachers, said what the school really needed was a clear mission statement. She talked about a statement that would capture the essence of what the school represented—one that was developed by students, staff, and members of the school community. A number of teachers agreed and the discussion shifted to how we should go about developing a mission statement for the school. The staff decided to strike a working committee to develop a process for us to use and report back to the staff. Ten staff members volunteered for the committee! One of the ways I felt that I could support the initial efforts was by providing release time for those on the committee. I was successful in obtaining some funding from the school division for this project.

The first meeting proved to be an important one for a number of reasons. The discussions we had that afternoon revealed much about us as teachers and individuals. Two teachers came prepared to write the mission statement that day; several saw this as a longer term project. Most felt that it was crucial to a renewal for the collegiate. Everyone agreed that we would need representation from students and parents on the committee.

The afternoon ended with consensus. We agreed to meet again to look specifically at the composition of the committee and the process we would follow for developing a mission statement. It was obvious that the committee wanted the school's mission statement to be more than an exercise. There was a sense that the school was ready for renewal and a mission statement would be an integral part of the renewal process. I am well aware of the challenge that lies ahead of us. The task will be a long and at times frustrating one, as we determine what we believe and what our school should represent. However, I can't help but be encouraged by the enthusiasm the committee has shown to this point. Clearly this is one of the first steps in creating the type of school culture and climate Barth (1990) suggests.

Perhaps the most encouraging thing I've noticed since coming to the collegiate are the dialogs between staff members and me and with one other. We talk to each other about what we are doing in our classrooms and in the school. As principal I have a responsibility to create opportunities for this type of discussion to take place.

Staff meetings are a good place to begin. Our staff meetings need to be more than simply times to transmit administrative trivia. This year we have structured time at meetings for discussion of professional articles and concerns. Teachers know beforehand the agenda of the meeting and they know that they will have an opportunity to express their views.

Our school division has, for the past few years, held early dismissals three times a year for professional development sessions for teachers. At the collegiate this year, we used this time to work together in teams to explore a number of areas of concern. Our teachers are well into planning common exams, investigating learning styles, portfolio assessment, and cooperative learning strategies. The teachers are very interested in improving their classroom practice, and structuring time for this to happen is important.

What Does this Mean?

What are some of the underlying principles that influence my work as a principal? Over the years a number of individuals have shaped my thinking and my understanding of educational leadership and management. In his book *Moral Leadership*, Sergiovanni (1992) discusses a new way of looking at leadership and the role of a principal. He suggests that the idea of leadership may have to be reinvented for today's realities. To a large extent management theory and leadership practice have attempted to distance themselves from values and beliefs; they have instead held to traditional methods of administrative science and deductive logic. The scientific approach to administration has dominated the discussion of leadership theory and practice for a long time. Sergiovanni suggests we may need to view much of the existing management literature, and its prescriptions for leadership practice, as more historical than functional.

Sergiovanni provides us with an alternative way of looking at leadership and management. He suggests leadership should be based on moral authority. He talks about *leadership by purpose*, referring to a continuous stream of action by the principal to induce clarity, consensus, and commitment regarding a school's basic purpose. He also discusses *leadership by empowerment*, the way power is divided and shared in a school.

The literature of educational leadership paints a distorted picture of the role of a principal in this process. Too often the principal is characterized as a visionary individual who will single-handedly lead the staff along the right path. Carl Glickman points out the problem with this ideal:

> ...the principal as all knowing, all wise, and transcendent in vision, who can lead the staff development council and the curriculum council, be an expert on group facilitation and organizational change, can spend 50% of his or her time in the classrooms with uncanny analytical and conferencing abilities, deal with all manner of students, staff, parents and communities, plus fill out all the necessary forms, run all the schedules...this is an incomprehensible idea. (Glickman, 1991: 7)

Both Glickman and Sergiovanni recognize the need to empower others to participate in accomplishing tasks that are meaningful and rewarding. Principals then become leaders who mobilize the expertise and talent of others in the school and the community. Students and teachers become leaders as Barth suggests in his book *Improving Schools from Within*.

Sergiovanni (1990) also discusses *leadership by outrage*. He points out that real toughness is always principled. He contends that leaders should be outraged when they see core values that define what the school believes in and represents violated. Leaders can not stand by and pretend not to see such indiscretions. They must act when the situation calls for it.

As principal of the school I am aware of my responsibilities as a leader. However, I do not see this as my responsibility alone. I am responsible for setting a framework for collaboration, but I must rely heavily on the efforts of others to help to guide our school's path. This process must be a collaborative one.

How Did I Come to be this Way?

I had three reasons for becoming a teacher. The first was my love for and interest in children. As I grew older, I began to seek opportunities to volunteer. I coached baseball and soccer at the community club, worked at the YMCA as a youth leader, and returned to my old high school to coach basketball. My teaching experiences were already well underway. The second reason was the teachers I had in school. I respected them for the passion they brought to their teaching. Mrs. Krindle, Mr. Arnold, and Mr. Biluk really inspired me, and indeed encouraged me to become a teacher. Finally, I believed I could relate well to young people and that I could make a difference to the lives of the students I taught. Looking back now those were three good reasons for becoming a teacher.

I began as a high school teacher. I soon discovered my formal training had barely prepared me to cope with a classroom of thirty-five students. I was focused on the curriculum, and for the first few years of my career probably worried too much about covering what was prescribed. Looking back I realize that by concentrating on the curriculum I totally missed the needs of many students.

My desire to try new strategies and techniques in the classroom led me into some interesting attempts at meeting students' needs. It also led me on a journey of learning—learning in the professional sense of courses and graduate studies as well as in personal awareness and growth. It forced me to take on a number of challenges where I was confronted with change both in my professional and personal life.

I've been teaching for nineteen years; the last ten in some administrative capacity. My teaching experience has been varied. I have taught grades four to twelve. I began in a high school, moved to junior high, and then to an elementary school where I began my administrative career. I remember well the reaction of many of my colleagues when I requested an elementary assignment. Many of them told me I was crazy and warned me that getting back to high school teaching would be difficult. There is still that notion that the high school is the place where the real teaching takes place! I'm glad I didn't heed them because my experiences have helped me tremendously to understand the complexities of how children learn and how different levels attempt to meet the individual needs of students.

Now I am the principal of a high school—the only high school administrator in our school division with elementary teaching and administrative experience. My experiences with younger children lead me to believe that high schools could learn from elementary school. Perhaps this is one of the reasons I believe a restructuring of high schools is long overdue.

There is a prevailing belief that teaching and education are really unproblematic, that everyone knows what a teacher does and what schools are about. This notion is at best misleading. As David Coulter suggests:

> the idea that we can unproblematically decide what schooling
> is about, determine how to go about accomplishing education
> for children and then hold everyone accountable for faithful
> replication of procedures and uniform results is misguided.
> (Coulter, 1991: 2)

I see the need for teachers, and all other educators, to join the highly political public debate about the purposes of schooling and the type of schools we want today.

How Might I do Things Differently?

Smyth's final question. As a principal I need to continue to challenge the traditional theories of educational leadership. I'm not comfortable with the old notions; as Sergiovanni suggests it might be time to look at different models of leadership.

I constantly struggle to keep educational issues on the front burner at our school. This means I need to continue to look for more efficient ways of dealing with the managerial and political aspects of my job.

I need to challenge the idea that a school can be led by non-educators as some people propose. I strongly believe that schools need leadership from principals who have been teachers and who continue to see themselves as teachers.

I am always looking for ways that will help me improve my administrative practice. Probably the most important thing I can do is what I'm now trying to do. An inquiry, a reflective look at *What I do? What that means? How I came to be this way?* and *How I might do things differently?* If schools are to be vibrant and inquiring places for our students and our teachers, then we must all enter into a critical study of our practices so we may have the opportunity to articulate what it is we believe and how we might go about improving our practice.

Barth, Roland. (1990). *Improving Schools from Within*. San Francisco: Jossey-Bass.

Coulter, David. (1991). The Purposes of Education. Seven Oaks School Division Paper. Winnipeg, MB: Seven Oaks School Division

Cuban, Larry. (1988). *The Managerial Imperative and the Practice of Leadership in Schools*. Albany: New York Press.

Deal, Terence. (1985). The Symbolism of Effective Schools. *Elementary School Journal*, 85: 601-620.

Glickman, Carl. (1991). Pretending Not to Know What We Know. *Educational Leadership*, 48(8), May: 4-10.

Hargreaves, Andy. (1994). *Changing Teachers, Changing Times: Teachers' Work & Culture in the Postmodern Age*. New York: Teachers College Press.

Newman, Judith. (1991). *Interwoven Conversations*. Toronto: OISE Press.

Oakes, Jeannie. (1990). Restructuring and Rethinking. Cocking Lecture. NCPEA Conference.

Sergiovanni, Thomas. (1987). *The Principalship: A Reflective Practice Perspective*. Boston: Allyn and Bacon.

Sergiovanni, Thomas. (1992). *Moral Leadership*. San Francisco: Jossey-Bass.

Smyth, John. (1992). Conflicting Conceptualizations. Seven Oaks Symposium Paper. Winnipeg, MB: Seven Oaks School Division.

CONTROLLING OR NURTURING?

Elizabeth Hughes

Throughout my teaching career I have been dealing almost exclusively with children from backgrounds that are probably best described as non-mainstream. This was more by accident than design, but that kind of teaching situation was where I found myself. Twenty-one years ago these children were referred to as culturally deprived, and many intensive efforts were made to help them enter the mainstream.

My first teaching position was as a Grade Two teacher in an inner-city school. I loved working with these children, but getting them to sit and listen, to do the work I had decided was on the day's agenda, was, to say the least, a challenge.

Basal reading series were in their heyday; the children's ability was assessed through achievement tests that accompanied these series and workbook assignments that accompanied the stories provided seat work to be done individually. This worked fine except that sometimes students couldn't read or couldn't remember the directions. And, with a few exceptions, didn't want to do the work much of the time. Those who were able to work independently did well, but for some reason I wasn't happy with the way students were spending their time.

Although I had done none of the reading that has influenced me recently, I felt these children were spending too much time doing pages of pencil and paper exercises that had nothing to do with reading. I felt I was committing an outrageous act when I told them, in mid-October, to answer the first question and then move on to the next story. I had an instinctive feeling that one learned to read by reading.

One reason behind my desire to attempt something different with reading instruction may be my own memories of learning to read in school. I clearly remember three experiences from my own literacy development. First, an acute feeling of disappointment when my Grade One teacher (as well meaning as I later was) kindly assured me that "yes, we had to review the primary readers to make sure we remembered all those words before we could start Grade One reading." I remember feeling I just wouldn't be able to stand this. Her kind manner with all forty of us sustained me, but rereading these non-stories was horrible.

As profoundly disappointed as I was to realize I had to wait to read something new in school, I was ecstatic when I found a yellow and white covered book on the shelf that contained really funny stories in which things happened. I was told to put it away, we would read that at the end of the year. The book, called *Open the Gate*, was labeled as an enrichment book not to be used until the regular program was completed. My teacher took these directions very seriously. Would I have been damaged in some way by reading them?

My third memory is from Sunday school, singing "Onward Christian Soldiers," while holding the song book, I suddenly connected the words on the page to the words I was singing. I remember thinking, "Now I can read!" I had been successful at reading in school, but this event outside of school was when I felt I had joined what Frank Smith (1988) calls "the club of readers."

At this time, in 1972, I didn't instinctively connect the powerful relationship between reading and writing. I took a small step further, however, by abandoning the workbooks for those I deemed my "bright" students. I prepared content questions so that they used reading to find information from each story. This worked so well I soon had all four of my reading groups, including the bottom one, which contained one specially cherished soul who struggled to retain any vocabulary at all. Dino did work to answer his questions. I kept hoping he would internalize some sentence structure through the repetition of the answer pattern from which I had him work.

I wish I had thought about responses such as "What did the story remind you of?" "How did you feel when you read this?" or "What did you think when you read this?" These questions would have let the children connect what they were reading to their own lives, letting them enhance the meaning they were making through reading. Of course I was dealing with a basal series, which at that time was not noted for its rich use of language. In fact I had waited three weeks for this highly recommended

Sheldon Series because it introduced vocabulary the most slowly of all programs then available.

This past year I encountered Shirley Brice Heath's research, in which she shows that children have a variety of ways for making sense from books, and relating their content to knowledge about the real world (Heath, 1982). She observes that most educators work on the assumption that taking from books is not a learned skill but a natural process. Her research clearly outlines learned patterns for taking from print, and it is obvious that the patterning procedures developed in middle-class homes are the design basis of basal reading programs. No wonder many of my students had difficulty when I tried to engage them with these books.

When I remember these children, as I do sometimes even now, I shudder to think of the stories we didn't read together, the writing that wasn't created. I remember Peter Elbow's contention, "You're always right and you're always wrong" (Elbow, 1976). I was right in that I was doing my best using the information I had at the time. I was wrong in that I stopped short of what I now appreciate I could have done for these children. My adventure with basal readers and content questions, however, pales beside my next good intention.

There were three noticeable behavior problems in the class; one particularly profound. I was a first year Grade Two teacher; I was eager about my job, and flattered to be asked to work with a psychologist interested in helping children get more work done through careful response to on-task behavior. Statistics generated in my classroom showed the power of positive reinforcement, as opposed to reprimands, in motivating children to complete assigned tasks. Two or three people, usually the psychologist and one or more university students, sat at the back of my room. Their job was to count the reprimands and positive comments I directed at my students. They also recorded the on-task behavior of the target students, chosen because of their behavior problems, or their inability to complete work. The observers at the back of the room established a baseline of on-task behavior and then we began.

Events described as behavior problems did decrease. My higher praise rates correlated with greater on-task behavior from them. My life was easier in the classroom. The children finished more work, the class was quieter. We were all pleased with ourselves.

The initial part of a behavioral academic program required reading lines and lines of nonsense rhymes—phonetic decoding—then a writing program was introduced. We published an article which dealt with the effect of timed writing intervals, immediate feedback on number of words produced, and public posting of results on compositional rates of Grade Two students. These three conditions were shown to double the rate of words produced and increase the subjective quality ratings of composition made by independent judges.

I couldn't help but feel pleased about such progress. I was relieved when a similar program was offered in math because trying to teach even more varied levels of achievement was exhausting. Timed math sheets fixed that! Charts showing increased rates of correct reading and math responses were posted in my room. This was accomplished through an apparent reward system, based on individual improvement, in which results were publicly posted. This system also created great competitiveness among the students.

Not much reflection marked my thinking as this behavior modification program mushroomed. When I now reflect on my past enthusiasm about this work, I realize that teacher reflection was not being reinforced! I was being conditioned to be more and more dependent on this program for controlling my class. The children's engagement with their work was achieved through competition.

As I describe this program, I think of Peter Elbow's comment, "No one has undermined behaviorism's main principle of learning: that reward produces learning more effectively than punishment" (Elbow, 1986:187-206). I just wish I had used positive reinforcement differently.

From my present stance, I see clearly the most appealing part of this program was that it took control of the children's behavior in a socially acceptable way and involved them with words, writing, and numbers; it helped them memorize some information. However, I doubt their potential as readers and writers was anywhere near tapped in light of what I now understand about the composing process.

Researchers such as Frank Smith (1982) and Sondra Perl (1983), for example, have described the writing process as a non-linear event in which the writer's thoughts are developed as writing proceeds. Smith says:

> No writer ever produces words (or phrases or sentences) in a
> mental vacuum, first contemplating what should be written

> without reference to what has previously been written, and
> then revising it before beginning to contemplate what is to be
> written next. (Smith, 1982: 104-105)

I really wonder how writing races foster contemplation or revision. In this same article, Smith also raises an issue that is hard to reconcile with speed writing, and that is that, "we have to look to see what we have written and may even find it is not what we expected or wanted to write."

Sondra Perl describes felt sense as "sense experience observed if one pays close attention to what happens when writers pause and seem to listen or otherwise react to what is inside of them" (Perl, 1983: 45).

I have difficulty marrying these ideas with speed—timed speed at that. Writing did happen with the behavioral approach, but what could have happened had I given these children an opportunity to write and an opportunity for the kind of response that I see nurturing my student's writing today?

This year I am teaching a class of twenty-six students who have been defined as learning disabled. They are old enough for high school, but they are not ready to handle a Grade Ten general program. Their reading and writing abilities are in many cases what I would have expected from Grade Three or lower. I have been quite humbled by this experience in a multitude of ways.

I thought I knew a technique that worked, but this group of students has opened my eyes to issues I hadn't considered before and, in conjunction with the graduate education courses I have been taking, my thinking has been pushed a long way.

A long history of school failure has left a mark on my students. Many of them have repeated at least one grade, often primary, and most have been in resource classes since Grade Six. Melvin told me I was the first person who ever told him he was smart. I hope this isn't true, but obviously he has not been washed with appreciation for his strengths. The class generate frequent comments about how stupid they are; that they are "speds."

The first question, in light of Heath's research, is whether the activities offered to a reluctant primary student should be examined rather than labeling the child as underachieving or not ready for school. I think a reflective stance on the part of the teacher is indispensable in most teaching situations, especially one like my current one. The fact that children grow academically and developmentally at different rates, just as they do physically, surely deserves consideration. I think this calls into question the wisdom of grades in elementary schools.

Anne Martin (1990) calls for dealing with students' wide variety of abilities by focusing on strengths and consciously supporting them. She recommends an examination of how the classroom could adapt to the child's difficulties. She describes learning styles that are not compatible with the testing situation; for example, her student David worked by "fastening on one challenge at a time and running it into the ground before moving on to something new. It was this quality that had got in his way in a test situation that required switching quickly from one thing to another" (Martin, 1988: 495).

How many students have been compromised by tests? Many parents put blind faith in the school's judgment, which based on such assessment is less then desirable. Martin feels the best support for learners happens within the classroom community. I see examples of this in my class. One morning I discovered that the janitor had rearranged our desks in groups of four. The resulting layout has made writing more infectious than when the students were sitting separately.

I enjoy teaching my class, or better, trying to create circumstances so students learn more than if I wasn't there. I like the challenge of trying to improve their self-esteem, mainly by convincing them that each of them has a voice worth hearing. My problem has been finding literature they will enjoy hearing, reading, and responding to. Some days I feel I do cartwheels; they won't listen if they aren't in the mood. This has shaped my behavior to the point that many days I have had my preamble on paper, have distributed it, and then traveled from table to table, interrupting student conversation as gently as I can to make sure they know what the task is. I offer suggestions, but the students are welcome to write about what they want to. Most do rely on my suggestions, but I include a bottom line so no one feels that he or she cannot write about something particularly compelling about which I am unaware. Sounds good doesn't it!

Despite my great creative energies and bottom lines, I have had many students engaged in throwing spit balls, walking, kicking under the table, and going to the bathroom. My anger did not engage anyone. I actually provided great entertainment for them,"Look, she's really losing it now!" Trips to the office were working up to expulsion for some, and I wanted them in class working happily, not out of school. I couldn't help remembering my clockwork Grade Two class of 1972. I had to admit to myself, however, that the behavioral program I had adapted so eagerly in 1972 did not deal with engagement, it was a curriculum based on control. My fleeting thoughts of the rows of student heads bent over timed worksheets did not engage me.

Actually a big worry was that I would be perceived by my peers as not being able to control these kids. But, in spite of some really low moments, I didn't want to control them. I wanted them reading and writing and loving it—a tall order. The problem was that writing requires thought. These students were great copiers from the board, skilled worksheet-doers, and looker-uppers of the answer on page whatever. I was asking for their voices on paper. I gave them the mental space to do this; time to write. The challenge for me was to make them feel they could, so that class time was filled with writing not the disruptive behaviors they retreated to.

How could I deal with their resistance? How could I best engage them, have them make connections to new ideas, gain new insights in every class?

This year I have explored Mayher's contention that writing development should proceed from fluency to clarity to correctness (Mayher, 1990). Many of us were schooled with an upside down version of writing— that one begins with correctness. Mayher shows the number of restrictions this creates for a writer, therefore what actually makes sense is getting ideas down first, clarifying them, and then polishing surface features like spelling and grammar. Because I want my students to feel they have a voice worth hearing, I don't correct their writing, I talk to them through it. I do not want the restrictions imposed by concern for correctness to stop them writing.

Michael Holzman (1986), in "The Social Context of Literacy Education," says:

> Resistance to the institutions of the dominant society, of which school is merely one, is a form group identification, a qualification for that material and emotional support from the community that makes life possible, if barely tolerable, at the margin. Once we realize these are not random perverse actions,

> we will seek to match the real material and social benefits of
> resistance to education...we will emphasize group work, we will
> integrate school life with life outside of school, the organization
> of literacy education (should be) based on human priorities.
> (1986: 32)

I thought about this when James told me that in spite of his participation during the first two terms, he has decided to do no more work in class. His reason was that our remedial class was not a credit course. Furthermore he believed his writing was as good as many students in the general Grade Ten program. Rather than have his resistance escalate into a confrontation, I suggested he write a letter to our supervisor, with copies to the principal, explaining his feelings. If I can be objective about this, James is correct. To encourage him to express his feelings politically may be the best thing I can do for him.

Palinscar and Klenk (1992) discuss programming for students labeled learning disabled. They argue that a problem for such students arises with intentional learning, as opposed to incidental learning, where they are forced to deal with the organization and structure of learning "for the purpose of recalling what has been learned and applying that information in the context of problem solving activity" (1992: 215). The argument is that skill-based instruction, intended to remediate these students' weaknesses, often compromises comprehension opportunities. "Consequently, these children do not receive the same instructional opportunities as their normally achieving peers to learn how to engage in the syntactic, semantic and schematic analyses of text that complement the use of graphophonic analysis." Students' experience with varieties of text structures is limited, as is the background and content information that promotes intentional learning. This happens to students, frequently, in spite of our best intentions. Palinscar and Klenk describe a procedure (reciprocal teaching: learning dialogues to enhance text comprehension)for improving students' understanding of text. They contend LD students do benefit from "strategy instruction occurring within classroom cultures that support collaborative discourse, the flexible application of comprehension strategies, and appropriate, meaningful opportunities for reading and writing."

I have been trying foster collaborative discourse with and among the students. A more heterogeneous social population would support more extended learning, but we do our best. The students in my room sit at tables arranged in a square. Usually there is an empty seat. One of my goals is to talk with students at each table, every class. I am interested in how they have connected to the proposed writing, but if they haven't, instead of reprimanding them I try to get some talk going.

Avoiding reprimanding is a major challenge for me. For example, one day Barryn did everything in his power to distract other class members and irritate me when he kept interrupting a short article I was reading to the class. I was determined to make it through without losing my temper. The question I was trying to answer as I worked through this episode was when is the need for nurturing superseded by a need for consequences.

I sat down, when I finished reading the piece, and started talking to Barryn, who to my surprise asked me about it. I began to read to him, to give him the gist of things, and he reprimanded me for skipping a paragraph. His need for individual attention is acute. It took some reflection for me to realize I might have to give up some control over exactly when the work is done, and that talk is a more valuable use of their time when they feel like this.

The direction that makes me most comfortable is one which deals with these students' literacy, not their learning disability. With sensitivity to their individual needs, LD students can carry on in classes with their normal peers, enjoying the rich discussion and development of ideas that is possible in a diverse body of learners. I suspect they would flourish at least as well as they do in special classes.

I look around the room—at this moment nearly everyone is engaged. The only sound I hear is the hum of energy as pens churn out pages and pages of articulate thought. Most days I feel I am engaging students. No one has asked me for quite awhile now, "Am I allowed to say...." Dennis told me he was glad to be in the class, that he felt he could now write a Stephen King novel. One day Scott, who generally wrote nothing, asked to join Dennis at another table. This social interaction resulted in Scott actually producing close to a page of writing. The fact that I remember Scott asking if he could join Dennis makes me reflect on how far I have come and how far I have to go in creating the community of learners I would like my students to experience.

David had been driving me crazy. He walked around constantly, with no writing completed at all. He interrupted other students. One afternoon, when I had decided I really needed more structure for the days when I had this group for two consecutive periods of English, I couldn't believe what I was seeing. David was sitting and writing and writing. Before class I had decided the time had come to phone his mother and tell her just what he wasn't doing.

Ian, who can be a real spitball specialist, said he wanted to write about his snow-shoveling enterprise. Two-and-one-half foolscap pages later, he looked up.

Sherman is working on a response for the book *Malcolm X*. He, who in September was involved in a classroom fist fight, has worked on this project for several half-hour periods; he has even worked on it in other classes.

Dennis told another teacher that now he feels he can really read.

Jim told me he used to read, but now he really likes it. He said he really got into his book about Pink Floyd and found it hard to put down.

Because I still find those double periods long, I decided, one day, to show a movie. I was intrigued that Dennis and Scott retreated to their writing corner and wrote for an hour. Pens and paper appeared on several desks. A feeling of calm settled.

The point I am trying to make with these vignettes is not that my room is now happy valley. I certainly am happier than I was in September because gradually I feel I am engaging more students with reading and writing. At the end of a class I don't think about how noisy they were but about how many actually read and wrote. I am usually encouraged.

Elbow, Peter. (1976). *Writing Without Teachers*. New York: Oxford University Press.

Elbow, Peter. (1986). *Embracing Contraries: Explorations in Learning and Teaching*. New York: Oxford University Press.

Heath, Shirley Brice. (1982). What No Bedtime Story Means: Narrative Skills at Home and School. *Language In Society* 11(1): 49-76.

Holzmann, Michael. (1986). The Social Context of Literacy Education. *College English*, 48: 27-33.

Martin, Anne. (1990). Screening, Early Intervention, and Remediation: Obscuring Children's Potential. *Harvard Educational Review*, 58(4): 488-501.

Mayher, John S. (1990). *Uncommon Sense: Theoretical Practice in Language Education*. Portsmouth, NH: Boynton Cook: 229.

Palinscar, Annemarie and Laura Klenk. (1992). Fostering Literacy Learning in Supportive Contexts. *Journal of Learning Disabilities* 25(3): 211-225.

Perl, Sondra. (1983). Understanding Composing. In J.N. Hayes et al. (Eds.) *The Writer's Mind: Writing as a Model of Thinking.* 43-51. Urbana, Ill.: NCTE.

Smith, Frank. (1979). *Reading Without Nonsense.* New York: Teacher's College Press.

Smith, Frank. (1982). *Writing and the Writer.* New York: Holt, Rinehart and Winston.

Smith, Frank. (1988). *Joining the Literacy Club.* Portsmouth NH: Heinemann Educational Books.

Backing Out of the Room

Jim Albright

Isabelle and Sara were talking about their writing. I happened to overhear their conversation as I rounded the corner of the set of desks they share with two other students. Sara had finished drafting a piece. She had decided to prepare a final good copy. As I passed their desks, I heard something that set me back. From Isabelle's remark I assumed Sara had proofread her draft, as best as she could, and she was now wondering if I would proofread the piece before she wrote her good copy. Isabelle replied, "He won't do that."

Recently I have begun paying closer attention to what student's say to one another while they are engaged with their reading and writing. As I begin to attend more carefully to what is being said, I am quickly beginning to realize that these conversations are important clues as to what issues the students and I need to tackle to better promote learning in the class.

During the year I had been careful to encourage students to write with greater fluency. "He won't do that," didn't mean I was busy at that moment. It revealed to me that I had shied away from clarity and correctness issues in my student's writing—not that that was an entirely bad idea. Sara and Isabelle had learned about fluency concerns from my demonstrations. But, they were now indicating they had a need as writers to deal with what Donald Murray (1986) calls "the third read."

Yet I wasn't fully satisfied with this interpretation for this incident. "He won't do that," pointed to something else I was doing in the class. My professional inquiry as a part of the graduate education program at Mount Saint Vincent University has recently led me to examine, more critically, my day-to-day practice in my classroom. I have become more questioning of the hidden assumptions which have guided my teaching. Over the last eighteen months I have no longer felt easy with a lock step view of the writing process in which every piece of writing winds its way from brainstorming to final good copy. I am no longer satisfied that I could assume that my mini-lessons, which took up the first ten minutes of each class, were appropriate for what my student-writers needed. There was something else missing which "He won't do that" revealed.

I teach in a reading/writing workshop with Grade Seven to Nine students in Lower Sackville, Nova Scotia—a predominately middle-class bedroom community of Halifax. A close associate, Maureen Gow, and I had begun the workshop early in 1989. In *The Annual, A Journal of the Nova Scotia Reading Specialists Association,* we celebrated the completion of the first year of the reading/writing workshop at our school. Maureen, our school's resource teacher, and I reported in our short article, "Resource in the Classroom," the success we felt we had in meeting the learning needs of all the students in our Grade Seven and Eight classes. We had worked from December to June in planning and running the workshop. Our work had earned grants and other funds to equip the classroom with a library of young adult novels, a rug, a filing cabinet to store student writing portfolios, and other materials necessary to operate a writing workshop.

All that activity during the first months of the writing workshop had a significant impact on our learning and the learning of the students. We reported, "Students chose their own novel, wrote what about what they knew, and worked at their pace to meet their goals for the term" (Albright and Gow, 1990: 17). Students were given a chance to reflect on their writing and reading; they were able to benefit from collaborating through journals and writing conversations with peers and teachers. We commented that we saw our role shifting in the classroom; we were not the only authority. Maureen Gow, Fran Anderson (who taught the "alternate" class), and I collaborated among ourselves and with the students.

We felt very satisfied with our efforts. The students were encouraged to take greater control and responsibility with what they did in the classroom. As teachers we also took greater responsibility for our learning. We reflected on what was happening with the class as a whole and about the needs of particular learners. We investigated professional literature about reading and writing, shared what we learned, and adapted it to the situation of the class.

A search to promote a higher level of engagement in our students had initiated us into this process of change. Reading Nancie Atwell's *In the Middle: Writing, Reading, and Learning with Adolescents* led to the establishment of the workshop. I had read the book in the fall of 1988.

During that time, Maureen and I discussed the possibility of collaborating on such a project. Over the Christmas holidays I prepared a synopsis of Atwell's work to present to our school administration for approval, which we received. We began to implement Atwell's model of a reading/writing workshop at the beginning of second term.

In the years that followed, the workshop received support and praise. A new curriculum consultant came to visit. He was skeptical and we wanted more money to purchase books for the workshop's library. As we were chatting at the end of the last period of the day, Leanne, a gregarious Grade Eight student, returned to the room to discuss a new author she had discovered. After a few minutes of conversation, the consultant was impressed with Leanne's response to her reading. We had our grant! Another time a supervisor of a student teacher who was working in the class noted his appreciation of how the workshop functioned. The professor commented that it seemed to run itself, like clockwork, and our conversation ran to Elbow's writing about the teacherless writing class (Elbow, 1976).

Early this year our new science teacher remarked that he thought the students at our school wrote better than the students he had taught at previous schools. Because of his teaching situation he had taught at five different junior and senior high schools in our district during the past six years. His comments were gratifying and they confirmed the general opinion held by the other teachers at our school about the language arts program. But they were unaware of the discomforting concerns I had about the reading/writing workshop. These concerns had begun in the early days of its operation.

Maureen Gow and I had set up the workshop to run as closely as possible to Atwell's model. One of the first questions we debated concerned the imposition of deadlines. We had noticed that while some students were actively engaged with writing, others seemed to take a long time to complete pieces. A few never completed any piece within the reporting period. Our only goal setting for the next term was to focus these students on the need to bring their writing to final good copy. This meant that some students published only once in two to three months. We debated the merits of setting deadlines for publishing pieces within a set period of time. Because this seemed to go against the notion of choice and freedom in our "doing Atwell," we rejected instituting deadlines in the workshop. Only later, after reading more extensively the literature on the writing process, did we discover that some authorities viewed deadlines an essential part of writing.

Issues about the writing process, publishing, and genre connected to our ambivalence with choice and freedom. Despite invitations to write a variety of genres, many students chose to write the same type of story over and over again. Some students never published anything. They found our invitation to read and write too broad. They had difficulty sustaining a piece of writing or reading a novel to completion. Others took all their writing in lock step fashion from brainstorming through first drafts, revision, editing, to final good copy. They read thousands of pages uncritically. Our slavishness to our model failed to extend fully the range of student engagement with writing.

While some students wrote as they had never done before, others wrote less. These students questioned the whole literacy enterprise. They challenged the whole notion of joining the literacy club. They insisted they could read and write but did not wish to identify themselves with the notion that these were valuable activities. They had better things to do with their lives.

Maureen and I had set up the classroom to model Atwell's as closely as possible. Some aspects we could not replicate. Atwell's timetable allowed a writing period and reading period each day—ten periods a week. At best we could offer eight periods a week for the Grade Seven classes and eight for Grade Eight. This year the timetable changed so that both grades now had only seven English periods over a six-day cycle. A Grade Nine class was added to the teaching load when there were cutbacks. This was considerably less time then was afforded Atwell in Boothbay.

When we set up the workshop we followed Atwell's model in allocating time for reading and writing—always giving more time for writing. I have recently come to question this division. As I have become more of a writer myself, I can see how my reading informs my writing. My students also need to experience this connection between reading and writing. Despite efforts to link the two in mini-lessons and writing conversations, this connection was hindered by the model's arrangement of separate reading and writing periods.

Giving choice to students to read or write during class has been popular. But, after teaching in the reading/writing workshop the first year, it seemed obvious that it might be hard to sustain the same freedom over two-and-one-half years of junior high. Some effort had to be made to keep the interest of our students while maintaining the overall structure of the workshop.

An important concern was the physical arrangement of the classroom. We were limited by the size of the room. Areas for writing supplies, reference, storage for finished writing, trays for submitting writing for response, book shelves, journals, and writing folders were considered and found. Desks were arranged to assist collaborating, but space for coming together and working individually without distraction seemed to complicate the planning. There seemed a constant tension between the conflicting needs for different groupings in the classroom. Students became familiar with our attempts to find a workable compromise and they were often involved in coming up with new classroom arrangements. While some students were able to store and use materials well, others had difficulty accepting responsibility for their use. The type and amount of writing supplies available to students was eventually limited and better monitored.

Some students had difficulty following workshop procedures. Mini-lessons which introduced and reviewed procedures took up much time. "Doing Atwell" we followed procedures for conducting each workshop class and for students and teachers to monitor the work of the class. Time for mini-lessons, status-of-the-class checks, and sharing at the end of class frustrated students who wanted to get on with reading and writing. These agendas seemed to be teacher led and did not reflect the needs of the students. The mini-lessons only sometimes addressed the immediate needs of the students. Usually, they connected with only some of the students in the class.

Students generally found tracking sheets difficult to use and not all found writing diary and editing sheets helpful. Only topic sheets were used regularly. Reading record sheets were kept because they directly affected term evaluations. Again many students saw these as part of the teacher's agenda. While we were concerned with choice and freedom, this appeared to be a mixed message for students. Many picked what they wanted to use and ignored the rest. These were some of our earliest concerns. Over time, mini-lessons were reduced, recorded status sessions were dropped, and sharing was done less formally.

Initially, students used Atwell's version of a dialog reading journal. They reported surprise at the amount of reading that they now did. But, as with writing, a few chose not to read, and the range between those who wrote many interesting and insightful journal entries and those who did not was wide. Since then I have tried several variations of journals, logs, and reflections. Some students found the change helpful, others did not.

Some students had distinct preferences to the kind of journal they liked to keep, but this did not necessarily correspond to how well they kept them. Of all these procedures, the student record sheet was the most useful for teaching and evaluation. Only later did I realize that it, and the use of a teacher's diary or log, helped with the day-to-day planning of and responding to the learning needs of the students.

I made some attempt to write with the students, but these occasions seemed too contrived—merely to make some point in a mini-lesson. Later, as the some procedures were dropped and the use of time became more flexible, writing alongside the students became more natural.

What was effective was the writing conversations which occurred individually, but there was an ambivalence with respect to who initiated the conversation. Some students gained much more from these than others because they regularly sought help with their pieces; others remained very reluctant to discuss their work.

The experience of teaching in the writers workshop led to a great amount of tinkering. I read professional writers—Calkins (1986), Murray (1986), Graves (1989), Romano (1987), Daniels and Zemelman (1988)— and frequently mined them for ideas to address the growing number of concerns arising from what was happening in the workshop. This experience, though, led to greater questioning of the workshop model I was using. What had begun as a copy of a single researcher's model of a reading/writing workshop evolved into something else. It was as if we had begun with a Ford and had installed, over time, a Chrysler transmission, a Volvo interior, and any number of other maker's parts. At times it ran surprisingly well, but it never did run like the description on the page. I now realize that this was not the most important issue. What has become more evident to me is that the flaw lay in looking at the reading/ writing workshop as a program which could be corrected with the help of someone else's hints.

What Sara's remark brought to my attention was that I had stepped too far back from the class. My resolve to be more attentive to students revealed that I had removed myself from the class and that the students were, to some extent, adrift with their writing. The remark allowed me to see that the students viewed me as being disinterested in their concerns about their writing. In "doing Atwell," I had allowed myself to be push-pulled out of the classroom.

Sara and Isabelle taught me an important lesson. In the coming days and weeks we needed to begin a closer dialog about clarity and correctness.

During that time I needed to become more attentive and responsive to what my students were saying and doing. I had to plan more carefully activities which would allow them to learn more readily what they needed to know. Another important lesson for me was that the students had to see me as a more active participant in their learning.

Along with working with and listening to Sara and Isabelle, my work at Mount Saint Vincent University helped me see what has happened with my teaching. In her book, *Interwoven Conversations*, Judith Newman frames the role of a teacher in the image of a coach—supporting, encouraging, and challenging students. As Maureen and I did in "doing Atwell," the teacher designs and extends invitations and prepares the environment for learning, but Newman points out, this is only the start. The teacher-as-coach must sustain this engagement, support student struggles, and celebrate student accomplishments. She needs to reflect on balancing taking control and backing out of the room (Newman, 1991: 57-58).

In presenting this view of teacher-as-coach, Newman relates the concern of her colleague, Allan Neilsen, who has been disturbed by how some have interpreted learner-centered education. Neilsen notes that the uncritical acceptance of the need for student choice and independence can lead to confusion about the teacher's legitimate role in the classroom. Neilsen argues that "independence is learned it just doesn't 'happen' by leaving students on their own" (Newman, 1991: 21).

It is instructive to see how common is this tendency to step back from the class. Pat Kidd, who teaches at a neighboring junior high in my school system, has also noted this problem of "backing out of the room." She writes that, upon reflection about her teaching over the past few years, she has come to think that her "respect of the learner's vulnerability, learning preferences, and space [has] merely demonstrated [her] isolation rather than her collaboration, and a lack of teacher interest [to students]." She wonders, "Have I written myself too far out of the script?" (Kidd, in Newman, 1991: 286).

This theme recurs throughout *Interwoven Conversations* as Judith Newman underscores the notion of teaching as coaching. It is a juggling act between freedom and control, with the teacher's eye focused not solely on the learner or the program, but on the learning that is taking place in the classroom. Newman's metaphor of teacher as an active coach, involved in the student's learning while equally engaged in his or her own learning, seems to be best voiced by Donald Schön (1983, 1987) in his work in defining the reflective practitioner.

In relying on a model, evident in the pride I felt in the clock-like manner in which the workshop functioned and my private unease when it did not work well, I had overlooked a fundamental reality of professional practice, which Donald Schön demonstrates in his research. My desire for a mechanistic solution to promote student engagement blinded me to the reality of everyday practice. Schön remarks in *Educating the Reflective Practitioner* that "the unique case falls outside the categories of existing theory and technique.... The case is not 'in the book'" (Schön, 1987: 5). The reflective practitioner must improvise, invent, and test in the context those strategies that she devises from reflecting upon past practice but, as well, from within her own present practice. Reading Schön has allowed me to see that the practice and design of my teaching must build out of the class situation organically. Imposing Atwell's model was to a large extent the same as older types of programming which focused on the content of the class. In this case, the content of our class, to a great extent, became "doing Atwell."

Newman comes to the same conclusion as she reflects on the summer institute which she taught in 1990. "We build theory out of practice. New understanding develops as we teach. It can come from a variety of sources— from critical reflection on instruction, by reflecting on learning, as well as from questions rising through reading and discussion" (Newman, 1991: 342). This is an ongoing process. In a written conversation with me, Judith reflected on her recent experience with a class of Grade Seven students.

> I leaped in expecting those kids to take some responsibility for themselves but two things were against me—1) the kids had been spoon-fed through elementary school and weren't able to initiate and sustain themselves, 2) they were being spoon-fed and forced to comply in their other classes—I needed to have set much smaller "activities" and paced the kids through them to slowly extend their ability to make decisions for themselves—my chunks were way too big (Judith Newman, Written conversation: 1/15/93).

Her reflection on her own teaching experience points to what Donald Schön sees as essential in teaching as coaching—focusing on the learning that is going on in the room. Schön writes that the practitioner needs to focus on the interactions in the situation—literally to ask oneself and the students what is happening. The teacher must try to sense and articulate her own tacit understanding of what is happening and then to reflect on the students' understanding of what is happening. This understanding then should be communicated and tested in practice. Then the process begins again.

Recently a fellow graduate student, Rosemary Manning, visited my class. She had some good insights about some of the students. We talked about the kinds of invitations that could be made to them and shared the realization that our best efforts may not be always good enough. As we reflected on our professional practice, we concluded that you are always right and always wrong. The ultimate decision for engagement resides with the learner. How I, the teacher, respond to this is what is important. It is my responsibility to come up with new invitations to support engagements—to keep trying. Reflecting on my practice as a teacher led me to consider the importance of paying attention to the contexts in which I teach. As a teacher I have to go through a process of unpacking the context in which I teach in order to reflect and then respond more effectively to it. The better I can do this the better I will be able to promote engagement in my students.

This may seem like an obvious sort of revelation. I and other teachers who have followed recent research in language arts instruction have been blinded to it by an oversight in much of the literature. An insight may lie in a recent collection of articles written by teachers in which researchers then drew observations. In Courtney Cazden's response to Sara Allan's "Student Sustained Discussion, When Student's Talk and Teachers Listen" (in Branscombe, Goswami & Shwartz, 1992), she notes that a problem researchers share is how to figure out how best to incorporate the practitioner's own role as an active teacher into an understanding of active learning. Cazden notes how British and New Zealand educators have remarked about the effect of current research on classroom practice—the focus has been on students. These overseas readers have observed that the research has not been accompanied by descriptions of how teachers can help build on student learning. Cazden reports that such one-sided research can "paralyze teachers and lead them to give up even reasonable and helpful aids" (Allan, 1992: 93). Cazden, in her response to Sara Allen's article, contributes to Allen's description of the daily practice of inquiry in her class. She notes how Allan entered into and sustained student discussion at crucial points, dealt with inequalities, evaluated and, at times, was quite directive in her teaching. Cazden's observations have taught me be more critical of research literature that overlooks the role of the active teacher.

My initial, by-the-book approach to the implementation of a reading/ writing workshop had treated Atwell's work as orthodoxy. My recent experience as both a student and a practitioner has led me to the conclusion that "whole language" is a stance not a program. As a teacher I need to develop what Schön calls "an epistemology of practice" to guide me in engaging students in learning (Schön, 1983: 20).

Writing this piece, I am very aware of how often I have referred to what I have learned over time through my practice in the classroom. It is my practice as a teacher, a reader, and a writer alongside students which informs and grounds my professional knowledge. I asked Sara and Isabelle to discuss this piece and comment on how my teaching has changed over this year. To their credit, they seemed quite comfortable in noting the kinds of invitations I now extend to students and the support I provide. Isabelle and Sara easily listed the changes to the class which dropped the focus on procedures and freed it up to work on various concerns as they arose. Their comfort and ease showed me that, over the next few years, we will continue to read, write, and learn together.

Albright, James and Gow, Maureen. (1990). Resource in the Classroom. *The Annual: A Journal of the Nova Scotia Reading Specialists Association,* 2: 17.

Allan, Sara. (1992). Student Sustained Discussion: When Students Talk and Teachers Listen. In N. Amanda Branscombe, Dixie Goswami, and Jeffrey Shwartz (Eds.) *Student's Teaching, Teachers Learning.* Portsmouth, NH: Heinemann Educational Books.

Atwell, Nancie. (1987). *In the Middle: Writing, Reading, and Learning with Adolescents.* Portsmouth, NH: Boynton/Cook.

Branscombe, N. Amanda, Dixi Goswami, and Jeffrey Shwartz. (Eds.). (1992). *Student's Teaching, Teachers Learning.* Portsmouth, NH: Heinemann Educational Books.

Calkins, Lucy M. (1986). *The Art of Teaching Writing.* Portsmouth, NH: Heinemann Educational Books.

Elbow, Peter. (1976). *Writing Without Teachers.* London: Oxford University Press.

Daniels, Harvey and Steve Zemelman. (1988). *Building a Community of Writers.* Portsmouth, NH: Heinemann Educational Books.

Graves, Donald. (1989). *Experiment with Fiction.* Portsmouth, NH: Heinemann Educational Books.

Murray, Donald. (1986). *Read to Write: A Writing Process Reader.* New York: Holt, Rinehart and Winston.

Newman, Judith M. (1991). *Interwoven Conversations*. Toronto, ON: OISE Press.

Newman, Judith M. (1993). Written conversation with James Albright, January 25, 1993.

Romano, Tom. (1987). *Clearing the Way*. Portsmouth, NH: Heinemann Educational Books.

Schön, Donald A. (1983). *The Reflective Practitioner*. New York: Basic Books.

Schön, Donald A. (1987). *Educating the Reflective Practitioner*. San Francisco: Jossey-Bass.

PART FOUR

RESISTING

The major impetus for teachers
examining their assumptions comes
from our students—particularly
students who reject school.

At some time or other we all face
students who resist what's going on in
the classroom. The traditional way of
dealing with their resistance is to
identify their behaviour as "bad" and
punish them for it. More effective,
however, is to attempt to understand
their resistance, then try to find ways of
inviting them into learning.

Sandra Millen, in THE WILD ONES, takes
a close look at several of her junior
high school students who reject school.
She discovers that by listening to
their stories she learns that there is
more to their behavior than meets
the eye. She comes to realize that
students resistance has many
origins and important implications
for her teaching.

It is not only students who resist the
institution of school. Teachers

commonly find ways of subverting administrative decisions that force them to act in ways that disenfranchise students. At the very least, we agonize over what we perceive are dictates that undermine the relationship building which is at the heart of teaching.

Marcia Harding, in JUSTICE FOR JUSTIN, describes the tensions she experiences around standardized testing, particularly for at-risk kids. She shares her anger over how the testing situation undermined Justin, a third grader, and how, in retrospect, she sees herself contributing to the problem by not resisting. This experience with Justin helped Marcia understand that inaction has political consequences.

Judith Newman, in SABBATICAL, explores the oppression rampant in junior high schools. Through her poetry she examines her personal response to the students' resistance.

THE WILD ONES

Sandra Millen

There are the boys in the class.
There are the girls in the class.
And then there are the *wild ones*.
They are strong.
They are courageous.
They are independent.
They heed no one,
They care for everyone.
They shout when they want to,
They co-operate when they choose.
These are the proud, indestructible *wild ones*.
These are children more *at risk* than others.
These are children who need love, understanding, caring
And a challenge to meet their own *wildness*.
Our challenge is not to tame them
But to discover their challenge.

I sat in the unfamiliar hall supposedly taking notes on the latest educational innovation being elaborated on by the speaker. My thoughts drifted back to the Grade Eight students in my classroom two thousand miles away. They worried me. And as I thought about the students I wrote a poem. The poem allowed me to see how a few of my students were getting to me. I needed to think about them differently. This was a turning point— I began to question what it was that caused some students to resist what others in the class seemed to accept (or endure) without question.

Prior to this particular junior high teaching assignment I had taught a variety of early adolescents, but for the most part my teaching experiences had been with Grade Seven and Nine students. Like Krogness (1994) I found Grade Seven students

> ...nice little critters whose eyes are wide with fear and expectation. By the time the school year starts, they've already heard about their big new school, certain teachers, and those mean eighth (and ninth) graders who are out to get them. During the first semester, the seventh graders' desire to please often keeps them in line.... In relative terms seventh graders—especially alongside eighth graders—are manageable. (Krogness 1995: 27)

Grade Nine, on the other hand, produced kids who had been in the school at least two years. They know the routine and are ready and willing to accept responsibility for many of the daily tasks the junior high culture expects of them.

I was assigned a homeroom when I returned to the classroom in 1991. It wasn't long before I became aware of some obvious differences in Grade Eight students. They were certainly not innocent or naive, although perhaps I was. They were eager to be independent yet unable to follow through on one idea before another one superseded it. They changed daily. This was the adolescent I met in Goodson's simile in Calkins' *The Art of Teaching Writing* (1994):

> Adolescence is like the flame in the ornery burner of a gas stove; the one that leaps ferociously one minute and then hardly makes a blue ring the next. Adolescence is a time of struggling between extremes: fast and slow, blissful and tortured, seeking and shunning. Perhaps crucial is the only word that applies unquestionably, because it is in adolescence that we begin to take responsibility for who we are. (Calkins, 1994: 157)

Over the last three years I have become curious and interested in the unseen obstacles impeding the learning of some Grade Eight students. What I did not know was whether these obstacles were self-imposed or whether they were due to external forces. I have loosely labeled this phenomenon "resistance." By resistance I don't mean the outward act of striving against, such as Everhart in *Reading, Writing and Resistance* (1983) has suggested, but the forces that hinder motion. In this case the forces in students' lives that cause them to be resistant hinder their educational mobility.

Everhart (1983) describes early adolescent resistance as stemming from students' desire "to control their fate in an environment that, quite unabashedly, views them as passive members of the organization" (p. 25). Albright (1994), contends "students' refusal to engage in the dominant discourse in schools and society can now be seen as resistant openings rather than oppositional endings" (p. 44). Taking a cue from the latter, I began to observe my *wild ones* more carefully and to listen to them more closely, looking for openings.

Resistance can include both external and internal school factors. Parental expectations, past school experiences, major life experiences, personal illness, desire for attention, peer pressure, temporary attitudinal changes, home problems, and learning difficulties are among those affecting most adolescents at one time or another. How did this resistance affect my students?

Jolee's father had been away for six months on a training program and had fallen in love with another man on the course. He came home and informed his family—wife, daughter, and son—of his new sexuality and his desire to live harmoniously with both families. Jolee's resistance, especially to anyone who might be expecting her to conform to the norm, was evident immediately through her actions—she began shouting out in class, crying, and talking to her friends rather than working on assignments. It also explained her expressions of isolation and her refusal to write anything personal in her journal or to share experiences with anyone.

Suddenly, about two months after this behavior started, she began writing about her experiences and feelings concerning her parents' difficulties. Often she would share her writing with me, tears pouring down her face. Slowly she became more able to accept the situation. A major breakthrough occurred when she realized that if she failed Grade Eight or left school at this point she would have a Grade Seven standing. "That would be so embarrassing!" she concluded.

Claudine is one of the most competent and capable students in my class this year. She arrived in September all smiles; she thought she knew what to expect because an older sister had been in my class two years earlier.

Her status with her peers was confirmed by her election to our class student council. She enjoyed writing and working on the creative book reports we were doing. Sometime in November there was a change. Assignments stopped coming in. Claudine talked during quiet time in class. She strode down the hall shouting out to friends one day and sat curled in a ball against her locker the next.

One afternoon after school I heard screams and crashing sounds coming from the girls' washroom across the hall. I can still see the look of total misery on Claudine's face as she flew around the room then crawled tightly onto the corner sink. She wouldn't tell me what was wrong but wailed to a friend who had come in behind me, "Nobody believes me! They're taking his side!"

The next day, Claudine wrote furiously and left a paper filled with headings, questions, and paragraphs on my desk at the end of class. The paper "Rape—It Happens!" concluded with the sentence, "I know, because it happened to me." I suddenly understood her behavior and her resistance to school. It was little wonder she was showing so much resistance to completing class assignments. How, I asked myself, does a teacher build space for kids like Claudine? How do I help a child like this?

Simon arrived late to school. He often comes in late and angry. He will open his writing book if I ask and he will write the date. Then he will write a few words and stop. Often he just sits quietly; he generally answers in monosyllables. I have learned that if I speak to him harshly, he shuts down altogether and withdraws into himself. He fought a good deal in Grade Three and got into trouble for it. In Grade Seven he "didn't do anything 'cause the teacher did it for him." Although he has no confidence, he will write if I offer some encouragement, but my positive comments take time to be processed. He always sounds surprised when I praise him.

Today, because Simon was in a receptive mood when I spoke to him, he worked on his poem in the hall with a teacher assistant. It is hard for him to assess his own likes and dislikes; although he appears to like working with this assistant. I visit him near the end of the class and he is looking pleased with what he has accomplished. Shortly afterwards, however, he returns to the room with a cloud on his face.

"What has happened?" I ask the teacher assistant. "He was smiling a moment ago."

She replies that the resource teacher, seeing Simon working quietly in the hall, had seized the opportunity to chastise him about his failing grade in French. I wonder how often in the past have Simon's rare educational successes been obliterated in this way. He has learned that not trying produces the same lack of success that trying does. So mostly he doesn't try; that's his form of protective resistance.

In mid-October Stanley arrived at the school with a history of violence. He enters the classroom with a swagger or a slouch depending on his mood. I look up and there he is sitting slumped in his chair, arms folded. I walk over to him each day and say good morning. Some days he replies; other days he grunts and turns away. As the other boys in his group arrive he slowly brightens. When the others begin to work, so does Stanley.

Stanley surprised us all when he brought in an AIDS video as part of his health class project. The video featured a man learning about the dangers of HIV from community health workers upon returning to his reserve after a stay in prison and living on the streets of Vancouver. I sit beside Stanley during part of the showing of this video. He asks, "Why do they laugh at the drum music? I like it." I agree with him and am rewarded with a shy smile.

The Jolees, Claudines, Simons, and Stanleys, have very different approaches to learning and have very different needs when compared to other students. How do I provide learning opportunities for students like these, experiences that will help them to experience success both educationally and socially? How do I recognize and meet the challenges of these *wild ones*? These questions nag at me as I prepare for class.

Calkins offers a partial answer to my dilemma:

> When teachers asked the author Avi, 'What do we do if our kids won't write?' Avi answered, 'First you have to love them. If you can convince your children that you love them, then there's nothing you can't teach them.' (Calkins, 1994: 17)

How does a Grade Eight teacher convince these "flames...that leap ferociously one minute and then hardly make a blue ring the next" that they are loved?

There was a point this year when I invited all of the teachers who worked with this class to meet. I knew the social worker was very knowledgeable about many of the kids in my home room so I invited her to attend the meeting, too. One by one the teachers expressed concerns and made suggestions for working with these students. After a length of time the social worker spoke up.

"You really should make the effort to know the backgrounds and families of these kids," she said. "Kids will do almost anything when they are convinced a teacher cares about them."

It was Avi's the message—"you must love them." To love them we must know their stories. How was I to learn their stories?

Slowly I began to change my approach to the Grade Eight curriculum. I read Nancie Atwell (1987), Maureen Barbieri (1995), Lucy Calkins (1994), Donald Graves (1985), Mary Krogness (1995), Tom Romano (1987), and I read and listened to Judith Newman (1991). I took classes in cooperative learning, learning styles, and portfolio assessment. My classroom sprouted a bookshelf that, over time, became two. The overhead projector became a device for sharing information rather than a tool for transmitting knowledge. I let the kids begin to choose what novels they would read, what topics they wanted to learn more about, and what they would write about. Our daily journals began to be used to record experiences, observations, and reactions. The students started using these jottings as prompts for longer pieces of writing.

I tried to shift from being an authoritarian teacher to providing a welcoming learning environment. Instead of rigid assignments, we read. We talk about what we read and about how the author writes. We write, share our writing and ask questions about our writing. We publish our work with the computer and display our publications on the bulletin boards in the classroom and anywhere else we can find space. Most days our literary circles are active. The resistance that comes from the many factors external to the classroom have become part of our conversations. Some of the conversations are quiet, one-to-one, some occur in small groups, and some involve the entire class.

Having abandoned a teacher-controlled classroom format, I have time to sit with a student, or a group of students, and talk about their current projects or just to listen to their stories.

Danica spoke little English when she came to class fresh from an ESL program in another school. By October she was in tears not wanting to return to her previous school. "I'm not ready," she cried. Paired with an emotionally needy but very accomplished student, Danica has gained greater control over the language and she has developed confidence in herself. In one of our conversations she shared how her father had not wanted her brother to be conscripted into the army in her country. The smaller children were sewn into duffel bags and the family wealth was hidden in the baby's diaper. They were loaded up and exported as baggage into a neighboring country where they lived for a year before coming to Canada. Her father recently returned from Vancouver and has now gone to Edmonton hoping to find a job there. Danica, as a result of our conversation, was then able to share these experiences with the rest of the class as a public speaking assignment.

Listening to the students stories has helped me to understand their resistance and to find ways of diminishing it.

Recently I began watching myself teach! I found myself thinking about the choices I was making in the classroom. It began while I was watching a lesson on literary genre the librarian was delivering to the classes. I watched while she used the overhead projector as a blackboard, flipping carefully prepared transparencies with the highlights underlined and circled for easy reference, while the students copied the information. As the librarian's lesson progressed, I circulated around in the room looking over shoulders and encouraging participation. The students were restless. They wanted to know exactly what to write in their notebooks. Some whispered to each other. Some gazed vacantly. Is this note taking? I asked myself. Something didn't feel right. What are the students learning, I asked myself. How to keep quiet and try to guess what answer the teacher wants?

Suddenly I saw myself teaching that same kind of lesson and I recognized how much my approach has changed. The contrast in the kids' behavior in that library lesson and in the classroom was evident. They are far more involved in the learning experience in my classroom than they used to be. Although the assignments haven't changed all that much and the material is the same, the students' engagement is different. They are discovering what I want them to know for themselves and sharing it with their classmates. At the same time, each student is learning what is needed to successfully complete each assignment. It's little wonder they were having such difficulty trusting their own capabilities to learn earlier in the year—I had been feeding them information instead of letting them learn how to take charge of their own learning. I've also noticed that as they become more responsible as learners they lose their fear of one other.

It is 8:15 AM. I round the corner near my classroom door, check my day book for last minute duties, check in officially at the office, then catch up on the latest over coffee in the staff room before the 8:45 when the kids arrive.

Chris is there with a gentle grin wanting to tell me about his latest asthma episode. We go into the room and I listen.

We are followed by Erin looking for chalk so she can change the date and the school day on the chalkboard.

Cristina saunters in next and drawls out her daily, "Mornin' Ms Millen. How's it goin'?"

Johann bounces in, book bag swinging and a hearty, "Hey, Ms Millen did you hear...."

And the day begins. I disentangle myself from their conversations long enough to check in at the office and pick up the daily notices and other administrative trivia from my mail box. There is no time for coffee and sharing with colleagues this morning; only hurried greetings as we pass in the hall. I return to the classroom to find Christina directing a group of six in a play she has just put together. "We're making a movie," they say.

"We're the crew," say another two. Four more are audience. Two more come through the door and join in.

More of the class arrive and find seats on the other side of the room. The 8:55 bell rings and I round up a few more from the hallway. These are usually wanderers or visitors whose friends are in other classrooms and bring us all the news of the school I was unable to get in the staff room. We don't miss much!

The nine o'clock bell rings and Jeff squeezes through the closing door. Mom has written a very nice note apologizing for his frequent lates, but she drives three boys to three different schools in the morning and sometimes it's difficult to get them all together in time, they will try harder.

"O Canada" comes over the intercom, the daily announcements are read, attendance is taken, and the day begins in the same structured, prescribed-by-the-public-schools-act way. External laws and curriculum give little consideration to the resistance students bring with them to the classroom. There are certain curricular standards to be met that do not account for the child who is feeling abandoned by her parents in their own time of need and separation. How can they all be expected to stay in the small lifeboat that school offers when there is a fragile lifeline, or no lifeline at all, provided from home?

Claudine is a child dealing with adult issues. She knows she has been hurt grievously and is prepared to testify in court. How does our curriculum adjust to allow her to overcome the resistance she feels to society in general and school specifically? Is it reasonable to expect her to conform to the external expectations for a Grade Eight student? The curriculum and expectations are both affected and therefore must be reflective of Claudine's experiences.

> Each of us operates on the basis of our 'action theories'. Our beliefs about learning and teaching are largely tacit. We operate a good deal of the time from an intuitive sense of what is going on without actively reflecting on what our intentions might be and what our actions could be saying to students. (Newman, 1987)

Not knowing the students' stories and not actively reflecting on what we are saying and how we are acting towards them, creates a resistance that goes beyond the individual situation and leaves us as teachers in the unenviable position of creating or perpetrating resistance rather than relieving it.

Eleanor Duckworth tells us that the kind of person we are striving to develop is "curious about the world, inventive of ways to find out about it, confident of his own ideas, respectful of others, and so on" (Duckworth, 1987: xiv).

She contends that the key to developing this kind of person centers on "the importance of taking children's knowledge and feelings into account as starting places, and the importance of teachers being aware of their own knowledge and feelings" (p. xv). Here Duckworth supplies the entry to Albright's "resistant openings."

The exhibitions of anxiety, the verbal outbursts, the physical withdrawal and isolation, inspired a need to know the stories of these *wild ones*. Becoming aware of my own knowledge and feelings about the situations these kids were finding themselves in and then choosing the starting place for overcoming their resistance has been an all consuming yet interesting task. The stories have provided me an opening to learn about and respond to this resistance.

For the girls the opening was made by taking into account their knowledge and validating them as individuals. The journey is not easy or short, but provided with their knowledge we can understand each other and face the school year one day at a time. With careful planning and sharing of information I can learn to deal with each student's life situation. I can begin to recognize how their life circumstances impact on their school lives and then attempt to accommodate for that in the curriculum and in the classroom.

It is more difficult to help Simon and Stanley. Their discomfort in a classroom, lack of interest in getting to school on time, or completing assignments seems to come from past school and home experiences. There are years of learned responses and resistance to confront. However, knowing their stories allows me openings to their resistance.

With these students it is necessary to take into account their knowledge and feelings when designing a program of study for them. These students also need to feel a part of the Grade Eight classroom. Their successes, no matter how small, must be celebrated. I am not suggesting that the goals for these students be lowered or that they be given modified programs that reaffirm their inability to do "regular" Grade Eight work. I am suggesting that they are given credit for what they do and are accepted as individuals in the classroom. We need to seek out their strengths.

Recognizing that resistance to school has many origins has implications for me as a classroom teacher. I need to take students' resistance into account when designing and implementing classroom activities. What seems to be most beneficial for these students is for me to provide the structures and the expectations and then to get out of their way—to act as a facilitator, always watching and alert for individual needs.

Progress may appear slow because gains are not as easily recorded as when a topic is taught and tested, but the learning appears to be deeper and more personal for each student. Even those who resist eventually, with patience and sometimes a little bullying, take some responsibility for their actions and their learning.

There are no easy solutions to the resistance that I encounter with Grade Eight students, but taking into account their knowledge allows them to become engaged in a learning process that is involving and meaningful and permits them to meet their own challenge.

❖

Atwell, Nancie. (1987). *In the Middle: Writing, Reading, and Learning with Adolescents.* Portsmouth, NH: Boynton/Cook.

Albright, James. (1994). *Literacy Conflicts: Who Needs Them?* Unpublished M.A. thesis. Mount Saint Vincent University, Halifax.

Barbieri, Maureen. (1995). *Sounds from the Heart: Learning to Listen to Girls.* Portsmouth, NH: Heinemann Educational Books.

Belenky, Mary Field et al. (1986). *Women's Ways of Knowing: The Development of Self, Voice, and Mind.* Basic Books, a Division of Harper Collins.

Calkins, Lucy McCormick. (1994). *The Art of Teaching Writing.* 2nd edition. Portsmouth, NH:Heinemann Educational Books.

Duckworth, Eleanor. (1987). *The Having of Wonderful Ideas.* New York: Teachers College Press.

Everhart, Robert. (1983). *Reading, Writing and Resistance: Adolescence and Labor in a Junior High School.* Boston: Routledge & Kegan Paul.

Graves, Donald. (1985). *Breaking Ground: Teachers Relate Reading and Writing in the Elementary School.* Portsmouth, NH: Heinemann.

Hewitt, Jean D. (1994). *Teaching Teenagers: Making Connections in the Transition Years.* Thornhill, Ontario:Willsdowne Press.

Krogness, Mary Mercer. (1995). *Just Teach Me, Mrs. K.* Portsmouth, NH: Heinemann Educational Books.

Mayher, John S. (1990). *Uncommon Sense: Theoretical Practice in Language Education.* Portsmouth, NH: Heinemann Educational Books.

Newman, Judith M. (1991). *Interwoven Conversations.* Toronto: OISE Press.

Romano, Tom. (1987) *Clearing the Way: Working with Teenage Writers,* Portsmouth, NH: Heinemann Educational Books.

JUSTICE FOR JUSTIN

Marcia Harding

A year had passed since the day the standardized testing incident had stripped Justin of his self-esteem, yet I still feel the tension. Was it my guilt that created the inner rage—the nagging feeling that I had forsaken my student when he most needed me to plead his case? I had not intervened when I should have. It seemed a strange coincidence that while I was reflecting on this tension in my teaching career Pamela should call with concerns about recently published standardized test results.

"Have you seen the report in the *Sunday Daily News* (Lightstone, 1993) on achievement test results?" By the tone of her voice I surmised our county had not fared well. "We are in the bottom 25% in everything! What are our schools doing wrong? Our kids are obviously missing out on quality education. Do you think we should publish these figures in our local paper so parents will be aware of the poor job our schools are doing?"

I shuddered. Her assumption was that these scores were an accurate and indisputable measure of the quality of education that our students were being offered. How could I explain in twenty words or less all the negative feelings I had about standardized tests? Pamela, like many conscientious parents, is legitimately concerned about the quality of our schools. She has been actively involved in fighting for improved services for struggling readers, working to raise money for books and equipment, and rallying public support to secure funding for a new elementary school to replace our century-old facility. She found these published statistics alarming and demoralizing. I suddenly realized I was experiencing first-hand some of the negative consequences that occur when standardized test scores are misinterpreted and accepted as objective evaluations of what really counts in education.

"A lot of people question the validity and reliability of these tests," I offered. "I personally don't believe standardized tests can measure the quality of education. Research has shown they are biased against minorities and lower socio-economic groups. Without more information about to what the numbers actually mean, the results tell us very little. Comparing urban and rural areas is unfair." I was struggling to put my views into simple arguments she would understand.

Pamela was perplexed. "I don't understand," she said. "Are you telling me I should not be upset when this report clearly indicates we are behind most other districts? Surely someone must believe these tests measure what counts. Why would the school board waste time and money on an instrument that does not do what people assume it does?" The conversation left me feeling hollow and anxious. I agreed to drop off some literature and copies of recent articles in *The Teacher* that addressed the political questions she had raised.

I reviewed some of the articles I had been reading. My research was an attempt to make sense of the whole issue of standardized testing. I wanted to know how other educators felt. I highlighted some passages for Pamela, hoping excerpts from various studies would prompt her to question the merits of standardized tests.

I included Johnson's (1992) summation:

> The more the public comes to define the quality of education in terms of the students' performance on these tests, the greater will be the effect on instruction. A consequence of this will be the instruction will be defined in terms of what is easily measurable in a controlled, timed, standardized setting, which will *exclude* such things as enjoyment of reading, diversity of reading, use of alternative information sources for research, use of study techniques, participation in discussions of literacy works, construction of alternative realities, and so forth (p. 296).

I included a quote from Edelsky and Harman's (1988) study contending that reading tests don't actually measure "real" reading because the test designers have a distorted conception as to what reading actually is. "Test-makers wrongly assume that reading is a complex mechanical activity made up of separable components.... The test only measures a simulation of reading" (p. 146). I copied a study of 1000 children by Altwerger and Resta (1986) which showed no particular relationship between students' actual reading and their scores on the California Test of Basic Skills. I wanted to alert Pamela to the danger that we might fall into the same testing frenzy as is occurring in the US. I noted some of the disturbing statistics quoted by Dennis (1993). "By one estimate, US students now devote 20 million school days taking 127 million separated tests a year."

Finally, I highlighted articles from *The Teacher* which further clarified my feelings that the recent interest in testing was incongruent with the department of education's espoused philosophies. I hoped Pamela would consider the opinions of reputable educators. Gerry Carty's article (1993) was a personal plea to the minister of education imploring him to reconsider his proposal to expand standardized testing. Carty argued that such an important education decision must be left to educators who have the expertise to carefully consider the potential harmful affects, the possibilities for abuse and misuse of test scores, and the negative repercussions of sorting and classifying students. Jim Grant (1993) voiced concerns of school administrators in Nova Scotia that conflicting messages were undermining teacher morale. Administrators believed espoused goals and values in the public school program (PSP) were incongruent with the recent interest in standardized testing. He lamented the fact that politicians do not seem to be aware of the incongruency in praising the implementation of more holistic language instructional practices on the one hand and, on the other, supporting a type of testing incompatible, if not completely inconsistent, with holistic teaching and assessment practices.

I passed the material on to Pamela and explained my concern that expanded testing programs will promote competition between students, teachers, and schools with potentially devastating results. Teachers, knowing their worth is judged on the basis of such unfair assessments, resort to coaching for tests in spite of their convictions that results do not reflect the quality of instruction in their classroom. If I could convince one concerned parent that the tests did more harm than good, it was a start.

Conversation with Judy, my daughter's Grade Three teacher, confirmed the negative effects on teacher morale when such impersonal tests are imposed on teachers who truly believe in a child-centered approach. I have witnessed Judy's competence as a dedicated and reflective teacher first-hand, having collaborated with her extensively during the past three years, enriching one another's practice by sharing ideas and materials. Judy devotes extended time and energy to creating a rich and challenging learning environment for her students. My daughter's enthusiasm and positive attitude, her varied projects and assignments, her love of books, her entertaining and creative writing, her journal entries, and her animated descriptions of school experiences, all convince me that she is participating in a meaningful and stimulating educational enterprise. As an interested parent, I am able to evaluate her learning daily. Surely this evidence is a more reliable measure of my child's learning than the numerical scores on some test. Judy was near tears describing her tensions during the recent standardized testing, "I felt so frustrated. I couldn't help them or clarify directions. The format was foreign and confusing for some kids. Setting the struggling students up for failure goes against everything I believe in, contradicts all the values I try to convey in my practice. It just doesn't feel right! I'm out of here if we are going to revert back to depersonalized competition. It's breaking my heart." Again, I felt a resurgence of anxiety as memories of Justin's defeated face reinforced my shared abhorrence of depersonalized, mechanistic methods of assessment.

This was the "sore" that forced me to critically assess the potentially harmful affects of standardized testing.

There was something different about Justin. The resource teacher heaved a sigh of frustration, "He's the most unmotivated child I have ever tried to teach!" Justin slid between us, his brown eyes downcast, shoulders slumped. I closed the door, sheltering him from her exasperated summation, "I can't get him to do a thing. He just doesn't seem interested in learning. I am dropping him from my caseload and taking a student who will benefit more from my efforts. These sessions are a waste of time for both of us!"

Justin was already ten in Grade Three. His red head towered above the other students. I knew it was critical that he make real gains this year and take a more active attitude towards learning. Her description was accurate, however. Justin was lethargic and listless. He couldn't read and he refused to write. He often played with his hands as if he were seeing things in another dimension. His mother had confided her frustrations, "Getting him to do anything is like pulling teeth. I try to help him at home but he just won't try. I bribe him, coax him, take away his TV time. Sometimes he will make a real effort and surprise me, but mostly I get so frustrated I wonder if I do more harm than good." Her worried eyes beseeched me not to give up on her son.

I, too, was baffled by Justin's apathy. He usually wore a broad smile in spite of his apparent disinterest in schoolwork. Sometimes he seemed to retreat within himself, oblivious to the stimuli in the world around him. I puzzled about whether his exclusion was by choice, habit, or the symptom of some deeper problem.

One day, while the other students were busy writing stories, I watched Justin as he played with his plastic dinosaurs. The rule was, if you play with toys during work time, I put them on my desk. But here was an opportunity to capitalize on his interest in prehistoric creatures. I crouched beside his desk and whispered, "Tell me about your dinosaurs, Justin. Where did you get them? Do you know their names?" Just as I had expected, Justin could tell me all sorts of amazing things about dinosaurs. He knew the scientific names, which were meat-eaters, and a host of other facts. After we chatted about his beasts, I asked him if he would like me to record some of the things he said. Justin enthusiastically dictated several sentences about the battle between a triceratops and a fierce tyrannosaurus rex. His description was vivid and full of action. I encouraged him to add an ending. It worked. This wasn't a miraculous transformation, but it was the beginning of real engagement. The following week I employed similar tactics to subtly inspire a report on how he captured iridescent beetles with a flashlight at night. He reveled in sharing his tactics with his classmates. Beautifully illustrated books on insects captured his attention and opened the door to reading. I had found an in—his fascination for science. I recalled Frank Smith's (1985) words of wisdom, "Find out what a child wants to know and help them learn it" (p. 143).

In group work Justin had typically been dragged along by his classmates. They often became frustrated with his ambivalent attitude. Kids knew intuitively that Justin was different and accepted his limitations. But patience and persistence brought its rewards. I was amazed by the positive power of two determined females who motivated a more active stance from Justin. Kristin and Carolyn gave Justin much support but made it clear that they expected him to pull his weight in a group project on Calgary. Discovering in the literature that Calgary had an amazing dinosaur park, the girls helped Justine write a letter requesting information. Thrilled with the pamphlets, Justin proceeded to build an impressive three-dimensional model of the park featuring his model dinosaurs. His oral presentation on fossils discovered in that area won rave reviews from classmates. The positive feedback from his peers boosted his self-confidence and launched him on the road to being a more active participant in the classroom. His hearty laughter echoed his involvement.

Many educators, myself included, have come to fully appreciate the power of group learning. Noel Jones points out the importance of teachers structuring and fostering group processes within the classroom (Stephens, 1990). Jones says group work may entail the most intense intellectual engagement of their lives. Newman (1991) writes, "I now recognize that collaboration is at the heart of learning. Learning is social" (p. 14). Certainly the peer influence had a positive and dramatic influence on Justin's attitude. He was finally making a real effort to read and write and engage in discussions. I had new hope for Justin. The supportive community of learners had provided a learning environment able to respond to his particular interests and cater to his special needs. I was elated to report to his worried parents that Justin was finally trying and making significant gains.

Then came the week of standardized tests. I had tried to minimize the kids' anxiety by playing the "these are not really important, but do your best" game. It didn't feel right. The kids were getting mixed messages. All regular classes had been canceled, even silent reading, and we never canceled that for anything. On the designated day a stranger appeared in a freshly pressed suit lugging a box of booklets. Desks were aligned in soldier-style formations with measured spaces between each one. The booklets were distributed face-down with explicit orders that they were not to be touched until the command was given. The children clutched their weapon-sharp pencils in their sweaty palms and watched the second hand of the wall clock tick its way to zero. The click of the stop-watch symbolized competition. The race was on.

Twenty-six tense little robots huddled over typed tests. My vibrant busy classroom, suddenly silent, had the ambiance of a morgue. I had the disconcerting anxiety that some invading power had conquered my realm and imposed its foreign rule. Now I stood on the sidelines like a guard feeling the frustration of their tired sighs. Students who were always willing to offer assistance and clarify assignments now tried to ignore the anxious stares of confused comrades. I was struck by the contrast of this sterile environment with the warm collaborative atmosphere we had established through sharing and caring. Now they sat divided, isolated by the competitiveness of the task, intent on proving to someone, somewhere, that they were knowledgeable human beings.

My thoughts drifted back to my days in Grade Three. Assigned to a seat, I faced the front, listened to the teacher, completed the tasks in workbooks, copied notes from the board, and counted my blessings that I wasn't one of the Justins sitting on the dunce chair. I left Grade Three not knowing my classmates much better in June than I had in September. There was no opportunity to communicate with peers—talk was forbidden. We were separate little souls confined in the same cocoon, but there was no real metamorphosis, we did not transform into beautiful butterflies. I learned that marks were the most important thing. Grades told me what I knew. They mirrored my self-worth and spelled out my potential. I was dependent on the teacher to tell me what to think and how to learn. There was no liberation, just conformity. I remember feeling sorry for Moyle who scuffed to the end of the line to pick up his report card. How did it feel to rank last in a class of thirty-three? Competition bred insensitivity not only in the teachers but in fellow students who taunted Moyle with chants of "dummy" on the playground.

I moved quietly up and down the aisles watching the children as they struggled with a test whose very design guaranteed failure. I thought about the positive changes in education during the last decade. In my early years of teaching I had slavishly followed the manuals and imposed poorly designed workbook exercises and inappropriate lifeless stories on the children without daring to question their merit. I assumed the experts who manufactured the texts knew better than me what was best for my students. I taught what they prescribed and swallowed the bitter medicine, only occasionally daring to put aside the guides to investigate something that engendered excitement and engagement. Over the years I gained confidence in my own ability to assess students and respond more confidently to their individual needs. As I relied less and less on packaged programs I experimented with more meaningful learning experiences and encouraged more input and participation from the students. The results were astounding! School became a happier more productive place where children participated more fully in enriched programs; teaching became an invigorating and rewarding challenge. Not easier, but well worth the extra effort. Now I pondered what it was that these tests measured. Did they really measure the quality of education in my classroom? How could testers quantify the things that really counted as knowledge? I questioned how multiple-choice questions could measure a love of literature, the ability to communicate thoughts and feelings through writing, social skills, empathy for fellow humans, appreciation for the beauty of the world, curiosity to uncover its wonders, and awareness of the social injustices. These were among the many things tests could not measure. Many questions surfaced as I circulated among the students on tiptoe.

I tried to comfort Willie with a reassuring pat on the back. But I sensed he felt betrayed. I recalled how his speech had been hardly intelligible the first day at school. An import from the nearby country school, Willie stood out like a sore thumb. Cruel, callous students teased him about his country clothes and afflicted speech. He stood alone in the center of the circle, epitomizing Andersen's description of the ugly duckling. Feeling humiliated and forsaken, he had sobbed in my arms. But group work in the classroom fostered friendship, tolerance, and respect for diversity. By working with Willie, the children came to appreciate his warm, affectionate personality. Willie shared his expertise as a fisherman, his knowledge of goats, and his encounter with a bear while out picking blueberries. Peers gained an appreciation for his rural lifestyle. Willie wouldn't do well on this test, but he had developed tremendous confidence in his ability to express himself through talking and writing. I thought about how different Moyle's memories of Grade Three might have been had he been given opportunities to interact with peers and share his life experiences. The test could not measure a child's social development, compassion, or tolerance.

I thought about the highlights of the year. The trip to Lunenburg when the guide complimented the children on their extensive knowledge about whales. I could still picture their proud faces as they boasted how they had made bracelets and popped popcorn to raise money to adopt Foggy, a humpback that visited the Bay of Fundy every summer. But the tests did not measure a child's concern for fellow creatures or his respect for the environment, topics we had worked on diligently and with great enthusiasm.

I remembered the tears of sympathy the day we heard the miners at Westray were buried underground. Coincidentally, we had just finished reading Joyce Barkhouse's wonderfully sensitive novel *Pit Pony*, and the children had come to understand the hardships and brutal realities of a miner's life. The letters my students wrote to the children in that community expressed the compassion they truly felt. Days later, when the news confirmed our darkest fears, we bowed our heads to honor the dead, and let Rita MacNeil's words seep into our souls. "And I never again will go down underground" had real meaning. Our subsequent studies on mining had depth deeper than the tunnels. I believe creating experiences to help children view the world from someone else's shoes makes them more tolerant, caring people better able to make fair and wise social decisions in a democracy. But the tests don't measure that.

I recalled the wonder in their faces the sunny fall day we watched the spider spin her web. We had gone to my house to watch the animated movie *Charlotte's Web*, a celebration of the reading of this wonderful classic.

During our walk into Wilbur's world, our classroom gradually came to reflect our involvement in the literature. Our classroom was full of sculptured pink pigs and fuzzy spiders that dangled from silver draglines suspended from the ceiling. Children had enjoyed the book immensely and extended the theme to study how food was produced on a farm. While picnicking on my patio, comparing and contrasting the book and the movie, Willie spied a spider spinning her web. The coincidence reinforced the magic and mystery of nature. Students decided they should become detectives and spy on spiders, noting details in their homework pads so they could compare observations in class. Responding to a teachable moment launched a class of curious scientists on the road to careful observation. But the tests do not measure observation skills or enthusiasm for learning.

I concluded that standardized tests do not, and cannot, measure the quality of education in my classroom.

The tester broke my reverie. "That little boy with the red hair. He is not doing a thing. He hasn't made a single mark on his paper."

Justin had retreated to his private dimension. He had that far away look I'd almost forgotten about.

"He won't do anything without assistance and support. He needs encouragement," I explained, trying to talk in spite of the lump in my throat.

"But we aren't supposed to help him. It's an independent effort." The examiner was sympathetic but perplexed by the problem. "How can I make him at least try?"

"You can't MAKE him do anything. He works if he has support. Otherwise he retreats into his own world."

The examiner, in silent resignation, just shook his head.

Justin's frustration manifested itself in disruptive behavior. He began to squirm and fidget, repeatedly dropping his pencil on the floor. He grunted and groaned in spite of the examiner's private reminders to be quiet lest he distract others. I felt enraged, powerless. It was the tester's domain; my authority had been eroded. All year I had tried to nurture this child's self-confidence, encourage engagement, ignite a spark. Finally Justin had responded. It was a critical time for reinforcement to perpetuate the momentum. These testing sessions were undermining all of our successes.

Everything I had led Justin to believe was now being contradicted. When he really needed a lifeline, I let him sink.

As I reflected on the incident I became more and more angry with myself. I should have taken Justin out, called his parents, made a plea to the principal to exclude Justin from the testing. But I passively accepted what I believed to be the board's mandate—all students will be tested.

What we did to Justin was criminal. We cried loud and clear for all to hear—"You are stupid! You are different! Look around you. Everyone else can perform. What's wrong with you?" Those were the messages our education system sent to Justin. All that talk about building a child's self-confidence; those curriculum documents saying we should recognize individual differences, respect children for their unique talents and capabilities, adapt our curriculum and strategies to accommodate special learning styles. Damn the pretentious packaged prescriptions. When it came right down to it, the individual child had no value, no special consideration, no rights. And I, as his teacher, had stood passively by as this demoralizing experience robbed Justin of his self-respect.

Shannon (1992) helped me understand that teachers are political whether they act or not. Doing nothing makes a statement about what one values. Shannon says:

> The inattention and lack of action perpetuates the status quo: policy makers and educators with vested interest in current practices and programs accept their silences as tacit endorsement of current practices and use it to argue against change. That is, teachers' political naiveté concerning literacy, teaching, and schooling actually contribute to their students' and their own predicament (p. 2).

Certainly my inaction opened no doors for negotiation or potential for change. I did not want to look at the political aspects of education this year at the Mount. I came back to university after nineteen years of teaching to revitalize myself and find ways to enrich the educational opportunities of children in my class. I wanted to find out more about how to help struggling students make sense of print. I wanted to expand my knowledge of children's books so I could nurture a love of literature and inspire my students to delve more eagerly into reading. In short, I wanted to find new strategies to enrich the quality of education in my classroom. I resisted looking at the political issues. "Why waste time and energy on the things

I can't do anything about?" I said. But Judith Newman encouraged me to take a more reflective stance. She wouldn't let me skirt the issue. She helped me see that even silence projects a political voice. Indeed, silence means compliance. And the price to be paid is too dear. My new insights and knowledge about how to foster literacy development in my classroom will all be for naught if educators, myself included, bow to political pressure and allow dictates to undermine the foundations of our educational system.

I couldn't express my concerns on the phone to Pamela in twenty words or less, but I have tried to voice some of my concerns in this piece. Many colleagues are as frustrated as I am. The solution is to address the issue of accountability. We must let parents know that we share their desire for effective evaluation, and gain their support in searching for improved and more meaningful assessment techniques that inform our practice and act as a catalyst to improve instruction. To earn their confidence and trust, we must invite parents into the schools and let them witness the progress we have made. Our assessments must match our values. As Linda Darling-Hammond (1991) argues:

> ... assessment cannot be a constructive lever for reform unless we invest in more educationally useful and valid measures of student learning.... Investing in the creation of authentic assessments of students' actual performance is a strategy with the potential to yield much greater benefits in the long run (p. 224).

We are not looking for easier ways to assess our children. We are searching for more effective, enlightening evaluations that foster a fair and accurate assessment of the child's wide range of talents, aptitudes, and capabilities. I ask Pamela and other parents to reflect on what is really important in education.

Ultimately our goal is to nurture happy, socially adjusted human beings who revel in the beauty of the world, appreciate the uniqueness of others, develop compassion for those less fortunate, and seek to expand their understanding of the world through talking, listening, reading, and writing. Isn't that what school should really be about?

❖

Altwerger, Bess and Virginia Resta. (1986). Comparing Standardized Test Scores and Miscues. Paper presented at the International Reading Association Annual Convention, Philadelphia, PA.

Carty, Gerry. (1993). An Open Letter to the Minister of Education. *The Teacher,* Jan. 29: 8.

Darling-Hammond, Linda. (1991). The Implications of Testing Policy for Quality and Equality. *Phi Delta Kappan,* 73 (3) 220-225.

Edelsky, Carole, with Susan Harman. (1991). One More Critique of Testing with Two Differences. In Carole Edelsky *With Literacy and Justice for All.* London: The Falmer Press: 141-153.

Grant, Jim. (1993). Standardized Testing and the Goals and Values of a Liberal Education. *The Teacher,* Mar. 12: 11.

Johnston, Peter. (1992). *Constructive Evaluation of Literate Activity.* New York: Longman.

Kelly, Dennis. (1993). Testing Chief Tallies the Results of a Long Career. *USA Today,* Mar. 11.

Lightstone, Michael. (1993). Education: Big Money, Big Question. *The Sunday Daily News,* March 14: 5.

Newman, Judith. (1991). *Interwoven Conversations.* Portsmouth, NH: Heinemann.

Shannon, Patrick. (1992). *Becoming Political.* Portsmouth, NH: Heinemann

Smith, Frank. (1985). *Reading Without Nonsense.* New York: Teachers College Press.

Stephens, Diane. (1990). *What Matters?* Portsmouth, NH: Heinemann Educational Books.

Sabbatical[*]

Judith M. Newman

The Witch

You think you see me
Here in front of you
But you're wrong.
There are really two of us—
Her and me.
You think it's me
Talking to you
But it's *Her.*
And I am as surprised by that as you are.
Instantly, uninvited
She was there.
Her whom I despise.

---

* These poems were written during the fall of 1992 during which time I spent a term teaching and observing in a junior high school. I had grandiose plans of writing about the struggles in junior high schools from the inside—I'd read Tracy Kidder's *Among School Children* (Boston: Houghton Mifflin, 1989) and was convinced I could do at least as well exposing the reality of life in schools, of making people aware of the politics of classroom teaching. So I arranged a placement in a junior high school. I became a member of the Grade Seven team attached to the 7B class, teaching the students language arts as well as pitching in as an extra pair of hands in the rest of 7B's classes. I also spent some time hanging out with students and teachers elsewhere in the school. This sabbatical experience made me question my understanding of the world and left me with an anger and a sense of futility and hopelessness that took a long time to resolve.

Where did she appear from?
I have no idea.
For twenty years I've fought to banish *Her*
And I thought I'd succeeded
But yesterday *She* suddenly appeared.
No warning.
No puff of smoke.
She just took control
Leaving me a helpless bystander.
Water won't dissolve *Her*
Like the Wicked Witch of the West.
Incantations, prayers have no power over *Her*.
I believed *Her* safely contained
But my chains were mere threads.
Now I'm terrified I will never be free of *Her!*

No Word

There is no word in English
For what I feel.
There's *misogyny*—
having or showing a distrust or hatred of women.
There's *misanthropy*—
a hatred or distrust of mankind.
But no word describing
What I feel for particular males:
males who strut,
who act as if women were theirs to use.
My antennae are so sensitive—
I bristle with rage
At a mere whiff of their contempt
And my Steffi Graf forehand is at the ready.
My _____ was roused
By some boys the other day.
Just children, really,
New grade sevens—
Small, immature, insecure

Protecting themselves
With a strutting insolence
But I sensed the men they could become
And my hatred erupted.

Two-Valium Morning

O——h G——o——d!
This feels like a two-valium morning.
The knot in my stomach
Shortness of breath—
A real anxiety attack
Fearing who I might be today.
Brandy would ease the tension
Instead I yoga breathe:
In—2—3—4
Out—2—3—4
I n h a l e
E x h a l e
R e l a x
R e l a x
Until finally I think I can cope.

Locked Doors

Some petty theft
A bit of vandalism—
not textbooks
(*who'd want those*)
not computers or software
(they're useful)
Just other kids' stuff
Gone missing
Graffiti
On blackboards and desks.

And our response?
Locked doors.
Shutting them out of the space
We say is theirs.
But kids know the truth:
Classrooms belong to teachers.

Resistance

It's war—
We've drawn the lines.
We proclaim:
No hats in public places.
They reply:
Hey, man. Hats are everywhere!
We declare:
No hats in class!
They retort:
Why not?
The combat is joined
And their resistance pays off—
Our gaze is diverted
From learning
To endless punitive measures
That in the end are for naught:
When they leave school
They'll wear their hats
Wherever the hell they please!

Mirror

Chaos confronted me
as I entered the hall:
kids running around
pulling stuff from one another's lockers.

I was standing there
hands on hips
when twelve-year-old Sally
sidled up
leaned close
and said,
"Pretty rowdy, aren't they?"
"Yes," I concurred, "like wild Indians."
She leaned closer—
"I'm part Indian, you know," she confided.
A friendly overture
reflecting an image
I was shocked to see.

Soaring

I want them soaring at a thousand feet
Finding their own wind
In balance.
But I'm fighting the turbulence
Here on the ground—
paying out slack,
hauling in line
So they won't dive and crash.
Climbing to where the wind is steady
Takes a great deal of patience and skill
I must wait for the right gust
To offer some lift
Then carefully maneuver—
in and out
out and in
Until suddenly they're off on their own.
Some days the gusts are simply too strong.
Just when they hover
A down-draft sends them crashing.
Sometimes, as they begin to climb,
The wind drops

And they slowly flounder back to earth.
But occasionally the wind is perfect—
steady and light
And together we soar
Riding the breeze with that solid tug
That makes us all feel joyful.

Like Grandmother

I discovered engagement
In my grandmother's kitchen
Her body supporting my four-year-old frame
Helping me shape bagels
And knead bread
For the whole family to eat.
I discovered engagement
On my grandmother's sofa
Her deft hands helping mine
Ply a crochet hook
Weaving garments for my dolls.
I discovered engagement
By my grandmother's side
Teaching her to spell
While she helped me
Become a woman.
My engagement brought
Independence and community
Wonder and responsibility.

But where's that engagement in school?
"First ya gotta control 'em,"
That's what I hear.
"They won't do anything unless ya make 'em."
So it's no lockers between class,
No trips to the bathroom.
It's late slips and detentions
And in-school suspension.

There's no working together, no adventure
Or excitement at learning something new.
"If it's aversive enough," I hear,
"They'll comply."
But compliance brings
Dependence and hostility
Resistance and rebellion.

I try so hard to be like my grandmother
Offering invitations to wonder and explore
But the confining walls we inflict on kids
Serve only to alienate.
My grandmother knew something we have forgotten
We must welcome them warmly into our adult world.

PART FIVE

BECOMING

❖

The point of teacher/action research
isn't to prove anything. The reason for
engaging in teacher/action research is
to confront the question "How might I
improve what I'm doing?"

Teaching is fraught with
contradictions. There is always a gap
between our intentions and our actions
as teachers. In some sense, we're always
'becoming' as teachers; that is, there's
always something new to learn—new
students present new challenges and
changing times require changing our
ways of teaching.

In ON BECOMING A BETTER TEACHER, I
attempt to show my own growth as a
teacher and as a teacher/researcher. In
this piece I share some of the tensions
in my own teaching. The question
always foremost in my mind is "How
is my teaching affecting my students?"
Only by observing my students, by
allowing myself to learn from them, am
I able to answer it.

ON BECOMING A BETTER TEACHER

Judith M. Newman

The assignment was to capture some critical incidents—moments
which catch us by surprise, which make us aware of an aspect of
what is going on that we haven't noticed before.

I'd distributed three by five index cards, six to everyone, with
instructions to make notes about events, or comments, or
observations on one side, leaving the back clear for our discussion
the following week. I'd handed out six cards because I wanted the
teachers to see critical incidents as arising from the commonplace.
One card would have said, "I'm looking for something B I G." I
wanted them, instead, to begin attending to the ordinary—to see
everything in their classrooms as potentially problematic and
worthy of notice.

Next class begins. Marilyn is obviously uncomfortable. She
becomes more fidgety as the evening progresses. Others relate
incidents that have caught their attention during the week. They
describe a variety of situations—student's comments that
surprise them, unexpected responses to an assignment, something
about their own reactions—Marilyn has nothing to say. Not like her,
really. She's usually quite vocal; but not that evening. It transpires
that she feels she has no story to contribute to the discussion.
I offer her encouragement before she leaves. "Listen to what the
kids are saying. Watch how they do things, how they interpret what
you ask them to do. You'll find surprises if you let yourself," I say to
her.

A week later, still nothing. Nor the following week. "I almost didn't
come to class this evening," she says. "I just don't have any

language stories. The kids are doing fine. I'm not seeing anything unusual."

Again she listens to the stories others relate about moments that surprise them. Again she fidgets. Again at the end of class I encourage her to keep observing what's going on.

The following week a different Marilyn arrives. She waves a card. "Finally, I've got one. At least I think it's a language story," she says.

"Let's hear," I encourage her.

"Robert did something interesting yesterday. He was busy writing and talking loudly to himself the way Grade One kids do. He was being quite boisterous, and I could tell it was disturbing some of the others nearby so I went over to him and asked if he would write a bit more quietly. I didn't want to tell him to shut up because I know verbalizing his thoughts is a good way of cueing himself; I just wanted him to do it more softly.

"Obviously, my request didn't faze him because he just carried on. Not five minutes later, however, while I was working with Jimmy, Tammy, and Paul at a table nearby, I got a tap on my shoulder. I turned, intending to snap, 'Can't you see I'm busy,' but I didn't get the chance. Robert was standing there and said, before I could say anything, "Would you mind working more quieter?"

"My immediate reaction was, "Who does he think he is? I'm the teacher. Kids don't reprimand teachers." Fortunately I caught myself before I said a word. I took a breath. "I'll try," I said and carried on with the others, making an effort to speak a little more quietly myself.

When she finished her story, I asked Marilyn, "What do you make of this incident? "

"Well, it raises the question of who has the right to ask what of whom in my classroom. If it's OK for me to ask Robert to work more quietly, can't he ask me the same thing? I'd never considered that before. I just assumed I was the teacher and I had the right to be as intrusive as I wanted to be. Robert made me think about that. I really never considered the working situation I set up and how my actions might be wrong for some kids."

"It's a wonderful story. The next step is to write the kind of things you just said on the back of the card. The point is to remind yourself why you made note of the moment then think about the issues it raises for you. I think you'll find yourself coming back to this story again and again. It has the potential to help you learn much about your teaching and about learning." (Judith Newman, Reflection: 3/7/87)

This incident occurred during my first formal foray into teacher/action research. Up until that time I had been working with a teachers' collective informally. The teachers and I met regularly to discuss classroom issues—we talked about creating a curriculum, about literacy instruction, about the political realities of their schools and their professional lives. We had published a book together, in fact, in which we examined several aspects of literacy instruction and learning. We hadn't named what we were doing teacher/ action research (Newman, 1985), but I now realize that it was really teacher/action research we were engaged in.

Then, during the winter of 1987, I had an opportunity to teach a graduate seminar on curriculum implementation in language arts. I thought that if we began with what the teachers were currently doing, if they examined how their instruction impacted on their students, we could enter into a conversation about change—change based on their observation of students as learners. I wanted the teachers to discover what worked for individual children and what interfered with their learning. Hence my invitation to begin collecting what I later came to call critical incidents.

While preparing for the seminar I happened to read a book by Chris Argyris (1976) in which he makes a distinction between espoused theories and theories in use. He contends it is not uncommon for there to be substantial contradiction between what we say we believe about the world and how we act in it. I decided to make uncovering the contradictions and tensions in our professional work the focus of this graduate course.

The question is how do you go about identifying tensions and contradictions? First we had to uncover some of our assumptions. We had to make visible our beliefs and values which normally are transparent. I thought that if we made an effort to record moments that puzzled us we'd be on to something. Over several weeks we attempted to capture events which offered insight into our teaching and into students' learning. I participated in the activity myself and made a systematic effort to keep track of the surprises, of the tensions, in my work with teachers. I made notes after classes and workshops. I fleshed out some of my stories and shared them with the graduate students.

> I was conducting an inservice session with some junior and senior
> high school teachers. I began the morning by creating what I hoped
> would be a critical incident. I had asked the teachers to make a list
> of the various kinds of writing they'd done that week themselves—
> its purpose, its audience, who initiated it, the constraints affecting
> their decision-making as writers. When they'd completed that list, I

asked them to develop a similar list for their students. My intention was to nudge the teachers to identify contradictions between the various attributes of writing in the "real" world and the restrictions they were placing on their students' writing.

When we began discussing the two lists a change came over the room. I could sense tension mounting. As we talked about their own writing I started hearing, "Yes, but...." Real resistance emerged when we got to the students' list.

What made most of the teachers uncomfortable was the comparison between the kinds of writing they themselves did in the course of a week, why it's done, what constraints affect it, and what they were expecting from their students. I overheard one teacher mutter as I was compiling the second list, "I don't like what I'm seeing here!" Others expressed open hostility. "I don't want to leave here feeling guilty!" "Why should I change how I think about assignments; teacher-assigned writing worked for me as a student."

This was a critical moment. I'd intended to use this first conversation about the constraints we place on students' writing to lead into an activity which would demonstrate how writing for different purposes and audiences could be used for making sense of a difficult text. We hadn't reached the activity yet. By raising the contradiction it was now apparent I'd run into a concrete wall.

What do you do at such a point? I had been invited by the curriculum supervisor to engage the teachers in an examination of their instructional practices, to help them ask themselves, "What if it could be otherwise?" I indicated people were free to leave if they weren't interested in exploring the question. There were other sessions going on—I would not be offended if they chose to go elsewhere. I paused so those wishing to leave could do so. No one left, which surprised me. Most even returned after the coffee break.

The teachers fought me throughout the morning. They wanted no part of what I was trying to help them see: that knowledge is individually constructed within an interpretive community, not a commodity passed from teacher to student; that learning involves the personal construction of knowledge; that active 'doing' is crucial for understanding. The teachers resisted my every suggestion to jot notes, make gist statements, brainstorm, to use writing in a variety of ways to help them make sense of the text. They behaved exactly like their own students ("This is boring!") until they found themselves actually beginning to make sense of the text.

Their resistance returned in full force, however, when I asked them to think about what they'd learned from the experience and what

questions it raised about their teaching. One person wanted to
know why we'd wasted so much time when I could have told him
what I wanted him to know in ten minutes. I decided not to answer
him directly. I asked, instead, if anyone in the group could respond.
One or two people tried.

I was exhausted by lunch time. I hadn't been prepared for the
intensity of their antagonism. Unlike another group with whom I'd
done something similar a few weeks ago, these teachers erected
barriers at the outset. The previous group had been open to the
contradictions evident from our comparison of the two lists and
used them to ask, "How could we redress the balance?" This group
immediately backed off.

As I drove away I wondered whether I'd helped anyone become
more receptive to asking the difficult questions I believe we all
should be asking. (Judith Newman, Reflection: 2/16/1987)

The stress in this situation arose from my desire to have workshop
participants critically look at their teaching and their reluctance to confront
contradictions. I was attempting to foreground the tensions between their
teaching and students' perception of instruction. I wanted them to consider
the various purposes and strategies they employed for reading and writing
in their own lives as a basis for thinking about what kids might need to
learn and how we might help them learn it.

The teachers' resistance to my invitation was much stronger than
anything I'd encountered previously. Asking them to compare their own
uses for literacy with the opportunities they were offering their students
inadvertently set a confrontation in motion. Given the brief time I had at
my disposal, I had no way of back-tracking to find somewhere more
comfortable for them to begin. I suppose I might have asked the teachers to
identify and analyze their concerns, to talk about the issues with which
they were struggling. Unfortunately that didn't occur to me at the time
and, even if it had, I'm not sure these teachers would have been willing to
candidly discuss any difficulties they were experiencing with their
students.

Sharing this experience with the graduate students, however, led to an
intense conversation about the assumptions and tensions inherent in school
change. My account of the workshop raised questions about understanding
the contradictions in our practice. We talked about needing to see things
from the students' perspective, and discussed the importance of thinking
about learning and about instruction that might make classrooms more
congenial. We began dealing with the tensions of teaching.

James Moffett (1985) argues that it's not a lack of research that holds us back from making curricular change, it's a whole host of political factors like resistance to change, concern about control, fear about liberating thought and behavior, administrative unwillingness to support teachers in any real decision-making that disrupts the status quo.

> We don't need special studies to tell us that the language opportunities offered in school are almost invariably inferior to those of an optimal learning environment or that if teachers would shut up and let children talk both groups would learn more. We already know perfectly well that such oral activities as small-group discussion and improvisations will pay off for reading and writing. (Moffett, 1985: 52)

The tensions of teaching center on these political issues. Most teachers know perfectly well their students aren't engaged. It doesn't take a rocket scientist to notice more and more kids (both junior and senior high students) stay away from school or behave in unacceptable ways when they're there. Research studies demonstrate that minority students, students living in poverty, or those without strong parental support have a hard time in school and many tune out. Life in classrooms is tough and getting tougher. It's difficult, understandably, for teachers to recognize and acknowledge that they contribute to the oppressive climate of the schools in which they work. Teacher/action research, I have found, allows us to discover and name for ourselves the institutional tensions and constraints that silence both students and teachers.

I was observing a lesson between Shelley and Brian (an at-risk third-grader). The book Shelley had chosen was a bit too difficult for him; Brian was having trouble reading it on his own. She was pointing out picture clues, prompting him to articulate the strategies he could use to figure out what the text was about, showing him how to figure out unfamiliar words.

I could see Brian backing away from the task—he tightly folded his arms against his body, the tempo of his feet, swinging back and forth under the table, increased. His escalating tension was very apparent, but Shelley seemed unaware of it. Afterward, however, when we talked about what she'd observed, she commented on Brian's anxiety. That was interesting. So why, I wondered to myself, did she persist? Why didn't she step back? Why didn't she just invite him into a shared reading? I asked Shelley, and her response changed my understanding of the pressures under which teachers perceive themselves to be working.

Shelley had observed Brian's tense body, she knew what it meant. She provided what in other situations might have been useful reading strategies, but in this instance her support was doing little to reduce Brian's anxiety—if anything it was increasing it. She was reading Brian's response accurately, but she was unable to respond to it appropriately because, as she explained to me, "I feel guilty providing that amount of support."

She had, she said, already read the book with him twice. She felt, at this point, he ought to be able to read it more independently. Her judgment call was based on her sense of what many of her other third graders could handle. I hadn't anticipated the impact Shelley's normative sense was having on her instructional decisions. In spite of Brian's obviously escalating anxiety in the situation, Shelley was unable to pull back and provide a different kind of support because, having done a shared reading twice, she felt this third grader ought then to be able to read independently.

We talked about external pressures which impact on the classroom and affect our decision-making, sometimes to the child's detriment. We talked about GUILT and how the only significant input which should determine our instructional judgments is that which we receive from the learner. (Judith newman, Reflection:: 3/18/1994)

My conversation with Shelley helped me understand the complexity of the climate in which teachers work. Conversations like this made me see I had to find ways to help teachers locate within themselves the power to make curricular decisions which support rather than undermine their students.

Once they begin collecting critical incidents, teachers become able to describe and name the tensions they're coping with.

For my whole teaching career I've been struggling between doing what I've been taught to do (cover curriculum) and doing what I believe teaching and learning to be. ...It's been a constant tug of war between these two ideologies....If I teach traditionally, I don't see the students learning anything of value. I hate what I am doing. I am bored and the drills drive me crazy. If I teach with an open curriculum, the room is active and exciting. However, I experience a constant nagging about "getting the students ready for next year's teacher," "making sure they have the skills they need for next year,".... I believe that some of my dilemmas would be resolved if I

had permission from the system to be someone other than the
trained professional who implements programs. (Kate Cummins,
Reflection: 5/23/1996)

Kate is addressing her anxiety about not being able to meet external
expectations. One of the objectives of teacher/action research is to strengthen
our professional knowledge so we can explain to ourselves and others
what we do. A teacher/action research stance allows us to enter the
professional conversation and to amass evidence that enhances our
understanding of learning and teaching. It helps us identify the
institutional pressures which make it difficult to be responsive to students.
In the end, the "permission" Kate seeks will have to come from within.
Permission to act must come from her observation of students—what's
really going on, what's allowing them to connect, and what prevents it.
She also has to read widely to become familiar with the debates in the
research literature. The better she understands the tensions affecting her
as a teacher, the more confident she will become about creating a curriculum
that engages her students.

Teachers are socialized to be dependent on external authority. They
are taught to consume knowledge fashioned by others, instead of creating
understanding for themselves. As undergraduates they are often expected
to memorize and regurgitate what experts have to say. As teachers they are
inundated with textbooks accompanied by manuals containing elaborate
lesson plans. They are buried beneath governmental curriculum guidelines
that lay out prepackaged courses of study. They attend professional
development sessions conducted by specialists who offer advice on various
aspects of instruction and behavior management. They work for school
districts that set up unending constraints. It's no wonder, then, teachers
rely heavily on others for making instructional decisions.

As I was leaving class last night, Ellen, one of the teachers,
stopped to talk. She described how her first graders were doing
quite a bit of writing—writing in journals, sending mail—but she
was bothered by the fact that they weren't using the writing center
for writing. They'd go to the writing center, take out the markers,
crayons, and paper, and draw like crazy, but they weren't doing
much writing. I suggested she remove the blank paper and
substitute lined paper instead. I predicted that the invitation
extended by lined paper would be different than that of blank paper.
"But I didn't think I was allowed to do that," she said.

Ellen's comment brought me up short—for her, learner-centered education means "hands off." In my view, I explained, teachers had an important role in the classroom, most aptly described by Montessori's notion of a "prepared environment." Montessori (Montessori, 1965; Lillard, 1973) believes teachers are responsible for creating a context which is actively responsive to the changing needs of the learner. That is, we have to know what we want to help students learn, then we have to create an environment which has the potential to foster that learning. It's a dynamic relationship; constantly changing as the children's responses to what's in the classroom change (Dewey, 1963).

I wanted Ellen to see we need to manipulate the classroom context to discover how we might influence and shape the children's activity and learning. Every material, every activity implies specific invitations. By introducing lined paper I'm attempting to increase the probability the children will write instead of draw. If making lined paper available didn't work, I'd try other ways of making my invitation stronger. I might photocopy wordless picture books for the children to write in. I might make shape books (small notebooks made with both lined and unlined paper and a cover of some sort, cut into different shapes: hearts, squares, Christmas trees, houses, etc.). I might try different writing implements.

Ellen and other teachers need to understand that it's perfectly fine to exploit the environment to encourage and support a specific activity. They need to know how to observe their students and how to feel confident about making instructional decisions based on their observations. (Judith Newman, Reflection: 2/9/1987)

I was again faced with the dilemma of helping teachers understand teaching in a different way. I was trying to show Ellen how she might take an active role in shaping the unfolding curricular agenda; I wanted her to comprehend that curriculum isn't something in books but the lived-through experience she shares with her students.

The most valuable insight I have had from my work with teachers is that they must explore the contradictions within their classrooms if they are to have any hope of changing their practice. Simply telling teachers about new curricular initiatives, asking them to take on new instructional methodology without helping them understand the assumptions they are operating from, is a waste of time. People might take away "nifty tips," but nothing really changes for students.

The power of critical incidents lies in the way they allow the tensions of teaching to surface. These stories bring us face to face with the reality of our professional work. That confrontation is disorienting, as one teacher explained in a written reflection:

> I have really felt this past two weeks that I have pulled the rug out from under myself. I feel as if everything I do in the classroom sits in a pile of ashes. Some things I suspect, I will resurrect from the ashes but with a different understanding or reason for doing them. Some parts of my practice will probably remain in the ash pile....
> (Heidi Delacroix, Reflection: June 6, 1996)

Heidi's comment reminded me of a piece written by another teacher, Michael Coghlan, "A Belief System Under Siege." In it he says

> The first shock was that I really had some underlying theory lurking around in my head, affecting the way I functioned in my classroom. Yes, I possessed a theory of learning—every teacher does. I had come to university to acquire one, and had found my own home-grown version fully developed within me; adopted unconsciously, unwittingly over the years in the classroom. Not me, you say, I don't pay any attention to that theoretical nonsense. Well, I discovered that I had indeed functioned with a very definite theory of learning, although I had not put much of it into words before. But actions speak louder than words, especially when dealing with students.
> (Coghlan, 1985)

It's necessary for teachers to uncover their action theories. Until we can name the metaphors we live by we can't do much to change them. So a big part of any teacher/action research agenda is using critical incidents, and any other evidence we can create, to uncover and describe the beliefs that drive our action. As Mike Coghlan discovered, he didn't need to jettison his entire scaffolding. He was able to reconfigure his edifice, using old bricks for new purposes. Heidi, too, will find the same thing.

As important as reflection on practice is, however, it is still not sufficient. Practice unconnected to the professional conversation remains largely atheoretical. We need to read what others write about their experience in order to name the tensions we face personally. Every article, chapter, or book (academic or literary) has the potential to let us see our professional work in a different way. I say potential because the questions aren't in any text but in our engagement with what an author has to say. By reading for helpful hints, as many teachers do, we may miss the opportunity a text affords us for thinking about our work in new ways. On the other hand, conversing with an author lets us see comparisons with our own work. As Patti Stock explains:

> Sometimes we begin by testing the dimensions of an anecdote one of us has told the others: Telling and retelling it, we place and replace it in contexts that enrich its meaning. As we add and subtract details, we translate the anecdote into an event, a significant occurrence within one of the larger narratives that define our teaching practice....We compare, contrast, sort, elaborate, and refine our anecdotes until we have identified those elements that name the family resemblances in them. ...We replay them, inviting colleagues who have not experienced those moments with us to examine them with us as we RE-SEARCH them....Drawing attention to those frames, we present our colleagues with problems for study. In so doing, we invite members of our research community to reach into their memories for analogous teaching-learning moments that have occurred in their classrooms and, in light of those moments, to join us in making such sense of them as we can in order that we may improve our teaching practice. (Stock, 1993: 185)

This is an example of what I call "thinking with." Our engagement with what Stock calls "the anecdotes" is what draws us into a reflective stance. Stock is arguing that anecdotal accounts are at the heart of understanding our professional practice. In order to make sense of our work we must RE-SEARCH our narratives—we must allow ourselves time and occasion to permit retrospective understanding to occur.

One of the graduate students made this point in a journal entry.

> I'm reading your article, Judith, for the first time in a few months, and I'm suddenly aware of how many layers of meaning are embedded in a text. Except on a relatively superficial level, the meaning of the text is almost entirely reader-dependent. Each reader picks out something different depending on what issues are dominating the scene in his or her life. And what the individual reader picks out...will change as the reader's thinking evolves.... I survey the physical evidence: different color inks, hurried scrawl, careful, neat script, and highlighter versus post-its. These tell the

> tale of at least three readings at very different stages in time, and in my way of thinking, and of making meaning. Each time, something different has crawled out of the woodwork of my understanding. (Karen Westridge, Reflection: 9/25/95)

This is an illustration of what Patti Stock has in mind. We need to revisit our own narratives, as well as the anecdotal accounts of others, in order to see ourselves with new eyes. The important difference between "thinking with" and a more traditional reading stance is one of purpose; instead of looking for teaching suggestions we're reading for connections and opportunities to see our work from a different perspective, to consider the questions which someone else's experience raises about our own. Karen has experienced first-hand how grappling with someone's published ideas affords a continuous unfolding of understanding.

The point of teacher/action research is to help us discover what's problematic with our teaching. The reason for engaging in inquiry is to understand better our relationship with our students as well as how to negotiate curriculum with them. I keep asking teachers, "What surprised you about...?" I do that because I want them to notice the unexpected, both in school and in their out-of-school lives. It's the moment of surprise, of being perplexed, that alerts us to something worth noting and provides an opportunity to make our assumptions, beliefs, and values visible. "What was I expecting?" people need to ask themselves. "Why was I expecting that?"

Another critical incident.

> One of the most difficult transitions I personally have had to make has been dealing with kids' resistance, their "not-learning" as Herb Kohl (1994) calls it. Just when I think I have some control over my responses I run into a kid who pushes me back into my instinctual, authoritarian way of responding. There's one like that in one of the third grade classes I've been visiting.
>
> In my experience when kids avoid engaging, offering some support brings about a small shift in attitude. Usually I can get a kid to "just try." I've learned that helping kids to be successful overcomes a great deal of their resistance. But I can't even get near this one, I'll call him Andrew. He cuts me off by turning away from me before I can offer help of any kind. His body language is real clear—stay away!
>
> Part of Andrew's problem is that he doesn't read or write very well. At age nine, that's starting to be serious. He's bright, so he

knows what the others can do and he can't. He behaves
aggressively: pinching, hitting, or jabbing his classmates with a
pencil. They don't want anything to do with him. His behavior keeps
them from discovering his shortcomings, but at a cost—by
isolating himself he is unable to build friendships.

I'm flummoxed. Andrew is showing quite clearly he won't learn
from me. And each time I attempt to engage him I seem to be
digging the hole deeper. Andrew evokes the "witch" in me. Although I
understand his antagonism, I react to it in a way that doesn't help
him. I find myself wanting to force him to try.

I have no trouble engaging Jake, who drives his classroom
teacher crazy. He doesn't make me bristle the way Andrew does.
What is it about the behavior that gets to me in Andrew's case
and not in Jake's. What in my own history is being triggered by
Andrew and not by Jake? I don't have an answer for that at the
moment.

Maybe it's the way Andrew rejects assistance. When he cuts me
off I just walk away. I've learned there's no point in attempting to
cajole him, and I have no authority to insist he do anything. But I'm
not happy walking away. I keep wondering what I'm doing that
evokes Andrew's resistance and what I could do that would permit
us to work out a different kind of relationship. (Judith Newman,
Reflection: 11/7/1995)

Writing about the problem helped me see that Andrew and I were
engaged in a power/control struggle.

I was rereading *Interwoven Conversations* (Newman, 1991) the
other day when I came across a critical incident about Danny—a
six-year-old who taught me to ask, "Do you need help?" before
barging in. I'm barging in with Andrew; he immediately raises his
barriers, which in turn angers me because it leaves me nowhere to
go. I guess I should at least be giving him some room to let me
know how I can help him before we're embroiled in his not-learning
game. I can see I should ask if he needs help and accept it if he
says "No." That gives him an out and me a way of leaving gracefully.
I'll try that tomorrow morning and see what happens. (Judith
Newman, Reflection: 11/14/95)

The next day, when I asked Andrew if he needed help, he considered
my offer and then told me precisely what assistance he wanted when I
followed up by asking, "What can I help you with?" That surprised me. I

discovered that asking if he needed help made it possible for him to retain control of the situation. It made it possible for him to engage in learning with me. My reflective writing helped me understand what was causing my struggle with Andrew and what I might do about it.

Bev, Andrew's teacher, and I had a conversation one afternoon in which she described how she learned to accept his clear signals that he wouldn't comply. She later wrote:

> The issue of power and Andrew's behavior was a serious issue. I found myself challenged by the dilemma of how to give Andrew the power he needed without "caving in" to his tyrannical behavior. How could I get out of the power struggle that I didn't want to be in and that Andrew continually created? One clue for me came when he told me one day that he didn't want to go to music and if I forced him to go he would misbehave so that he would be sent out of the room. At that moment I knew he had it figured out—he was in control and he knew it. I had to learn ways of negotiating activities with him, allowing him acceptable choices. Instead of reacting in an authoritarian way I had to find ways of allowing him to choose to engage. Andrew has taught me that I can't make anyone do anything he doesn't want to; external power has limited impact, it's internal power that makes a positive difference. (Bev Castle, Reflection: 4/21/95)

Bev learned how to negotiate with Andrew. Her important insight was that Andrew was always in control and that she would never get anywhere trying to force him to do anything. Because she has become adept at reading his signals, he's become much more involved and proficient at reading and writing and his behavior is considerably less resistant. My coming to understand the dynamics of my interaction with Andrew allowed me to talk with Bev about his resistance and avoidance of learning. In turn Bev was able to restructure her relationship with Andrew.

It isn't only our professional lives that serve as a source of critical incidents. A year ago I started taking hang-gliding lessons. Being a learner in totally foreign territory has yielded powerful insight into the tensions of learning and teaching.

> Since the weekend before last I have been intending to write about a hang-gliding experience. Kimberly Hill, setting up my glider and having trouble tensioning the king-post wires. I asked Eric, my instructor, for help. He immediately saw what was wrong—I had inadvertently hooked one of the reflex bridles under a batten tip

and hadn't noticed it. That's the second time I've done that. Eric handled the situation in his usual brutish manner—ridiculing me for not being more careful. I understand his rationale—my life depends on how carefully I set up and pre-flight the glider. However, the way he pointed out the problem made me feel stupid; it affected my flying, I could do nothing right that morning. I came away from the hill feeling very frustrated.

Wednesday evening we were towing at the flight park. Eric wants me to take more responsibility for making decisions so I try. The problem is that I still can't orchestrate all the variables, either on the ground or in the air. When I fail to meet his expectations he's abusive and then I freeze; I fear taking any initiative. I'm now finding myself in what Gregory Bateson (1972) refers to as a double bind—"Don't do x until I tell you to;" "I expect you to do x without being told." Both injunctions are followed by responses which immobilize me or leave me feeling intimidated.

Unlike kids in classrooms, I have strategies for getting myself out of this bind. First, I understand what is happening. Second, I can confront Eric. He doesn't understand the problem, but letting him know what I'm experiencing helps free me from his control. I am also contemplating asking a couple of the experienced pilots to assist me—both Mark and Brian have a much more collegial way of sharing what they know. But kids don't have the same options—I suppose they could, but only if we redress the power imbalance to make it possible for them to tell us what's happening for them. (Judith Newman, Reflection: 5/10/96)

The fact that I'm much older than Eric alters the traditional teacher/ student power relationship. I can tell him to get lost if I choose to. There are also no serious life consequences if I decide to quit flying. That's not the case, however, for my graduate students or for their students. School traditionally creates such a rigid authoritarian regime that students really can't risk taking on the teacher. They are effectively silenced in a situation where someone else holds the power over the evaluation and the outcomes of their learning. This incident harks back to Marilyn's concern arising from her incident with Robert. Who has the power to ask what of whom? A crucial question we teachers need to be asking ourselves.

Saturday I took another tandem flight, but I was badly overcontrolling the glider again and Eric's impatience came through loud and clear. His comments stopped being supportive. He finally took over the control bar to show me what I was doing wrong in such a way that I just gave up.

Tuesday evening I did some low level towing—the launches were OK, but I was still overcontrolling the glider in the air and my landings were much too hard—on the fifth landing I broke the basetube on the training glider! I set up my own glider after that, however, and tried again. Two flights! Two great flights! Solid launches, good control in the air, and soft rounded-off wheel landings. I felt terrific. Later Nes asked me what had been different—I suddenly understood that on those last two flights I'd been able keep my eyes on a reference point.

There are two things to learn in hang-gliding—light grip on the control bar, establish a reference. Both are actually quite difficult. I am beginning to get the light grip, but I have been so information-overloaded that I have not been managing to establish a reference point. I have been flying virtually blind—as if my eyes were closed. On those last two flights (they were real flights!) I had enough control over the other stuff—balance, wind direction, air speed, angle of attack—that I could consciously establish a reference and stay with it; and to my surprise all the rest fell into place, I was able to keep level, maintain air speed and altitude, and compensate for the turbulence all because I had a reference point and could make judgments about the glider altitude and speed relative to the ground.

But back to Eric and our teaching/learning relationship. As soon as I was successful his impatience evaporated. His excitement improved my flying. On the second flight I felt more confident, less inept, more willing to be aggressive and take charge for myself. What this all makes me think about is how I may inadvertently be conveying impatience to my students. I don't think I feel frustrated by any of them but that doesn't mean they aren't interpreting some of my responses that way and it could be closing them down just as Eric's exasperation does to me. (Judith Newman, Reflection: 6/21/96)

Teaching is like hang-gliding—light grip on the control bar, establish a reference point. Whatever the situation, learning involves more than acquiring some specific knowledge and a few learning strategies—it involves the development of an ability to make sound judgements.

My dilemma as a teacher is that I can't teach good judgement; I can only create circumstances which make it possible for learners to experience the consequences of their own decisions....my role is to structure conditions so that learners are willing to risk engaging in the experience and exploring the unfamiliar. And when students run into difficulty, when they don't understand what's happening, when they encounter something they aren't sure how to handle, I need to be on hand to ask questions, to offer suggestions, or just to provide moral support. (Newman, 1991: 19)

Teaching/learning, therefore, involves a very complex reciprocal relationship between student and teacher. In order to provide the kind of learning environment that supports the development of judgment, I have to face the fact that some of my own interpretations and decisions are likely to be wrong. If I've learned nothing else during my twenty-plus years of teaching, I've learned that I can't control how students interpret my intentions and actions. No matter what I do, it will be supportive for some but definitely interfering for others (Newman, 1991). The crucial thing for me as a teacher is to discover when my instruction creates barriers.

Several of the teachers in my current graduate class have also shared "out-of-school" experiences which have allowed them to think about their teaching. One teacher wrote about an incident involving her horse. She described a training session with a visiting instructor which went badly for the horse. The clinician was too aggressive—at one point the horse attempted to bolt. Tethered, however, she reared and then fell back unable to recover her footing; the horse was hurt quite badly. Anita writes:

Of course the parallels to the classroom are many. The subsequent events have been educational as well. The difficulties of time management, of negotiating curriculum, of the need to understand the causes of refusal and failure, of how difficult it can be to work as a team when the team members do not share some common philosophies. These are some of the issues which have arisen. As curriculum leader, this incident with Chessie so closely parallels some of my experiences in school this year.... (Anita Levine.: 5/24/ 1996)

This is a typical instance of a non-school situation turning our gaze on our work. Much of what goes on in our lives offers us reflective moments and permits us to see tensions in new ways.

Loreen, another teacher, explored her learning during a computer workshop.

> I am surrounded by serious technophiles, the monitors are flashing
> madly, the language is strange and intimidating and I have chosen
> to go to someplace ...familiar—ClarisWorks (for dummies like me).
> This scenario is speaking volumes to me about myself as a learner. I
> am feeling uncomfortable about my neophyte status. I am also
> working hard to quell my anxiety. One of the strategies I am using is
> to tune out that which is way beyond my ken...and tune in to the
> sounds that have some meaning for me. Aha, that is why my
> students and my kids tune me out! (Loreen Baldwin, Reflection:
> 5/24/96)

Observing ourselves learning can offer important insight into our students' behavior and help us think about teaching that supports learning as opposed to teaching that interferes or undermines.

In teacher/action research, understanding is often a retrospective enterprise; many events/experiences make sense only some time later, when life and circumstances permit a reframing (Conroy, 1991).

> When I was sixteen I worked selling hot dogs at a stand in the
> Fourteenth Street subway station in New York City, one level
> above the trains and one below the street, where the crowds
> continually flowed back and forth. ...I felt isolated with no one
> to talk to. On my break I came out from behind the counter and
> passed the time with two old black men who ran a shoeshine
> stand in a dark corner of the corridor. It was a poor location, half
> hidden by columns, and they didn't have much business. I
> would sit with my back against the wall while they stood or
> moved around their ancient elevated stand, talking to each
> other or to me, but always staring in the distance as they did so.

> As the weeks went by I realized that they never looked at
> anything in their immediate vicinity—not at me or their stand
> or anybody who might come within ten or fifteen feet. They did
> not look at approaching customers once they were inside the
> perimeter....their behavior was so focused and consistent they
> seemed somehow to transcend the physical. A powerful mood
> was created, and I came almost to believe that these men could
> see through walls. (Conroy, 1991: 68)

Perhaps ten years later, after playing jazz with black musicians in various Harlem clubs, Conroy began to learn from them something of the various ways in which different people get through life in the ghetto. "Only then," he says, "did I understand the two shoeshine men."

> Their continuous staring off was a kind of statement, a kind of dance. Our bodies are here, went the statement, but our souls are receiving nourishment from distant sources only we can see....
>
> The light bulb may appear over your head, is what I'm saying, but it may be a while before it actually goes on(p: 68). Education doesn't end until life ends, because you never know when you're going to understand something you hadn't understood before....For me, the magic dance of the shoeshine men was the kind of experience in which understanding came with a kind of click, a resolving kind of click. (p: 70)

The critical thing about retrospective understanding is that we can never know when a light bulb might go on. In teacher/action research, we collect stories but we may not understand what they are about, or how they relate, until something unexpected allows us to make a connection.

> This incident occurred when I was a graduate student. I was teaching an eleven-year-old spelling. We were examining some ways that meaning (not sound) is reflected in how words are spelled. I suddenly became schizophrenic—it was as if I were standing across the room watching the action—when something Frank Smith had written (which I had read perhaps two years earlier) suddenly struck me—that the one difficult way to make reading easy was to make it easy!
>
> It was clear from Martin's response that he was connecting with the words he and I were writing on the blackboard and what had been difficult for him before suddenly made sense—he could see the meaning patterns which are retained in how words are spelled, and that changed in quite a profound way his sense of himself as a speller; and I understood that most reading/spelling instruction which deals with decontextualized words makes reading/spelling difficult, when what learners really need is to be making sense. This was a clear instance of retrospective understanding. (Judith Newman, Reflection: 5/19/96)

One of the teachers wrote about how, sometime after the fact, she thought about an incident involving her Grade One students at the park. Marion mentions how Devin and Jerome asked for a push on the swings and how she announced, "I don't push." As she explains,

> I WANT those kids to make decisions on their own and look after themselves, in situations where this would be appropriate.

So she didn't push them, although she did show them what to do and offered lots of encouragement.

> Latoya had been on the monkey bars and had wanted to be lifted off. Again, I explained, "I don't lift kids off the bars." Another 'park' rule, I said to her.

Marion next considered Latoya and her writing. She described how Latoya had just begun putting her thoughts on paper. In the process of helping her tidy up her writing Marian had attempted to have Latoya flesh out her story a bit more. She got nowhere herself so Marian suggested that she ask Nancy to read it, hoping Nancy might persuade her to include more details. No luck; Latoya insisted, "I don't want to do that." Marian considers the two episodes.

> I asked myself why I wouldn't push the swing or help on the monkey bars....Then I think about Latoya's writing. Although I was willing to let her ignore the advice of her friend...I was uncomfortable; I still felt that she needed to make some additions to her story before it could be published....So sometimes I do push. (*Marian Andrews, Journal:* 5/24/1996)

"Pushing" is an important part of teaching. It involves setting challenges. Even though Marian declined to push the children on the swings, in fact she was still pushing—pushing them to become more self-reliant. She obviously engages in different kinds of pushing. Her challenge to Latoya was offered as encouragement to flesh out her writing; that invitation was rejected on this particular occasion, which left Marian feeling uneasy.

> I wonder about these episodes as I consider the article by Darling-Hammond (1993). She paints a very powerful picture of the

dichotomy of thinking that is ruling the education community. I agree with her that

the teacher's job is no longer to 'cover the curriculum' but to enable diverse learners to construct their own knowledge and to develop their talents in effective and powerful ways (p: 754).

I do not think of my students as "blank slates," in fact I have a lot of respect for the thinking that my Grade Ones are able to do. However, in the current political climate, I feel afraid for these same kids....
    The description given by Darling-Hammond of the other model of school reform certainly describes what's happening in our province.

Similar reforms during the 1970s had tried to 'teacher-proof' schooling by centralizing textbook adoptions, mandating curriculum guides for each grade level and subject area, and developing rules and tests governing how children should be tracked into programs and promoted from grade to grade (p: 754).

I do think that we are in a stage of competing models, and I do think that we progressive educators are in the minority.
    So what does this mean for me, a teacher of young children in a conservative school, a teacher who desires to give more power to my students and in some way must educate their parents that what I'm doing is best for their children? And how can I be sure that I am in fact helping to create an atmosphere of balanced power. Where kids can stretch their wings and fly. Where the teacher is a leader, a facilitator of learning. I wonder, too, how long it will be before the long arm of that other model of school reform affects my classroom. Or perhaps it already has. (Marian Andrews, Reflection: 5/24/96)

What interested me was Marian's analysis that one of the pressures affecting her decision to push Latoya was other people's expectations about what counts as instruction. Her understanding of how these external pressures were affecting her teaching had surfaced from her reading of the article by Linda Darling-Hammond. Her description of competing models of educational policy created a "Conroy" moment for Marian.

Freeman Patterson, a Canadian photographer whose work I admire greatly, writes something which I think makes some of the tensions of teacher/action research explicit. In *Photography and the Art of Seeing* (1979) Patterson enumerates barriers to seeing.

> First letting go of self is an essential precondition to real seeing. When you let go of yourself, you abandon any preconceptions about the subject matter that might cramp you into photographing in a certain, predetermined way....when you let go, new conceptions arise from your direct experience of the subject matter, and new ideas and feelings will guide you as you make pictures. (p: 9)

> Another barrier to seeing is the mass of stimuli surrounding us. We are so bombarded with visual and other stimuli that we must block out most of them in order to cope. Instead of seeing everything, we select a few stimuli and organize these. Then, once we have achieved order in our lives, we stick with the realities we have established....We develop tunnel vision, which gives a clear view of the rut ahead of us, but prevents us from seeing the world around us (p: 10).

> A third major sight barrier is the labeling that results from familiarity. ...we stop visualizing things freely, and put word labels on them instead (p: 10).

Patterson allowed me to understand that if I can get beyond my current labels I might see things quite differently. If I manage to step outside the comfortable order I've established, the taken-for-granted, I might discover new ways of observing the worlds in which I live.

There are many different forms of teacher/action research. Each version provides useful tools for taking a critical look at our professional work. I wrote the following synopsis for one of my graduate classes.

> Narrative inquiry (Connelly and Clandinin, 1988) allows us to explore our personal histories in an effort to understand how who we are impacts on what we value and what we do. The "evidence" consists of narrative accounts of significant moments in our past which helps us understand our values and provide insight into current decision-making. There may be elements of documentary evidence, but on the whole the evidence consists of the narrative reconstruction of incidents which we believe to be important for understanding who we are.

More traditional teacher research (Ruddick and Hopkins, 1985) compiles different sorts of evidence. It doesn't ignore narrative accounts, but it includes documentary evidence of various sorts—journal entries, students' work, policy documents from school divisions and province, newspaper accounts.... In this kind of work, the tensions of teaching are examined by identifying the constraints and pressures which impact on people's daily work. Here, too, the point of this inquiry is to understand the various influences on our decision-making as teachers and education professionals.

Critical inquiry (Smyth, 1992; Boomer, 1987) has a more overt political flavor from the outset. Narrative inquiry and more traditional teacher research are also political, in that we are working to uncover the pressures that impact on what we do and how we do it. But normally people don't see that aspect of their work until they're well into the later stages of putting things together. With critical inquiry, we know we're going to be exploring political issues from the outset. The evidence can consist of policy documents, correspondence of all kinds, newspaper sources, students' work.... The difference here is that the analytic tools are openly those that take a political view of schooling, learning, and teaching.

There are case studies too (Winter, 1986). A careful examination of an individual student or a small group of students can be the basis of a teacher/action research project. Here the point of the work is to learn from the situation how to act in it—to discover the kinds of decisions we make and to think about the theoretical reasons for making them. Evidence can consist of personal reflections, lesson plans, students' work, student/parent/colleague interviews, etc. In case study work, which would qualify as teacher/action research, the gaze is on attempting to uncover the assumptions driving our teaching; to learn from the learners how to make teaching a learning enterprise. (Judith Newman, Reflection: 1/22/96)

Notice that in all of these variations of teacher/action research the gaze is ultimately on the researcher. It doesn't matter which methodology we elect to use; in the end the account becomes a laying out of our personal understanding, our sense of the political realities which support or constrain our work with students. We come out of all of these experiences with an expanded appreciation of the complexity of learning, of teaching, and a stronger sense of how external realities affect what we can really do.

I had a lengthy chat with my friend Ann Vibert Friday evening; we
were discussing postmodern thought and how our work attempts
to implement these ideas. Ann said something interesting. "Judith,"
she said, "as long as I've known you you've always answered
questions with 'It depends!' That," Ann said, "is as contextually
embedded as you can get. It used to frustrate the hell out of me,"
she continued, "when you'd refuse to give me a simple answer. But I
came to understand that every learning situation is unique,
decisions/judgments are complex; there are no simple answers. You
taught me that!" Ann was a student of mine in 1984. (Judith
Newman, Reflection: 10/31/95)

The tough thing about this whole interpretive framework is trying to
find ways of balancing individual interpretations with the interpretive
community. When literacy/language folks contend that all learning is
social, we're arguing that all meaning making is embedded in our cultural
history and that most of who we are is tacitly absorbed both from our
immediate community as well as the wider community. Every
understanding is mediated to a large extent by the culture of the times, by
what we see on TV, what we read, by the conversations we engage in and
eavesdrop on every day. Our ways of making interpretations are influenced
by the various interpretive communities to which we belong. But in spite of
these communities and the social influences on our interpretations, we do,
in some senses, still make sense as individuals.

Such a theoretical perspective is important as a basis for action research.
It focuses our attention on interpretation—it makes us think about contexts
and how they affect our judgments and our interpretations upon which
those judgments are based. For me, it grounds the research in the ongoing
narrative of our professional activity. Because our judgments are based
largely on our tacit theories, on values and beliefs that are culturally
determined and not explicitly articulated, the act of creating a narrative
permits us to distance ourselves from our judgements a bit and affords an
opportunity to make the basis of our work open to inspection. The act of
creating the narrative sets us up to be detectives; the narrative offers clues
to the kinds of cultural values affecting our judgments. Hence the need for
critical incidents, for tracking the surprises in the daily work we are doing.

Melissa wrote something in her reflection that caught my
attention: "While getting the research question right becomes
critical, equally vital is how the study is conceived." I felt compelled
to respond to her in the margin: There is no "right" question,

certainly not at the beginning—nor will you necessarily be able to conceive of the study at the outset. This kind of research begins with the mess of being in the middle. The writing in the end will identify questions and will tell an organized story but the process leading to that is higgledy-piggledy. Be prepared for that.

We don't necessarily start with a question, and if we do, it likely isn't the question we will end up with. We're really dealing with journeys here—personal journeys into new understanding, new insight into the professional work we are doing. We can focus on our work in classrooms, with the teachers' union, with clinical cases, all sorts of different situations. But the glue which binds this work together is the inner-directed gaze, the inquiry into what sense we're personally making of what's going on and how our perceptions are changed by the situation, by our contact with the professional, scholarly, research literature, and with what other people think—which takes us back to the notion "thinking with." (Judith Newman, Reflection: 1/8/96)

John Smyth (1992) contends, it's not enough to just reflect, but that reflection has to go somewhere—instead of simply being a means of focusing upon ends determined by others the reflection becomes an active process of contesting, debating, and determining the nature of those ends. Ultimately all research is reflective; that is, the researcher does have to stand back from the data and make new sense of them. What differentiates teacher/action research data from traditional quantitative data is that the narratives, the stories, the anomalies, allow the researcher to cast his or her gaze back on his or her own assumptions and ask "so what?"

I was intrigued with Smyth's process: describing, informing, confronting, and reconstructing. His confronting questions mirror the questions I've been asking myself about critical incidents:

- What do my practices say about my assumptions, values, and beliefs about teaching?
- Where did these ideas some from?
- What social practices are expressed in these ideas?
- What causes me to maintain my theories?
- What views of power do they embody?
- Whose interests seem to be served by my practices?
- What acts to constrain my views of what is possible in teaching? (p: 299)

> But notice how the process begins with description—with the
> anomalies, stories, or critical incident narratives that bring the
> problematic into view. (Judith Newman, Reflection: 10/16/95)

Roger Simon (1987) extends the political argument—we must, he contends, ask questions about power and about whose interests are served. A "pedagogy of possibility," as he calls it, starts with descriptions which lead to some unexpected and difficult questions. What neither Simon nor Smyth make clear, however, is that we aren't looking just for single incidents.

> In my experience, it takes many small stories together before a
> pattern emerges which lets me understand, which serves as
> Conroy's "light bulb." That's why I've been encouraging you to begin
> collecting critical incidents. In the end you may share only a few
> narrative moments because later you will be able to identify those
> which are illustrative of the larger questions you're exploring, but
> when I'm starting out I have no idea what patterns could be
> present, I have little sense of the assumptions, the tensions,
> constraints, which are driving my teaching. So I begin with those
> anomalous moments, the surprises, the unexpected and by building
> a collection of stories/moments/ events/encounters I begin to ask
> a different sort of question about what's going on. (Judith
> Newman, Reflection: 10/16/95)

Now I circle back to Glenda Bissex (1988) and the question that perplexed her: "And what does that prove?" (p. 773). Conventional wisdom holds that educational research is supposed to prove something. I don't believe it can. I contend that all researchers can ever do is offer their experiences and interpretations against which readers can test their own, to raise questions for us to consider. Research (both quantitative and qualitative) is useful not because it provides answers but because it can be generative and lead to new inquiries (Stephens, 1997).

Teacher/action research is not about proving anything. The purpose of this kind of inquiry is to help us gain insight into teaching. By examining my assumptions, by thinking with various published authors, I make explicit the tensions and constraints which impact on me and on my students. By relating my stories and those of other teachers I am inviting readers to think about whether these same tensions and constraints are also affecting them. When I describe how I have come to my current questions, when I show what remains unresolved for me, I nudge readers to think about these same issues for themselves.

Maggie summed it up nicely in her poem last week:
freeze the frame,
learn from the moment—
freeze it so that other eyes may look upon it
and make sense of the changing, shaping, altering
of our perceptions and beliefs
(Judith Newman, Reflection: 10/16/95)

If reflective activity serves only to entrap us in maintaining the status quo of schools, then far from being emancipatory it undermines our teaching and who we are as teachers. The purpose of adopting a reflective stance on our work, then, is that it permits us to ask questions about what is worthwhile in teaching and why. It allows us to challenge the taken-for-granted.

Being reflective means more than merely being speculative; it means starting with reality and beginning to overcome that reality by reasserting the importance of learning. The question we must always be asking ourselves is "What am I learning?" That inevitably leads to others: "How is what I'm learning affecting my teaching?" "What evidence do I have that what I'm now doing is impacting on students' learning?"

This last question is the crucial one because ultimately the goal of engaging in teacher/action research is to become a better teacher.

Argyris, Chris. (1976). *Increasing Leadership Effectiveness*. New York: John Wiley & Sons, Inc.

Bateson, Gregory. (1972). *Steps to an Ecology of Mind*. New York: Ballantine Books.

Bissex, Glenda. (1988). On Learning and Not Learning from Teaching. *Language Arts*, 65(8): 771-775.

Boomer, Garth. (1987). Addressing the Problem of Elsewhereness: A Case for Action Research in Schools. In Dixie Goswami and Peter Stillman (Eds.), *Reclaiming the Classroom: Teacher Research as an Agency for Change*. Portsmouth, NH: Boynton/Cook Publishers, Heinemann: 4-13.

Connelly, Michael and Jean Clandinin. (1988). *Teachers as Curriculum Planners: Narratives of Experience*. Toronto: Ontario Institute of Education Press.

Conroy, Frank. (1991). Think About It: Ways We Know, and Don't. *Harper's Magazine*. Nov: 68-70.

Coghlan, Michael. (1985). A Belief System Under Siege. In Judith M. Newman (Ed.), *Meaning in the Making*. Halifax, NS: Mount Saint Vincent University; Centre for Reading and Language Education: 33-34.

Darling-Hammond, Linda. (1993). Reframing the School Reform Agenda. *Phi Delta Kappan,* June: 753-761.

Dewey, John. (1963). *Experience and Education.* New York: Collier Books.

Kohl, Herbert. (1994). I Won't Learn from You. In *I Won't Learn from You.* New York: The New Press: 1-32.

Lillard, Paula Polk. (1973). *Montessori: A Modern Approach.* New York: Schocken Books.

Moffett, James. (1985). Hidden Impediments to Improving English Teaching. *Phi Delta Kappan,* September: 51-56.

Montessori, Maria. (1965). *The Advanced Montessori Method.* Adyar, Madras, India: Kalakshetra Publications.

Newman, Judith M. (Ed.) (1985). *Whole Language: Theory in Use.* Portsmouth, NH: Heinemann Educational Books.

Newman, Judith M. (1987). Learning to Teach by Uncovering Our Assumptions. *Language Arts, 64(7):* 727-737.

Newman, Judith M. (1991). *Interwoven Conversations: Learning and Teaching Through Critical Reflection.* Toronto: Ontario Institute for Studies in Education Press.

Patterson, Freeman. (1979). *Photography and the Art of Seeing* . Toronto: Van Nostrand Rinehold Ltd.

Ruddick, Jean and David Hopkins. (Eds.) (1985). *Research as a Basis for Teaching.* London: Heinemann Educational Books.

Simon, Roger. (1987). Empowerment as a Pedagogy of Possibility. *Language Arts* 64(4): 370-382.

Smyth, John. (1992). Teachers' Work and the Politics of Reflection. *American Educational Research Journal,* 29(2): 267-300.

Stephens, Diane. (1997). Beginning with Research. Unpublished manuscript.

Stock, Patricia Lambert. (1993). The Function of Anecdote in Teacher Research. *English Education, 25(3):* 173-187.

Winter, Richard. (1986). Fictional-critical Writing: An Approach to Case Study Research by Practitioners. *Cambridge Journal of Education,* 16: 175-182.